THE EVERYTHING® RICE COOKER COOKBOOK

Dear Reader,

When I first moved to the United States in 2006 I was easily excited by an omelet breakfast, a pasta lunch, and a burger dinner. However, the exhilaration for such food did not last long. Perhaps because I was raised in a culture where rice is common for dinner, lunch, and even breakfast, or perhaps because my taste buds have been stubbornly implanted with something called "familiarity," I started looking back to my comfort staple: rice.

    I was lucky to be living in California, where the rice cuisine is flourishing due to the diversity in culture. So what was missing? Home-cooked food! No matter how enticing dining out is, and how convenient takeouts are, we crave simple and non-greasy home-cooked food, something we are familiar and comfortable with. And if those nutritious and healthy meals do not take too much time to prepare and cook, even better.

    Enter the rice cooker. The rice cooker is a popular convenience tool found in many Asian homes, and it is steadily finding its way into more American homes. You have to explore this lean, mean machine to know what it is capable of, and trust me, it is not as intimidating as it may seem. Before you know it, the rice cooker will be an additional helper in your kitchen. Enjoy this journey.

Hui Leng Tay

Welcome to the EVERYTHING® Series!

These handy, accessible books give you all you need to tackle a difficult project, gain a new hobby, comprehend a fascinating topic, prepare for an exam, or even brush up on something you learned back in school but have since forgotten.

You can choose to read an *Everything*® book from cover to cover or just pick out the information you want from our four useful boxes: e-questions, e-facts, e-alerts, and e-ssentials.

We give you everything you need to know on the subject, but throw in a lot of fun stuff along the way, too.

We now have more than 400 *Everything*® books in print, spanning such wide-ranging categories as weddings, pregnancy, cooking, music instruction, foreign language, crafts, pets, New Age, and so much more. When you're done reading them all, you can finally say you know *Everything*®!

QUESTION
Answers to common questions

FACT
Important snippets of information

ALERT
Urgent warnings

ESSENTIAL
Quick handy tips

PUBLISHER Karen Cooper
DIRECTOR OF ACQUISITIONS AND INNOVATION Paula Munier
MANAGING EDITOR, EVERYTHING® SERIES Lisa Laing
COPY CHIEF Casey Ebert
ACQUISITIONS EDITOR Katrina Schroeder
DEVELOPMENT EDITOR Brett Palana-Shanahan
EDITORIAL ASSISTANT Ross Weisman
EVERYTHING® SERIES COVER DESIGNER Erin Alexander
LAYOUT DESIGNERS Colleen Cunningham, Elisabeth Lariviere, Ashley Vierra, Denise Wallace

Visit the entire Everything® series at www.everything.com

THE EVERYTHING® RICE COOKER COOKBOOK

Hui Leng Tay

Avon, Massachusetts

To my family, friends, and visitors at Teczcape—An Escape to Food
www.teczcape.blogspot.com

Copyright © 2010 by F+W Media, Inc. All rights reserved.
This book, or parts thereof, may not be reproduced
in any form without permission from the publisher; exceptions
are made for brief excerpts used in published reviews.

An Everything® Series Book.
Everything® and everything.com® are registered trademarks of F+W Media, Inc.

Published by Adams Media, a division of F+W Media, Inc.
57 Littlefield Street, Avon, MA 02322 U.S.A.
www.adamsmedia.com

ISBN 10: 1-4405-0233-1
ISBN 13: 978-1-4405-0233-0
eISBN 10: 1-4405-0234-X
eISBN 13: 978-1-4405-0234-7

Printed in the United States of America.

10 9 8 7 6 5 4 3 2 1

Library of Congress Cataloging-in-Publication Data
Tay, Hui Leng.
The everything rice cooker cookbook / Hui Leng Tay.
    p. cm.—(Everything)
Includes index.
ISBN 978-1-4405-0233-0
1. Cookery (Rice) I. Title.
TX809.R5T393 2010
641.6'318—dc22
                      2010009951

This publication is designed to provide accurate and authoritative information with regard to the subject matter covered. It is sold with the understanding that the publisher is not engaged in rendering legal, accounting, or other professional advice. If legal advice or other expert assistance is required, the services of a competent professional person should be sought.
—From a *Declaration of Principles* jointly adopted by a Committee of the American Bar Association and a Committee of Publishers and Associations

Many of the designations used by manufacturers and sellers to distinguish their products are claimed as trademarks. Where those designations appear in this book and Adams Media was aware of a trademark claim, the designations have been printed with initial capital letters.

*This book is available at quantity discounts for bulk purchases.
For information, please call 1-800-289-0963.*

Contents

Introduction vii

1 Boot Up the Rice Cooker 1
2 Essential Basics. 11
3 Sensational Starters 19
4 Soup du Jour 38
5 The Mighty Rice 56
6 Comfort Congee (Rice Porridge) and Grains 81
7 Pasta Fusion 90
8 Oodling Noodles 104
9 Fish 124
10 Shrimp, Scallops, and Clams 142
11 Chicken 159
12 Pork. 177
13 Beef 191
14 Legumes and Beans 205
15 Eggs 218
16 Tofu. 232
17 Vegetables 243
18 Mushrooms. 259
19 Desserts 272
20 Tips, Leftover Tricks, and More 283

Appendix: Basic Rice Cooker Features 289
Index. 290

Acknowledgments

To the team at Adams Media, for giving me the opportunity; without their support, this book would not have been completed. To my husband, Khim Hong, for being understanding, patient, and supportive at all times. He wants me to be happy in whatever I do. To my parents and siblings, for standing by me, always ready to show care and concern. To Ari and Stella who have encouraged me to persevere. To other friends who have shown their care for me and the progress of this book—I cannot possibly list all your names here but you know who you are and you have my appreciation.

Introduction

OFTEN YOU DO NOT realize that life's basic conveniences are just beside you. I am not referring to store-bought frozen pizza or that tub of ice cream, but technologies that are created to make life easier. The rice cooker was considered a kitchen revolution when it was invented in Japan in the 1950s as it changed the lives of many homemakers in that country, where cooking rice in traditional ways was time-consuming. However, the use of rice cookers for anything other than rice was considered a sign of laziness and moral corruption that is characteristic of those who cannot be bothered with getting their wok down.

However, when it comes to home cooking, the rice cooker is indeed a kitchen revolution, and not just in Japan. Being able to whip up nutritious, healthy, and tasty meals without wasting a huge amount of time is still the key. The rice cooker can help achieve that. True, the rice cooker is not the only cooking tool that could do this, and its versatility may have been overshadowed by the one-pot cooking often talked about with slow cookers. But, the rice cooker can be your one-pot cooker too! It is a simple machine to operate and can bring you nutritious, healthy, and easy cooking, using the fresh ingredients and basic pantry items that are the linchpins of a good diet.

How versatile is the rice cooker? You can steam, stew, stir-fry, braise, sauté . . . almost like a portable stovetop! You can cook in the rice cooker the same way you cook with a pan on the stove, since the rice cooker can generate its own heat. Many of your daily recipes can be easily adapted to rice cookers. In fact, much home cooking is gradually moving away from the rigidity of traditional recipes and advocating improvisational cooking as an even quicker and easier way to make everyday meals. Building on successful meals is not difficult as long as the dishes can be deconstructed into basics: ingredients, taste, balance, flavors, and the correct techniques. Similarly, rice cooker cooking also starts with building a foundation—the correct technique; then you can make changes by experimenting. Such little experiments in each recipe will allow you to learn new flavors every day, and hopefully allow you to improvise and be creative in the process of working with your new tool.

This book's goal is to empower you with the knowledge of how to use the rice cooker more than to teach you perfect recipes. The focus will be on the technique and process. Rice cooker cooking is really a lot about careful planning and the sequence during cooking. Most (if not all) of the cooking in this cookbook has been done in the rice cooker. This is to really bring out the "real deal" in rice cooker cooking, which is that the cooker can stand alone, playing a primary role in your kitchen.

For those who already own a rice cooker and are already using it, mainly to cook rice and simple dishes, there is a much larger variety of recipes to explore, from nourishing soups to hearty meals. For those who do not yet own a rice cooker and are thinking of getting one, this can be a good starter guide on how to use the rice cooker for simple and appetizing recipes. Enjoy!

CHAPTER 1

Boot Up the Rice Cooker

This book does not advocate the rice cooker as the *only* appliance you should own in the kitchen, completely replacing your stovetop cooking or one-pot slow cooker. Rather, it hopes to present the rice cooker as a complementary tool in the kitchen, an additional helper that assists you as you whip up a new repertoire of simple home-based recipes. The process of rice cooker cooking should be enjoyed. It cannot be emphasized enough that this style of cooking is really about techniques, including the cooking sequence, knowing the ingredients well, experimenting, and building the experience. With that, this book starts you with a precious grain of rice and leaves you with an open mind toward the possibilities of your rice cooker.

Have You Eaten Your Rice Today?

It is not strange to hear this greeting, as a friendly, cheery form of "Hello" in Chinese communities around the world. It is also common to hear workers protecting their "iron rice bowl," meaning their stable occupation. The popular Seven Necessities that Chinese people considered important in a household are firewood, rice, oil, salt, soy sauce, vinegar, and tea. It's not difficult to explain the importance of rice in the sequence! Rice has been associated with many traditions and cultures around the world. In Sanskrit, the word for "rice" also meant "sustainer of the human race." Indeed, rice is a staple for a large part of the world's population, especially in Asia, where more than 75 percent of the world's rice is harvested.

The precise origins of rice are lost to history, but it is believed that rice was probably domesticated, after wheat and barley, in a few places such as the Yangtze Valley in China and India, in 6500 B.C. It finally became a staple crop in the United States in the late 1600s. During this time journey, rice also reached Japan, Southeast Asia, the Middle East, and Europe. Today each region utilizes rice either as part of cultivation, or as a staple in the diet.

> Rice is easy to digest, naturally sodium- and cholesterol-free, and contains only a trace of fat. It is also rich in proteins, with a good balance of the essential amino acids required by the human body systems. The amount of essential amino acid—lysine—is one and a half times that of wheat, and twice that of corn.

The freshest and healthiest grains go through many steps from the point of harvest to finally being sold on the shelves. These include sieving (a destoner to remove gravel, magnet to remove metal bits, and color sorter to remove seeds and fragments); hulling, to remove the husk; milling, to go from brown to white; polishing, to ensure the rice is shiny and attractive, and cleaning, to extend storage life.

Rice Surprise

Rice has a far richer diversity than the average supermarket shelf suggests. There are more than 40,000 different varieties of rice, but not all are grown commercially. Different types of rice may also have different levels of starch, causing one type of rice to be "stickier" or "looser" than another. Rice is generally categorized into whole-grain or white rice, as well as by the length of the grain. Whole-grain rice is minimally processed and so retains a nutrient-rich husk. Since whole-grain rice is not husked, the cooking time typically is longer than that for milled white rice. Whole-grain rice tends to be more flavorful, aromatic, and colorful. The most common variety of whole-grain rice is brown rice; the lesser-known types are black rice and red rice.

Black rice is a rice grain that looks like wild rice when dry. It turns deep purple when cooked and has rich and nutty flavors. The glutinous variety is the black sticky rice, which is used mainly in many Chinese and Southeast Asian desserts. Red rice is unpolished, and the color of the bran is typically maroon-red with the smell of husk. Also known as red cargo rice, it has a chewy texture compared to white rice, and tastes nutty when cooked.

White rice is often referred to as "polished" since the outer husk is removed, and the layers of bran are milled until the grain is white. White rice requires less cooking and has a milder flavor. It also has less nutritional value than the whole-grain variety.

Milled white rice is versatile and can be eaten plain, served with curries and vegetables, or cooked as flavored rice. The popular aromatic or Jasmine rice variety exudes a mild fragrance when cooked. White glutinous rice is short and plump with a chalky white, opaque kernel. When cooked, it loses shape and becomes sticky. It is very starchy, often cooked by steaming, and typically used in desserts.

Rice can also be defined by the length of its grain:

- **Long-grain rice** has a long, slender kernel, four to five times longer than its width. When cooked, grains are separate, light, and fluffy. Jasmine rice, a popular Thai variety, tends to be more moist and clings together, when compared to the Indian basmati rice, which cooks to separate grains that are drier and fluffier. Basmati rice maintains its distinct shape when cooked and is ideal with curries and stews.
- **Medium-grain rice** has a shorter, wider kernel than long-grain rice. Cooked grains are more moist and tender, and have a greater tendency to cling together than long grain. Arborio rice is an Italian short- to medium-grain variety often used when making risotto and paella dishes. Such grains absorb cooking liquid and remain dense without losing their distinct shape.
- **Short-grain rice** is short, plump, and has an almost round kernel. Cooked grains are soft and cling together. This variety of sticky rice is eaten as a staple in Japan and Korea. It is also commonly used when making sushi rice as the starch released produces the stickiness that is required when making sushi rolls.

Parboiled rice is unhusked rice that has gone through a steam-pressure process before milling, giving the rice a stronger flavor. This procedure also gelatinizes the starch in the grain, and ensures a firmer, more separate grain. This rice is favored by consumers and chefs who desire extra fluffy and separate cooked rice.

Rice and Cuisine

Rice traces back to the pastoral traditions and historical lifestyles in different parts of the world. Notably, rice has shaped and defined the varied cuisines of Asia. As the keeping of livestock was not historically the lifestyle in parts of Asia, such as in the East and Southeast Asia, there were fewer opportunities to consume meat and dairy products. These parts of Asia became rice-growing regions, and the local diet relied heavily on rice for nutrition. Rice became the main ingredient and centerpiece of every meal, often complemented with vegetables. Quite typically, a meal without rice was not considered a full meal. This important grain still is often served in the plainest way possible, with accompanying side dishes at each meal to provide a variety of flavors and more complete nutrition.

In parts of the world where animals were domesticated as part of a farm, rice does not necessarily accompany every meal as the main carbohydrate food for energy. Especially in the western Euro-Asian communities, including Western Asia and Europe, rice is usually flavored, generally cooked with flavorings, and often prepared using milk, cheese, or other dairy products.

In different regions of India, rice can be cooked plain or seasoned with ghee and spices as a base for *pulao* or *biryani*. In Sanskrit, *pulao* means "a bowl of rice" and refers to rice boiled with seasonings. Most *pulao* and *biryani* dishes are made with not just rice, but meat, vegetables, and beans. In many cases, the rice is sautéed in oil or butter with seasonings or spices before boiling. This same method of preparation was introduced to the Iberian Peninsula by the Arabs, where it became "paella," the saffron rice for which Spain is famous. The Spaniards brought this method with them to the Caribbean, where it further evolved in the context of Creole cuisine, as in the jambalaya of New Orleans. Meanwhile, rice cultivation had begun in the Po River Valley of Italy in the fourteenth century, where rice is boiled with meat and vegetables in a bouillon soup. This dish is known as "risotto."

Congee

Another rice dish that remains popular in most of Asia is rice gruel or rice porridge. Congee, or *Jook*, as it is referred to in different parts of Asia, is almost considered Asia's comfort food. Such a dish is easy to prepare—rice is cooked in plenty of water or broth and becomes a thick rice soup—and is regarded as most satisfying. Like cooked rice, plain rice porridge can be complemented with other flavorsome dishes. Congee is a comfort food, typically a breakfast food, and also was the basis for therapeutic treatment in ancient China.

ESSENTIAL

Congee is also prepared and used for religious ceremonies and festivals. For example, a Chinese congee, called *Laba Zhou*, is named to honor the eighth day of the twelfth moon, the day Buddha received enlightenment. On this day Buddhist temples prepare this congee with cereals, peas, dates, chestnuts, lotus seeds, and dried fruits. When this dish is prepared on other days, it is called eight-treasures porridge.

Similar to making flavored rice in the West, the water and broth can also be flavored when cooking congee, and there is almost no limit as to what ingredients, toppings, or condiments can be added. Chinese communities the world over would typically add ginger, green onions, and cilantro, while the Koreans sweeten their rice soup with honey, dates, and nuts. The Japanese flavor it with mushrooms and nori seaweed, while the Vietnamese prepare theirs with fish sauce and roasted peanuts. Typically, if a stronger-flavored broth base is desired, meat such as chicken, pork, or beef, or seafood such as shrimp and scallops, are used.

QUESTION

Why is congee or rice porridge often considered undesirable and less luxurious?
Rice porridge remains popular in most of Asia. Since this dish requires less rice than plain boiled rice to feed the same number of people, it is considered a poor man's meal in China. Because of this, on the first day of Chinese New Year people eat cooked fluffy rice for all meals. To eat rice porridge on this day is thought to mean hard times for the future. Further, due to the large proportion of water used, the final soft texture of the rice, and its nutritional value and ease of digestion, this dish is preferred for feeding babies, the elderly, and invalids. These factors all contribute to the less luxurious image of congee.

Cooking Rice Perfectly

One traditional way of cooking rice that still remains today is to bring rice and a small amount of water to a boil over the stovetop and simmer it over low heat until the water is almost gone; then let it stand and allow the remaining steam to be absorbed or to escape. The invention and commercialization of the rice cooker brings modernization and convenience to rice cooking, bypassing the stovetop. Traditional or modern, the basics of rice cooking remain essentially the same—the amount of water required depends on the type of equipment (or pot) used.

The degree to which you rinse the rice depends on how well you know its source. Typically, modern industry standards assure that rice is clean before it is packaged and sold on the shelves. Thus, there is no need to overdo the cleaning. Rinsing it sufficiently to remove any residual debris and foreign particles that may impact the flavor of the rice will be enough. To soak or not to soak the rice depends on the rice variety and sometimes the recipe you are using. For example, you will typically find glutinous rice dessert recipes that ask for the rice to be soaked to allow the grains to absorb enough water to be steamed dry. Additionally, soaking also helps to remove excess starch in glutinous rice.

The bran layer of whole-grain rice such as brown rice contains fatty acids, and when not protected from the air, the outer layers of the kernel go rancid relatively quickly. It is recommended that you store your brown rice in the fridge in airtight containers, and use within a year. White rice can be stored at room temperature for up to a year.

Back to the most important element—water. There is really no perfect recipe when it comes to cooking rice. The standard measure when cooking long-grain white rice in the rice cooker is 1½ to 2 cups of water to 1 cup of rice. However, each type of rice requires a different amount of liquid due to different water absorption rates, so falling back to the cooking directions on the rice package or rice cooker might be a best bet. For instance, the medium- or short-grain variety of white rice may require less water than long grain, with the short-grain variety possibly requiring just up to 1 cup of water to 1 cup rice. As a general rule, you can reduce the amount of water used for long grain by ¼ to ½ cup per cup of rice when cooking medium or short grain. As already mentioned, whole-grain rice such as brown rice requires more water (2½ to 3 cups water to 1 cup of rice) and about a 60 to 70 percent longer cooking time than white rice.

Do not lift the lid to check on the rice when it is cooking. The cooking process depends on the development of steam inside the pot, so allowing the steam to escape by opening the lid may result in improperly cooked rice.

Instead of measuring with "cups," there are also graduated marks on the inside of many rice cookers indicating how much rice and water should be added. As these measures can never be accurate enough, there are also the popular "orthodox" (or rather, "unorthodox") ways of measuring the amount of water required for white rice: the 1-segment finger rule, the knuckle rule, the palm rule, or whatever you call it. For example, in the 1-segment finger rule, you measure rice into the pot, add what seems to be enough water, and place your pointer (or index) finger at the top of the rice. The water should just cover the first segment (crease) of your pointer finger. Accurate? Not exactly. Rather, these "rules of thumb" can be used as a guide to countercheck the amount of water used when cooking rice. Ultimately, it will still depend on the kind of rice you are cooking, the equipment you are using, and simply, how you prefer your rice.

The Miracle Cooker

The first commercial rice cooker was invented in Japan as recently as the 1950s. While the rice cooker does not have a very long history, it has certainly brought convenience to many homes around the world. No longer do you have to stand behind a stove and monitor rice cooking. A revolutionary device that boiled rice on its own—it was a miraculous invention! But you can do even more miracles with it.

If you disassemble an automatic rice cooker, you will find that it is little more than an aluminum pot sitting on top of an electric heating element. When given power (electricity), this device will progressively heat, simmer, boil, and finally, cook whatever is placed inside the pot. What does this sound like? A slow cooker? Cooking in a pan over the stovetop? Yes, indeed, there is heat to cook the food inside the rice cooker just as you would cook via stir-frying, sautéing, steaming, or stewing. The tricky part is how to control the heat during the interval between raw and cooked food. But aren't all other cooking methods similar? Many people, even those who have owned a rice cooker for years, are misled by the name and assume that a rice cooker is only useful for cooking rice. Quite the opposite is true. It is possible to cook an entire beef stew in a rice cooker, assuming you keep in mind that unlike a regular stew pot on a stove, the rice cooker has basically two temperatures: on and off. However, it is all about control and mastering the techniques.

Use a nonstick spoon that will not scratch the inside of the pot when "fluffing" the rice after it is done or stirring other food while cooking. The best tool for this purpose is a plastic rice paddle, which comes with most rice cookers. You can also use a wooden ladle. To keep the rice from sticking to the paddle, dampen the paddle with cold water.

Due to the simplicity, versatility, and size of rice cookers, they are popular especially among students living in college dormitories and people whose kitchens have only a limited workspace. However, it has also penetrated into the homes of many others due to its convenience. As is true of any other kitchen appliance, you need to know your rice cooker well. Not all electric slow cookers are created equal. Some cook hotter than others on the same settings, so "low" or "high" in one pot may not be the same as in another. However miraculous, the rice cooker really can't do (quite) everything. Most rice cookers are designed to accommodate temperatures of 100°C to 120°C (212°F to 248°F), with some electric cookers able to manage up to 140°C (284°F). In other words, it is not made for high-temperature cooking, and thus it is not advisable to roast or deep-fry in a rice cooker.

CHAPTER 1 **BOOT UP THE RICE COOKER**

Types of Rice Cookers

Although there seem to be many options on the market, there are essentially only a few basic types of cookers, grouped into two categories: on/off rice cookers and fuzzy logic rice cookers. Although all are electronic rice cookers, the on/off models may be referred to as direct heat rice cookers, while the fuzzy logic models may be referred to as electronic rice cookers.

The two common types of on/off rice cookers are the "cook and turn off" and the "cook and keep warm." The "cook and turn off" cooker cooks the rice, and then automatically shuts off the unit. This is the least expensive version of the appliance. There is no light indicator that indicates when the rice is done. The on/off switch simply flips to the off position when the rice is done. These basic cookers do not normally offer nonstick pans or steamer units, but if you only want to cook rice, it will serve the purpose.

The "cook and keep warm" rice cooker cooks the rice, then reduces the heat when the rice is done, maintaining it at a warm temperature (the way to switch it off completely is to unplug it). These rice cookers are considered the most flexible and allow adjustable heat control for cooking (steaming, stir-frying, and stewing) other food.

Then there is a very sophisticated version called the fuzzy logic rice cooker. This type cooker has sophisticated electronic features such as a porridge-cycle button, reheat function button, quick cook function button, cake function button, and even texture setting button. All you have to do is press the button. It is a great machine, but expensive compared to other similar kitchen appliances (or pots) such as the slow cooker. This type of model buys you more convenience, but because it is operated by fuzzy logic sensors, it is hard to guess or even know how the heat is progressing, or how to control the heat while cooking. Nothing beats the flexibility of the basic on/off cooker and the variety of dishes that can be prepared in it—with user interaction, of course.

> Some rice cookers are designed to accommodate a basket above the rice. This basket is generally used to steam vegetables, holding them in the steam coming off the rice. Most types of dumpling and buns can also be cooked this way.

CHAPTER 2

Essential Basics

Long-Grain White Rice
12

Brown Rice
12

Sushi Rice
13

Rice Congee
14

Warm Oats
14

Pasta
15

Marinara Sauce
15

Chicken Stock
16

Pork Stock
16

Shrimp Stock
17

Vegetable Stock
18

Soybean Stock
18

Long-Grain White Rice

The standard measure for cooking long-grain white rice is 1½ cups (12 ounces) water to 1 cup (8 ounces) rice. Countercheck with the "knuckle method": The water should come up to the first knuckle of your index finger.

INGREDIENTS | SERVES 2

1 cup long-grain white rice
1½ cups water

Rice Rinsing Tips

When rinsing rice, gently swirl the rice in the pot with 2 or 3 changes of water, draining off the water each time. It is not necessary to rinse until the water is completely clear, as nutrients may be lost in the rinsing process.

1. Rinse rice well by gently swirling the rice in the rice cooker pot with 2 or 3 changes of cold water. Drain rice.

2. Add the 1½ cups water to the cooker pot. The water should cover the rice by about ½ inch. Place the pot back into the rice cooker, cover, and set to Cook. Time to cook varies with the type of rice cooker used.

3. After rice is cooked, do not open the cover immediately. Let it sit for 5 to 10 minutes to vent off the remaining steam. Fluff up the rice before serving.

Brown Rice

Brown rice has a thick bran layer that is coated with a waxy layer, and it is difficult for moisture to penetrate these layers. The cooking time for brown rice typically increases, while the cooking process remains the same.

INGREDIENTS | SERVES 2

1 cup brown rice
2 cups water

1. Rinse rice well by gently swirling the rice in the cooker pot with 2 or 3 changes of cold water. Drain rice.

2. Add 2 cups water to the cooker pot. Water should cover the rice by about ¾ inch. Place the pot back into the rice cooker, cover, and set to Cook. Time to cook varies with the type of rice cooker used.

3. After rice is cooked, do not open the cover immediately. Let it sit for 5 to 10 minutes to vent off the remaining steam. Fluff up the rice before serving.

Sushi Rice

A Sushi Oke (or Hangiri) is a large, flat-bottomed wooden mixing tub, traditionally used when seasoning sushi rice. A nonmetallic container prevents interaction between rice vinegar (seasoning for sushi rice) and any metallic surfaces. The large mixing surface allows the hot rice to cool rapidly.

INGREDIENTS | YIELDS 4 TO 5 CUPS COOKED RICE

2 cups Japanese sushi rice
3 cups cold water
½ cup rice vinegar
¼ cup white sugar
1 teaspoon salt

Before Rolling Your Sushi

Before rolling your sushi, "fan" the rice by folding the rice frequently to cool it and remove moisture from the rice. This process gives sushi rice its signature sticky texture and glossy shine. When cooled, keep the rice at room temperature (not more than 2 hours), covered with a clean, damp towel. Do not refrigerate the rice, as it will harden.

1. Rinse rice well by gently swirling the rice in the cooker pot with 2 or 3 changes of cold water. Drain rice.

2. Add the 3 cups cold water to the cooker pot. Place the pot back into the rice cooker, cover, and set to Cook. Time to cook varies with the type of rice cooker used.

3. While the rice is being cooked, prepare the vinegar mixture in a pan on the stovetop. Add rice vinegar, sugar, and salt into the pan and mix well, until the sugar dissolves. Pour the vinegar mixture into a small bowl; set aside to cool.

4. Spread the cooked rice into a large nonmetallic plate or bowl. Sprinkle the vinegar mixture over the rice and fold it into the rice with a plastic rice spatula in a spiral pattern, starting from the outside. Be careful not to smash the rice. Continue in this fashion until all of the vinegar is used.

CHAPTER 2 **ESSENTIAL BASICS**

Rice Congee

This is a type of rice porridge eaten in many Asian countries. In different parts of China, rice congee is enjoyed sweet or savory. Congee is also common as breakfast food in many places, such as Japan, Hong Kong, Singapore, and Malaysia.

INGREDIENTS | SERVES 2

1 cup long-grain white rice

3 to 4 cups water, according to desired consistency

A Healthy Mix of Rice Grains

You can use different rice grains (red, brown, and white) when cooking rice or rice congee to introduce different flavors and texture. However, cooking two or more kinds of rice grains together can be challenging, as they will require different amounts of water and different cooking times. Combining grains is easier when making rice congee, because the proportions of rice and water are not as strict as they are for cooking rice used in other dishes.

1. Rinse rice well by gently swirling the rice in the cooker pot with 2 or 3 changes of cold water. Drain rice.

2. Add 3 to 4 cups water to the pot, cover, and set to Cook. When you hear the rice cooker making noises and see over-bubbling of fluid at the lid, lift up the rice cooker cover, stir the congee, and continue to cook for about 15 minutes with rice cooker lid tilted slightly to vent the steam pressure.

3. Continue cooking and adjust water amount depending on whether you prefer thick or soupy rice congee.

Warm Oats

Garnish cooked oats with fruits and nuts to add color and variety. Bananas do not require further cooking and work well with cooked oats.

INGREDIENTS | SERVES 1 OR 2

5 cups water (adjusted as needed during cooking)

3 cups rolled oats

1 tablespoon honey

1. Add water to rice cooker, cover, and set to Cook. When the water boils, lift up the rice cooker lid, stir in the oats, then the honey, and stir continuously to combine.

2. Cook for about 5 minutes, until oats are cooked through. Add water as necessary, depending on preference for final consistency.

Pasta

The use of salt when boiling pasta enhances the flavor of the pasta. The recommendation is about a tablespoon of salt per gallon of boiling water.

INGREDIENTS | SERVES 2

6 to 8 cups water
½ pound pasta
1 to 2 teaspoons salt, to taste

The "Sticky" Issue

If your pasta is sticky, do not add oil and stir it more! Oil will not prevent the pasta from sticking and in fact, may have the undesired effect of coating the pasta, preventing it from combining well with your sauce. Pasta tends to stick together if it is not stirred during the critical first moments of cooking.

1. Add the water to the rice cooker, cover, and set to Cook. When the water boils, lift up the rice cooker lid, add the pasta and salt, and stir the pasta gently to prevent pasta sticking to the base of the pot.

2. Cover the rice cooker and allow pasta to cook for about 8 to 12 minutes, until al dente or done to your taste.

Marinara Sauce

The base for this sauce is made from olive oil, ripe tomatoes, garlic, and herbs. Add some red chili pepper flakes to spice up the sauce.

INGREDIENTS | SERVES 2

2 tablespoons extra-virgin olive oil
1 medium-sized onion, chopped
3 cloves garlic, finely minced
1 (14½-ounce) can diced tomatoes, with liquid
½ cup water or stock
Salt and freshly ground black pepper, to taste
½ teaspoon dried oregano
½ teaspoon dried basil

1. Add oil to the rice cooker, cover, and set to Cook. When the base of the inner pot gets warm in about 3 minutes, add the onions and fry for about 5 minutes until onions are slightly soft.

2. Add garlic and fry for about 1 to 2 minutes until fragrant.

3. Stir in tomatoes and liquid, water or stock, salt, and pepper. Cover rice cooker and allow to cook for about 5 minutes. Switch to Warm when the mixture bubbles vigorously and continue on Warm setting for another 5 minutes to allow the sauce to simmer.

4. Sprinkle in dried oregano and basil and mix well. If serving immediately with precooked pasta, add the pasta to the pot and mix well.

CHAPTER 2 ESSENTIAL BASICS

Chicken Stock

Depending on your family's typical usage, you can divide the chicken stock into smaller airtight containers, then either store in the fridge (keeps about 3 days) or store in the freezer (about 1 to 2 months).

INGREDIENTS | YIELDS ABOUT 4 CUPS

5 cups cold water, or enough to immerse the chicken
2 pounds chicken parts (bones, back, necks)
1-inch piece fresh ginger, sliced
4 green onions, cut into finger-length pieces
Salt, to taste

1. Add water, chicken parts, ginger, and green onions into the rice cooker. Cover and set to Cook.

2. When the water boils, switch the rice cooker to Warm, and allow the mixture to simmer.

3. After 1 hour of cooking, lift up the rice cooker lid and skim the top of the stock. Add the salt, cover rice cooker, then continue to simmer on Warm for another hour.

4. Remove the solids and discard them. Strain the stock before transferring to containers.

Pork Stock

Chicken bones are sometimes added when making pork stock to introduce more flavors and depth to the base stock.

INGREDIENTS | YIELDS ABOUT 4 CUPS

5 cups cold water or more as needed to immerse the pork bones
2 pounds pork bones
3 stalks celery, coarsely chopped
2 carrots, coarsely chopped to bite-sized cubes
1 onion, coarsely chopped
Salt, to taste

1. Add water, pork bones, celery, carrots, and onions into the rice cooker. Cover and set to Cook.

2. When the water boils, switch the rice cooker to Warm and allow to simmer.

3. After 1 hour of cooking, lift up the rice cooker lid and skim the top of the stock. Add the salt, cover the rice cooker, and continue to simmer on Warm for another hour.

4. Remove the solids and discard them. Strain the stock before transferring to containers.

Shrimp Stock

Add some shrimp stock to boost the flavor of seafood-based noodle and rice dishes.

INGREDIENTS | YIELDS ABOUT 3 CUPS

1 tablespoon vegetable oil

1 tablespoon finely chopped pancetta or bacon

Heads, shells, and tails from 2 pounds shrimp (see note below)

4 cups water

1. Add oil to the rice cooker, cover, and set to Cook. When the base of the inner pot gets warm, add the pancetta or bacon and fry for about 1 to 2 minutes, until fragrant. When fried, the pancetta or bacon will release more oil.

2. Add the shrimp heads, shells, and tails and fry in pot for about 2 to 3 minutes, covering rice cooker occasionally in the process of frying. Add the water, cover rice cooker, and allow stock to come to a boil.

3. Once boiling, switch the rice cooker to Warm, and simmer covered for 30 minutes. Remove the solids and discard them. Strain the stock before transferring to containers.

Save Up for Shrimp Stock

Whenever you eat shrimp, remember to save (and freeze) the leftover shells in small batches (sealed in airtight containers or bags). A family of two typically takes at least 2 months to accumulate enough leftover shrimp shells to make 3 cups of shrimp stock!

Vegetable Stock

This stock is useful when preparing vegetarian dishes, and when cooking dishes that would be overpowered by the strong flavors of meat-based stocks.

INGREDIENTS | YIELDS ABOUT 3 CUPS

4 cups cold water or more as needed to immerse the vegetables
3 stalks celery, stems coarsely chopped, retaining leaves
1 medium-sized onion, sliced
2 carrots, coarsely chopped into cubes
2 bay leaves
Salt, to taste

1. Add the water to the pot, cover, and set to Cook. When the water boils, add all the ingredients except salt; cover rice cooker, and bring everything to a boil again.

2. Switch to Warm, add salt to taste, cover rice cooker, and simmer for 1 hour. Remove the solids and discard them. Strain the stock before transferring to containers.

Soybean Stock

Plain boiled soybeans are amazingly delicious and nutritious. The cooking liquid is another alternative to vegetable stock.

INGREDIENTS | YIELDS ABOUT 4 CUPS

½ pound dried soybeans, soaked in water overnight, drained and rinsed before using (see note below)
5 cups water
Salt, to taste

1. Pour the 5 cups water into the rice cooker, cover, and set to Cook. When the water boils, add the prepared soybeans. Cover rice cooker and boil for 30 minutes. Stir occasionally and skim off the foam that rises to the surface of the water.

2. Switch the rice cooker to Warm and simmer to soften and cook the beans for about 1 hour, until tender.

3. Stir in salt, to your taste. Remove the solids and discard them. Strain the stock before transferring to containers.

Cooking Tip

Soaking the dried soybeans shortens the cooking time and improves their flavor and texture. Let the soybeans soak in water (about 5 cups water per ½ pound of beans) at room temperature for about 6 to 8 hours, or overnight. Before cooking, drain and rinse the beans. Or, to accelerate the soaking process, cook the soybeans in boiling water (about 5 cups water per ½ pound of beans) for 5 minutes, then allow the beans to soak in cooking water for about 1 hour. Before proceeding with the recipe, drain and rinse the beans.

CHAPTER 3

Sensational Starters

Fish Cakes
20

Tuna-Cheese Patties
21

Salmon Patties
22

Mini Fish Kebabs
23

Fish Salad
24

Chicken Satay
25

Bacon, Onion, and Potato Hash
26

Potato, Bell Pepper, and Mushroom Hash
27

Mashed Sweet Potatoes
28

Savory Taro Patties
29

Mini Ham and Corn Omelets
29

Stuffed Tomatoes
30

Hotshot Sweet Corn
31

Dim Sum: Steamed Meatballs
31

Dim Sum: Healthy Chicken Siu Mai
32

Dim Sum: Steamed Tofu
33

Mini Indonesian Potato Cakes
34

Seafood Napa Cabbage Rolls
35

Tofu Cabbage Rolls
36

Spicy Fish Custard
37

Fish Cakes

A croquette is essentially a fried cake of mashed potato, meat, or fish, often coated with flour or bread crumbs before frying. You can use either cooked fresh fish or canned fish for this recipe.

INGREDIENTS | YIELDS 4 TO 5 CAKES

1 medium-sized potato, unpeeled
1 fish fillet, snapper or sea bass
½ tablespoon butter
1 teaspoon lemon juice
½ cup chopped parsley
3 to 4 tablespoons flour (enough to coat the fish cakes)
1 egg, lightly whisked
3 tablespoons vegetable oil

Cooking Tip

Do not over-mash the potatoes; a good fish cake should not be mushy. A smooth and slightly chunky mixture of fish and potatoes provides the perfect texture and bite.

1. Fill the rice cooker pot with water to about the 4-cup mark (or sufficient amount to immerse the potato). Cover the rice cooker and set to Cook. While the water is heating, put the fish on a plate that will fit in the steamer basket or insert. Cover the fish with plastic wrap to prevent excess condensation.

2. When the water boils, add the potato. At the same time, place the steamer insert or basket that holds the plate of fish into the rice cooker. Cover the rice cooker and steam for 6 to 8 minutes. Remove steamed fish and drain excess liquid from it. Remove the potato.

3. Peel the potato and mash it gently with the back of a fork, stirring in the butter at the same time. Flake the steamed fish and add it, the lemon juice, and the parsley to the mashed potato and mix well. Shape into round cakes and then chill for 30 minutes to help them firm up.

4. When ready to fry, dip the fish cakes in the flour, then dip into the whisked egg and flatten the cake.

5. Clean out the rice cooker and wipe dry. Add oil to the rice cooker and set to Cook. When the base of the cooker pot gets warm, add the fish cakes and pan-fry for about 5 minutes on each side, until golden brown and cooked through. Be sure to cover rice cooker while frying.

Tuna-Cheese Patties

Patties, cakes, and croquettes are similar, though differently named. A patty, which usually is circular and flat, is made of a combination of chopped or minced ingredients, and usually is not dipped in bread crumbs before cooking.

INGREDIENTS | SERVES 4

2 tablespoons butter
¼ cup flour
¼ teaspoon salt
½ cup milk
1 (6-ounce) can tuna in water, flaked
3 ounces shredded mozzarella cheese
½ cup finely chopped cilantro
1 egg, lightly whisked
3 tablespoons oil for pan-frying

1. Add butter to the rice cooker, cover, and set to Cook. When the butter melts, add the flour and salt and mix well.

2. Slowly add the milk, stirring, until mixture thickens.

3. Add the tuna and cheese and mix well, until cheese melts. When cool enough to handle, slowly add in the milk mixture into the egg (gradually tempering the egg), then add cilantro, mix well, and form into patties and chill for 30 minutes.

4. Meanwhile, clean out rice cooker and wipe dry. Add oil to the rice cooker and set to Cook. When oil is hot pan-fry the tuna patties 3 to 5 minutes each side, being sure to cover the rice cooker while cooking each side, until golden brown.

Salmon Patties

You can use finely chopped parsley, basil, or even green onions instead of cilantro.

INGREDIENTS | SERVES 4 AS A SIDE DISH

1 egg, lightly whisked
2 (6-ounce) cans salmon, flaked
¼ cup finely chopped cilantro leaves
Salt and freshly ground black pepper, to taste
2 tablespoons vegetable oil
4 small lemon wedges

Leftover Tips
Grilled fish leftovers tend to become dry under subsequent reheating. If you had grilled fish leftovers from the night before, you can break the leftover fish into flakes for use in these patties.

1. Stir half of the whisked egg into the salmon, add cilantro, and mix well. Continue to add remaining egg to mixture and mix well until the egg is absorbed by the salmon and the mixture can be formed into firm patties. Season with salt and pepper.

2. Add oil to the rice cooker, cover, and set to Cook.

3. When the base of the cooker pot gets warm, form flat patties (about 1½-inch diameter) from the mixture and add to the rice cooker. Pan-fry the patties (about 2 to 3 minutes per side), until their surface turns brown and slightly crisp, making sure to cover the rice cooker while frying. Serve with squeeze of lemon.

Mini Fish Kebabs

Skewer the fish cubes with green onions, pineapples, and green or red bell peppers to add variety and color.

INGREDIENTS | YIELDS ABOUT 10 TO 14 MINI SKEWERS

2 whole cloves garlic, peeled and crushed
2 teaspoons grated ginger
½ teaspoon turmeric
1 teaspoon fish sauce
2 tablespoons lime juice
1 teaspoon brown sugar
¼ teaspoon red chili pepper flakes
3 tablespoons extra-virgin olive oil
2 fish fillets (threadfin, snapper), sliced into 1-inch cubes
1 tablespoon vegetable oil
2 to 3 lime wedges

1. Combine garlic, ginger, turmeric, fish sauce, lime juice, brown sugar, red chili pepper flakes, and olive oil in a bowl. Add fish and marinate for 10 minutes in the fridge.

2. Thread marinated fish onto short skewers about 4 inches in length (or a length that can fit the diameter of the rice cooker), about 2 fish cubes per skewer.

3. Add oil to the rice cooker, cover, and set to Cook. When the base of the cooker pot gets warm, add the skewered fish (work in batches) and pan-fry the fish for about 5 minutes on each side until golden brown and cooked through, being sure to cover the rice cooker while frying. Use kitchen tongs to help hold the skewer and turn the fish, if necessary.

4. Transfer the mini skewers to a serving platter and serve with lime wedges.

Fish Salad

Lettuce and cucumber tend to contain more moisture and may make the entire salad wet and unappetizing. Drain excess liquid while preparing the ingredients, including the liquid from the steamed fish.

INGREDIENTS | SERVES 3 OR 4 AS A SIDE DISH

2 fish fillets (snapper, salmon, or mackerel)

5 or 6 lettuce leaves, finely sliced into thin shreds

1 shallot, thinly sliced

½ cup medley of finely chopped fresh herbs (fresh mint, basil, and cilantro)

1 small cucumber, sliced

Dressing for Fish Salad

Combine 1 tablespoon fish sauce, 2 tablespoons lemon juice, ½ teaspoon sugar, and 1 stalk lemongrass (bruised white part) in a bowl. You can drizzle this light and refreshingly tangy dressing over the fish salad before serving.

1. Fill the rice cooker pot with water to about the 4-cup mark. Cover and set to Cook. While the water is heating, put the fish on a plate that will fit in the steamer basket or insert. Cover the fish with plastic wrap to prevent excess condensation during steaming.

2. When the water boils, place the steamer insert or basket that holds the plate of fish into the rice cooker. Cover the rice cooker and steam for 6 to 8 minutes, until the fish cooks through.

3. Remove the fish and set it aside to cool. Once cool, break it into bite-sized flakes. Drain excess liquid.

4. Toss the fish flakes with lettuce, shallots, herbs, and serve with cucumber.

Chicken Satay

Satay is a popular street food in parts of Southeast Asia, such as Indonesia, Singapore, Malaysia, and Thailand. This dish typically is seen as a skewer of marinated chicken, mutton, or beef strips, grilled or barbecued over a charcoal fire and dipped in spicy peanut sauce. Turmeric gives satay its signature yellow gloss.

INGREDIENTS | YIELDS ABOUT 16 TO 20 MINI SKEWERS

2 teaspoons curry power
1 teaspoon turmeric
½ teaspoon salt
1 teaspoon brown sugar
½ teaspoon grated garlic
1 teaspoon grated fresh ginger
3 to 4 tablespoons vegetable oil, divided use
2 boneless chicken thighs, cut into 2½-inch long × ½-inch thick strips

Serving Suggestions

Pan-frying the satay is an alternative cooking method for homes that do not own an outdoor grill and do not like to deal with the mess of charcoal and smoke. Serve the satay with sliced red onions, sliced cucumbers, rice cakes (also known as *ketupat*), and Peanut Sauce (page 287).

1. Combine curry powder, turmeric, salt, brown sugar, garlic, ginger, and 1 tablespoon of the oil in a gallon-size plastic food bag. Add the chicken pieces, seal the bag, and turn the bag a few times to make sure the chicken pieces are coated with the marinade. Refrigerate and allow to marinate for 2 hours.

2. Thread the chicken pieces onto short skewers (about 4 inches long, or a length that can fit the diameter of your rice cooker).

3. Add remaining oil into the rice cooker, cover, and set to Cook. When the base of the cooker pot gets warm, add the skewered chicken (work in batches) and pan-fry the chicken for about 5 minutes on each side until browned and cooked through, being sure to cover the rice cooker while pan-frying. Use kitchen tongs to help hold the skewers and turn the chicken over, if necessary. Serve with Peanut Sauce (page 287).

Bacon, Onion, and Potato Hash

*To "hash" means to chop foods into small pieces.
A standard hash is a great way to use up leftover meat and potatoes.*

INGREDIENTS | SERVES 2 AS A SIDE DISH

2 potatoes, whole and unpeeled
1 tablespoon extra-virgin olive oil
1 medium-sized onion, thinly sliced
4 slices bacon, roughly chopped
1 clove garlic, finely minced
Salt and freshly ground black pepper, to taste

1. Fill the rice cooker pot with water to about the 4-cup mark (or sufficient to immerse the potatoes). Cover the rice cooker and set to Cook.

2. When the water boils, add the potatoes to the water, cover the rice cooker, and cook for about 10 minutes.

3. Remove the potatoes and allow to cool. When cool, peel and cube the potatoes. Set aside.

4. Clean out the rice cooker and wipe dry. Add the oil to the rice cooker, cover, and set to Cook. When the base of the cooker pot gets warm, add the onions and fry about 5 minutes until onions are slightly tender.

5. Add the potato cubes. Continue frying for about 3 minutes, covering rice cooker while cooking.

6. Add bacon, garlic, salt, and pepper and fry for 5 minutes, covering rice cooker while cooking and stirring occasionally, until potatoes are golden and tender.

Potato, Bell Pepper, and Mushroom Hash

This is a vegetarian version of hash. Vary the kind of vegetables according to your personal preferences. Pumpkin can be a good lower-carbohydrate alternative to potatoes.

INGREDIENTS | SERVES 2 AS A SIDE DISH

2 potatoes, whole and unpeeled
1 tablespoon extra-virgin olive oil
1 medium-sized onion, thinly sliced
½ green bell pepper, seeded and sliced
½ red bell pepper, seeded and sliced
4 to 6 white mushrooms, sliced
1 egg, lightly whisked
Salt and freshly ground black pepper, to taste

Potato Tips

Potatoes can be broadly grouped into starchy (most starch), waxy (less starch), and medium starchy (in between starchy and waxy). Starchy potato varieties, such as russets, are good for frying, and therefore for use in this recipe, because they break up slightly during frying and absorb flavors quite well.

1. Fill the rice cooker pot with water to about the 4-cup mark (or sufficient to immerse the potatoes). Cover and set to Cook.

2. When the water in the rice cooker boils, add the potatoes to the water, cover the rice cooker, and cook for about 10 minutes.

3. Remove the potatoes and set aside to cool. Once cool, peel and cube the potatoes. Set aside.

4. Clean out the rice cooker and wipe dry. Add oil to the rice cooker, cover, and set to Cook. When the base of the cooker pot gets warm, add the onions and fry about 5 minutes until onions are slightly tender.

5. Add the potato cubes and pan-fry for about 3 minutes, being sure to cover rice cooker occasionally while cooking.

6. Add bell peppers, mushrooms, egg, salt, and pepper, and fry for about 5 minutes (scramble the eggs into smaller pieces), being sure to cover the rice cooker occasionally while cooking. Continue to cook, stirring occasionally, until potatoes are golden and tender.

CHAPTER 3 **SENSATIONAL STARTERS**

Mashed Sweet Potatoes

Sweet potatoes have a buttery flesh and sweet taste, making these tubers enjoyable simply mashed.

INGREDIENTS | SERVES 2 OR 3

2 medium sweet potatoes, peeled and cut into 2-inch chunks
2 tablespoons butter
1 tablespoon brown sugar
½ cup milk
Salt and freshly ground black pepper, to taste

1. Fill the rice cooker pot with water to about the 4-cup mark. Cover and set to Cook. While the water is heating, place the sweet potatoes on a plate that fits into the steamer insert or basket.

2. When the water boils, place the steamer insert or basket that holds the plate of sweet potatoes into the rice cooker. Cover the rice cooker and steam for 15 to 20 minutes, until the sweet potatoes cook through. Remove and set aside to cool in a large bowl.

3. Clean out the rice cooker and wipe dry. Cover rice cooker and set to Cook. Add the butter and sugar to melt. Slowly stir in milk and cover rice cooker for about 30 seconds.

4. When mixture starts to boil, stir well and switch off the rice cooker.

5. Ladle the milk mixture into the sweet potatoes and mash until smooth. Season with salt and pepper and serve warm.

Savory Taro Patties

In Singapore, Malaysia, and other Southeast Asian countries, "yam" and "taro" mean the same vegetable. In the United States, however, sweet potatoes are sometimes mistakenly referred to as yams; which would be different from taro.

INGREDIENTS | YIELDS 4 TO 6 PATTIES

3 cups finely shredded taro
½ teaspoon salt
½ teaspoon ground white pepper
2 green onions, finely chopped
1 tablespoon toasted sesame seeds
2 tablespoons vegetable oil, divided use

Cooking Tip
Prior to adding oil or water to the rice cooker, you can use the cooker to "dry fry" or toast the sesame seeds on the Cook setting for a few minutes until slightly fragrant. Just take care not to burn the seeds.

1. Combine taro, salt, pepper, green onions, and sesame seeds in a deep mixing bowl; mix well.

2. Add 1 tablespoon oil to the rice cooker, cover, and set to Cook. Shape the taro mixture into flat, round patties (press firm with palms).

3. When the base of the cooker pot gets warm, pan-fry the patties (work in batches) for 2 to 3 minutes on each side until golden brown and crispy on the surface, being sure to cover the rice cooker while cooking. Serve warm when ready.

Mini Ham and Corn Omelets

If you don't have time to work in batches to create individual mini omelets, create a regular-sized omelet and then use a cookie cutter to cut out presentable bite-sized appetizer omelets.

INGREDIENTS | SERVES 3 OR 4 AS A SIDE DISH

3 slices deli ham, finely diced
2 cups fresh corn kernels
2 tablespoons finely chopped green onions
2 eggs, lightly whisked
Salt and freshly ground black pepper, to taste
3 tablespoons vegetable oil, divided use

1. In a bowl, combine ham, corn kernels, and green onions. Add whisked egg; stir and combine well. Season with salt and pepper.

2. Add about half the quantity oil to the rice cooker, cover, and set to Cook. When the base of the cooker pot gets warm, make the mini omelets: Working in batches (adding remaining oil only when first batch of oil is used up), evenly space out 2-tablespoon amounts of the egg and corn mixture across the base of the pot. Pan-fry each side for about 2 minutes, until the edges of each mini omelet turn brown and crisp, being sure to cover the rice cooker while frying. Serve warm.

Stuffed Tomatoes

Replace the tomatoes with red or green bell peppers and make stuffed peppers when you wish.

INGREDIENTS | SERVES 3 OR 4

2 tablespoons extra-virgin olive oil
1 medium-sized onion, finely diced
2 cloves garlic, finely minced
1 teaspoon grated ginger
¼ teaspoon freshly ground black pepper
1 teaspoon curry powder
½ pound ground beef
3 tablespoons water
1 green chili pepper, seeded and thinly sliced
1 tablespoon finely chopped cilantro leaves
4 large tomatoes

Leftover Tip
Left with tomato flesh after the tomatoes are scooped out for stuffing? Use it to make Marinara Sauce (page 15).

1. Add the oil to the rice cooker pot, cover, and set to Cook. When the base of the pot gets warm, add the onions and fry for about 2 minutes or more, until onions become soft.

2. Add garlic, ginger, pepper, and curry powder and fry the mixture for 2 to 3 minutes.

3. Add the ground beef (break up into smaller bits) and fry for 2 to 3 minutes until uniformly browned.

4. Add the water, mix well, cover the rice cooker, and allow to cook for about 8 minutes. When mixture bubbles vigorously, switch to Warm and continue to cook for 8 more minutes, or until beef cooks through.

5. Lift the rice cooker lid, switch to Cook setting, add the green chili and cilantro, and fry for about 2 minutes, mixing well with the beef mixture. Dish out and set aside.

6. Cut the top off each tomato and scoop out the flesh. Spoon the beef mixture into the tomatoes and serve warm.

Hotshot Sweet Corn

Add Szechuan peppercorns if you want a spicy, tongue-numbing kick. You can also use cooked corn on the cob for this recipe. Simply fry the mixture and before serving, slather the buttered green onion–chili mix onto the corn on the cob.

INGREDIENTS | SERVES 4

½ tablespoon butter
4 green onions, finely chopped
1 teaspoon red chili pepper flakes
1 teaspoon freshly ground black pepper
¼ teaspoon salt
½ teaspoon brown sugar
1 (15-ounce) can whole kernel corn, drained

1. Add butter to the rice cooker, cover, and set to Cook.

2. When the base of the cooker pot gets warm, add the green onions, chili flakes, pepper, salt, and brown sugar, followed by corn kernels; fry for 2 minutes. Mix well. Cover the rice cooker and cook for about 2 minutes.

3. Serve on warm toasted bread, or even with steamed rice.

Dim Sum: Steamed Meatballs

If you have a bamboo steamer at home, line the base of the steamer with whole lettuce leaves and place the food item to be steamed on the leaves. This will prevent the food, especially meat items, from sticking to the bamboo material of the steamer.

INGREDIENTS | SERVES 2 OR 3

4 ounces ground beef
2 ounces ground pork
4 fresh shiitake mushroom caps, finely chopped
½ teaspoon salt
½ teaspoon white pepper
½ teaspoon sugar
1 teaspoon sesame oil
1 tablespoon Chinese cooking wine
1 tablespoon corn flour
2 green onions, finely chopped
¼ cup finely chopped cilantro
6 to 8 whole lettuce leaves

1. Combine the beef, pork, mushrooms, salt, pepper, sugar, sesame oil, Chinese cooking wine, corn flour, green onions, and cilantro. Set aside to marinate in the fridge for 1 hour.

2. After 1 hour, shape the mixture into round balls (about the size of golf balls) and set aside on a plate that fits into the steamer basket or insert.

3. Fill the rice cooker pot with water to about the 4-cup mark. Cover the rice cooker and set to Cook. When the water boils, place the steamer insert or basket that holds the plate of meatballs into the rice cooker. Cover the rice cooker and steam for 12 to 15 minutes until the meatballs are cooked.

Dim Sum: Healthy Chicken Siu Mai

Dim sum literally means "a touch of heart" in Chinese. Dim-sum items are usually served in small portions. Siu Mai is typically three dumplings steamed and served in a small bamboo steamer.

INGREDIENTS | SERVES 4 TO 6 (YIELDS ABOUT 10 TO 12 DUMPLINGS)

½ pound ground chicken
1 cup blanched (frozen) spinach, thawed and drained of excess liquid
½ teaspoon salt
½ teaspoon ground white pepper
1 teaspoon light soy sauce
½ teaspoon sesame oil
1 egg
10 to 12 wonton wrappers
Water, for wrapping purposes

Cooking Tip

Pork Siu Mai is common in most Chinese restaurants that serve dim sum. The pork fats incorporated into the filling make the Siu Mai juicy and moist. If you substitute chicken, the result will be quite different, as chicken is a leaner meat. The use of spinach in this recipe helps to introduce some moisture into the filling so that the final Siu Mai does not turn out too dry.

1. Mix ground chicken and spinach in a bowl with salt, pepper, soy sauce, sesame oil, and egg. Combine well to a moist yet firm consistency.

2. Lay one wonton wrapper flat on your palm and try to gather up the sides of the wrapper slightly with your fingers, shaping the wrapper into a "cup." Use your finger to moisten the edges of the inside of the wrapper. Spoon about 2 teaspoons of filling onto the middle of the wrapper, maintaining the shape of the "cup."

3. When filled (filling should almost be at the brim of the wrapper), gather up the wrapper and fold the edges so that the filling "sticks" on the wrapper and the Siu Mai is able to stand by itself when you flatten its base (the bottom should be about the size of a quarter). Place the Siu Mai on a plate that fits in the steamer insert or basket. Cover the plate with plastic wrap to prevent excess condensation during steaming.

4. Fill the rice cooker pot with water to about the 4-cup mark. Cover the rice cooker and set to Cook. When the water boils, place the steamer insert or basket that holds the plate of Siu Mai into the rice cooker. Cover the rice cooker and steam for 12 to 15 minutes until the chicken cooks through.

Dim Sum: Steamed Tofu

The dim-sum menu in Chinese restaurants has become quite extensive over the years. Steamed dim-sum items such as Siu Mai (page 32) and Char Siew Bao (Steamed Pork Buns) remain very popular among dim-sum patrons. This steamed tofu item is also quite popular and is easy to prepare at home.

INGREDIENTS | SERVES 2 OR 3

1 egg tofu, cut into ½-inch thick slices
4 ounces ground chicken
1 cup blanched (frozen) spinach, thawed and drained of excess liquid
½ teaspoon salt
½ teaspoon white pepper
1 teaspoon light soy sauce
½ teaspoon sesame oil

Egg Tofu

In supermarkets, especially Chinese supermarkets, you can find egg tofu in the same section as soft and firm tofu. However, egg tofu is typically packaged in a long cylindrical tube, whereas soft and firm tofu is packaged in square or rectangular boxes. You can also use soft tofu for this recipe by slicing the tofu into smaller blocks and then scooping small "wells" as directed.

1. Using a teaspoon, scoop out a little "well" in the middle of each tofu slice, reserving the scooped-out tofu in a bowl. Set aside the slices on a plate that fits into the steamer insert or basket.

2. Mash the reserved tofu and combine with chicken, spinach, salt, pepper, soy sauce, and sesame oil. Shape the filling mixture into uniformly sized balls, using about 2 teaspoonfuls of filling for each. Place one ball into the "well" of each slice. Cover the plate with plastic wrap to prevent excess condensation during steaming.

3. Fill the rice cooker pot with water to about the 4-cup mark. Cover the rice cooker and set to Cook. When the water boils, place the steamer insert or basket that holds the plate of tofu into the rice cooker. Cover the rice cooker and steam for 10 to 12 minutes until the chicken cooks through.

Mini Indonesian Potato Cakes

These are also called begedil *in Malaysia and* perkedel *in Indonesia. Essentially, they are fried potato cakes made with ground beef.*

INGREDIENTS | SERVES 4 AS A SIDE DISH

2 potatoes, boiled and peeled
½ cup vegetable oil, divided use
4 shallots, finely sliced
½ pound ground beef
2 tablespoons water
1 cup finely chopped cilantro leaves
Salt and ground black and white pepper, to taste
2 eggs, lightly whisked

Time-Saving Tip

Use make-ahead Fried Golden Shallots (page 284) and add them when mixing the mashed potatoes, cilantro, and fried beef mixture. The potato cakes will definitely taste different from the ones used in this recipe (still good, if not better) and will be more fragrant.

1. Mash the boiled potatoes gently using the back of a fork. Set aside.

2. Add 1 tablespoon oil to the rice cooker, cover, and set to Cook. When the base of the cooker pot gets warm, add the shallots and fry for about 5 minutes until they turn slightly soft and caramelized.

3. Add the beef and fry until browned and cooked through.

4. Add the water, cover the rice cooker, and cook for 6 to 8 minutes. If the mixture bubbles too much, switch to Warm for the remaining cooking time (6 to 8 minutes total). Dish out and set aside.

5. In a large mixing bowl, mix mashed potatoes, cilantro, fried beef, shallots, salt, black pepper, and white pepper; combine evenly. Shape into round cakes, flatten slightly, and set aside on a plate.

6. Add the remaining oil to the rice cooker, cover, and set to Cook. When the base of the cooker pot gets warm, dip the potato cakes individually in the egg mixture to coat. Add the cakes to the rice cooker and pan-fry the cakes (work in batches) for 3 to 5 minutes on each side until golden brown and crispy on the surface, being sure to cover the rice cooker while frying.

Seafood Napa Cabbage Rolls

You can also use round cabbage instead of napa cabbage. However, round cabbage leaves may take longer to cook (or to soften). You can either adjust the steaming time accordingly or blanch the leaves for a longer time during preparation.

INGREDIENTS | SERVES 4 TO 6 AS A SIDE DISH

- 4 cups water or more, to immerse the cabbage leaves
- 10 to 16 napa cabbage leaves
- 6 to 10 medium-sized shrimp, peeled and deveined
- 1 fish fillet (snapper, threadfin, cod)
- ¼ teaspoon salt
- ¼ teaspoon white pepper
- ½ cup frozen vegetables (peas, corns, or carrots), cooked and cooled
- 1 teaspoon Chinese cooking wine
- ½ teaspoon sesame oil
- 1 egg white

Benefits of Cabbage

The antioxidants in cabbage are considered indirect antioxidants. Indirect antioxidants stimulate the body's natural antioxidant systems and act as a defense mechanism, triggering long-lasting effects on free radicals.

1. Add water to rice cooker, cover, and set to Cook. When the water boils, add the napa cabbage, blanch 15 seconds (just to soften the leaves for easy wrapping), remove, and set aside to cool. Leave the water inside the rice cooker for steaming later.

2. Mince the shrimp. Transfer to a bowl and set aside.

3. Mince the fish, and add to the shrimp. Mix well with salt, pepper, vegetables, Chinese cooking wine, sesame oil, and egg white. The final paste should not be too watery, and just slightly sticky.

4. Lay the cooled cabbage leaves on a flat surface (you can use 2 leaves so they partially overlap each other to increase the length of the roll). Spoon 1 to 2 tablespoons of seafood paste on the cabbage leaves (1 tablespoon for 1 leaf, 2 tablespoons for overlapped leaves). Fold up the edges and roll up the cabbage leaves to enclose the seafood mixture. Set aside on a plate that will fit in the steamer insert or basket. Cover the plate of cabbage rolls with plastic wrap to prevent excess condensation during steaming.

5. With the water from Step 1 still in the rice cooker, cover the rice cooker and set to Cook. When the water in the rice cooker boils, place the steamer insert or basket that holds the plate of cabbage rolls into the rice cooker. Cover the rice cooker and steam for 8 to 10 minutes until the filling is cooked through.

6. When ready to serve, slice the rolls into smaller pieces.

CHAPTER 3 **SENSATIONAL STARTERS**

Tofu Cabbage Rolls

An alternative fuss-free way of blanching whole cabbage leaves is to leave them immersed for 5 to 8 minutes in a deep bowl of hot water until the leaves soften.

INGREDIENTS | SERVES 4 TO 6 AS A SIDE DISH

1 teaspoon oyster sauce
2 tablespoons water
Salt and pepper, to taste
1 tablespoon vegetable oil
1 cup finely diced brown mushrooms (or shiitake)
1 cup finely diced celery
1 pack (about 12 ounces) regular firm tofu, completely drained
1 teaspoon corn flour
10 to 16 napa cabbage leaves, blanched (see page 35)

1. Mix oyster sauce, water, salt, and pepper in a bowl.

2. Add the oil to the rice cooker, cover, and set to Cook. When the base of the cooker pot gets warm, add mushrooms and celery and fry for 2 to 3 minutes until the vegetables become tender, covering rice cooker occasionally in the process of frying.

3. Add the oyster sauce mixture, cover the rice cooker, and simmer for about 1 minute until sauce reduces completely. Dish out and set aside to cool.

4. Mash the tofu in a deep mixing bowl. Add the cooked mushrooms and celery and the corn flour, and mix well. Drain final mixture thoroughly.

5. Lay the cooled cabbage leaves on a flat surface (you can use 2 leaves so they partially overlap each other to increase the length of the roll). Spoon 1 to 2 tablespoons of tofu mixture onto the cabbage leaves (1 tablespoon for 1 leaf, 2 tablespoons for overlapped leaves). Fold up the edges and roll up the cabbage leaves to enclose the tofu mixture. Place the cabbage rolls on a plate that fits into the steamer insert or basket. Cover the cabbage rolls with plastic wrap to prevent excess condensation during steaming.

6. Clean out the rice cooker and wipe dry. Add water to the rice cooker to about the 3-cup mark. Cover the rice cooker and set to Cook. When the water in the rice cooker boils, place the steamer insert or basket that holds the tofu cabbage rolls over the boiling water. Cover the rice cooker and steam for 5 minutes.

7. When ready to serve, slice up the rolls into smaller pieces.

Spicy Fish Custard

This curried custard, known as Ho Mok Pla in Thailand, can be served either as an appetizer or as a snack. Made from fish, or sometimes seafood, the custard is steamed in little "cups" made from banana leaves. To make a fuss-free version at home, small ramekins can be used to steam the fish custard.

INGREDIENTS | SERVES 4 (IN 4 SMALL RAMEKINS)

½ cup finely shredded cabbage
6 cups water
1 Thai chili pepper, seeded
1 tablespoon curry powder
2 kaffir lime leaves, shredded (see note)
1 egg
½ cup coconut milk
1 teaspoon fish sauce
1 teaspoon corn flour
1 fish fillet (snapper), cut into small bite-sized chunks

Kaffir Lime

Kaffir lime and kaffir lime leaves are almost indispensable in Thai cooking and cannot be substituted with other kinds of citrus. The leaves impart a sweet, lemony scent and a unique flavor to many soups, salads, curries, and stir-fried dishes in Thai cuisine. You can find these leaves in ethnic or specialty Thai and Vietnamese grocery stores, some Whole Foods locations, and also on the Internet.

1. Add water to rice cooker, cover, and set to Cook. When the water boils, add the cabbage, blanch about 20 seconds (just to soften the leaves), remove, and set aside to cool. Leave the water inside the rice cooker for steaming later.

2. Slightly blend chili, curry powder, kaffir lime leaves, egg, coconut milk, fish sauce, and corn flour in a food processor.

3. Line each ramekin with cabbage and place fish chunks into each ramekin.

4. Gently pour the curry mixture over the fish, allowing for a little expansion space at the top of the ramekin. Place the filled ramekins on a steamer insert or basket.

5. Fill the rice cooker pot with water to about the 4-cup mark. Cover the rice cooker and set to Cook. When the water boils, place the steamer insert or basket that holds the bowls of fish custard into the rice cooker. Cover the rice cooker and steam for about 15 minutes until the fish cooks through and the curry gravy has set into a custard-like consistency.

CHAPTER 4

Soup du Jour

Cabbage and Tomato Soup
39

Spinach and Tofu Soup
40

Bean Sprouts and Tomato Soup
40

Meatballs and Napa Cabbage Soup
41

Chicken Soup with Sweet Corn and Carrot
42

Chicken and Daikon Soup
42

Seaweed Soup with Enoki and Meatballs
43

Hot and Sour Soup
44

Chinese Fish Soup
45

Fishball (Dumpling) Soup
46

Halibut and Asparagus Soup
47

Coconut Chicken Soup
48

Chicken Herbal Soup
49

Miso Soup
49

Green Tea Miso Soup
50

Tom Yum Soup
51

Kimchi Tofu Soup
52

Minestrone
52

Cream of Mushroom Soup
53

Curried Carrot and Ginger Soup
54

Potato, Cabbage, and Spicy Sausage Soup
55

Cabbage and Tomato Soup

Substitute fresh ripe tomatoes for the canned if you wish, depending on what you have on hand and what is in season.

INGREDIENTS | SERVES 3 OR 4

4 cups water, divided use

½ (14½-ounce) can diced tomatoes, with juice

1 small head (12 to 16 ounces) cabbage, thinly sliced

Salt and freshly ground black pepper, to taste

½ teaspoon dried oregano, for garnish

Cooking Tip

Lycopene, found in tomatoes, is a phytochemical with antioxidant properties that maintains and supports healthy cells. Lycopene is insoluble in water. It can only be dissolved in organic solvents and oils. Therefore, when you lightly sauté tomatoes in oil, you receive more health benefits because the lycopene is released.

1. Add 2 cups of the water into the rice cooker pot, cover, and set to Cook. When the water boils, add the cabbage and tomatoes, stir well, and continue to cook for about 5 minutes.

2. When the soup starts to boil vigorously, switch the rice cooker to Warm and add the remaining 2 cups water. Stir well.

3. Switch back to the Cook setting and allow to return to a boil. Once boiling, switch to Warm, cover the rice cooker, and simmer for about 15 to 20 minutes until cabbage becomes tender. Add salt and pepper to taste. Keep at Warm and garnish with oregano before serving.

Spinach and Tofu Soup

Do not overcook the spinach. Add it in last, when the soup is just about ready to be served.

INGREDIENTS | SERVES 4

½ pound ground pork
¼ teaspoon salt
¼ teaspoon white pepper
¼ teaspoon sesame oil
¼ tablespoon corn flour
4 cups water
4 fresh shiitake mushroom caps, thinly sliced
Salt and white pepper, to taste
3 cups tightly packed fresh baby spinach
1 (10½-ounce) pack soft tofu, cut into 0.6-inch cubes

1. Mix the ground pork with salt, pepper, sesame oil, and corn flour. Leave to marinate while preparing the rice cooker for the soup.

2. Add the water to the rice cooker pot, cover, and set to Cook. When the water boils, make little balls out of the marinated pork and add to the rice cooker.

3. Add the mushrooms, cover the rice cooker, and allow to boil for 15 minutes.

4. When the soup is bubbling vigorously, switch to Warm and allow to cook for 15 minutes until pork cooks through. Add salt and pepper to taste, stir in the spinach and tofu, and allow to simmer for about 5 minutes with the rice cooker covered. Serve warm.

Bean Sprouts and Tomato Soup

If you prefer more crunch to the bean sprouts, simmer the soup for only 5 minutes after adding the sprouts to the pot.

INGREDIENTS | SERVES 4

1 tablespoon extra-virgin olive oil
½ cup sliced lean pork
1 fresh tomato, diced
4 cups water
3 cups bean sprouts
Salt and ground white pepper, to taste

1. Add the oil to the rice cooker, cover, and set to Cook. When the base of the cooker pot gets warm, add the pork and fry for 2 to 3 minutes, covering rice cooker occasionally in the process of frying.

2. Add the tomatoes and fry for another 2 to 3 minutes, covering rice cooker occasionally in the process of frying.

3. Add the water and cover the rice cooker. When the soup starts to boil vigorously, switch the rice cooker to Warm, add the bean sprouts, stir well, and allow the soup to simmer, covered for about 10 minutes. Serve warm.

Meatballs and Napa Cabbage Soup

Egg whites are usually mixed with the ground pork when seasoning and marinating Chinese meatballs. The egg whites bind the meat mixture and give a smooth texture to the meatballs.

INGREDIENTS | SERVES 3 OR 4

½ pound ground pork
¼ teaspoon salt
¼ teaspoon white pepper
½ teaspoon grated ginger
¼ teaspoon sesame oil
¼ tablespoon corn flour
4 cups water
1 small head (12- to 16-ounce) napa cabbage, large leaves sliced into halves
1 (3½-ounce) package enoki mushrooms, 1 inch of the stem bottom removed
Salt and white pepper, to taste

1. Mix the ground pork with salt, pepper, ginger, sesame oil, and corn flour in a bowl. Leave to marinate while preparing the rice cooker for the soup.

2. Add the water to the rice cooker, cover, and set to Cook. When the water boils, add the napa cabbage, cover the rice cooker, and cook for 3 to 5 minutes until mixture returns to a boil.

3. When soup mixture boils, make little balls out of the marinated pork and add them to the soup. Add the enoki mushrooms, cover the rice cooker, and allow to boil for about 10 minutes.

4. When the soup is bubbling vigorously, switch to Warm and allow to cook for about 15 to 20 minutes until pork cooks through. Add salt and pepper to taste. Serve warm.

Chicken Soup with Sweet Corn and Carrot

This soup is a popular Chinese home-cooked meal since it is nutritious and easy to prepare. Fresh corn on the cob works best in this soup.

INGREDIENTS | SERVES 2 OR 3

3 to 4 cups water (enough to immerse the chicken)
2 chicken legs
1 ear corn (leaves removed), cut into 3 pieces
1 medium-sized carrot, coarsely chopped
Salt and ground white pepper to taste

1. Add the water into the rice cooker pot, cover, and set to Cook.

2. When the water boils, add the chicken, corn, and carrots, then cover the rice cooker and return to a boil.

3. When the soup starts to boil vigorously, switch the rice cooker to Warm and allow to simmer for about 2 hours. Add salt to taste.

Chicken and Daikon Soup

Daikon adds a natural sweetness to this soup. You can substitute carrots or use a mixture of each.

INGREDIENTS | SERVES 2 OR 3

3 to 4 cups water (enough to immerse the chicken legs)
2 chicken legs
1 medium-sized daikon, coarsely chopped
½-inch piece ginger, slightly crushed
Salt, to taste

1. Add the water to the rice cooker pot, cover, and set to Cook. When the water boils, add chicken, daikon, and ginger. Cover the rice cooker and return to a boil.

2. When the soup starts to boil vigorously, switch the rice cooker to Warm and allow to simmer for about 2 hours. Add salt to taste.

Cooking Tip

To get clear chicken soup, you can parboil the chicken first by immersing in a pot of boiling water for about 5 to 8 minutes to remove part of the fat. Alternatively, you can boil the chicken in the rice cooker for about 5 to 8 minutes with the rice cooker covered and discard the first change of cooking liquid.

Seaweed Soup with Enoki and Meatballs

Which kind of dried seaweed to use in this soup is up to your personal preference. You can use Chinese dried seaweed or Korean dried kelp. In either case, make sure you read the directions on the package to know how much to use.

INGREDIENTS | SERVES 3 OR 4

½ pound ground pork
¼ teaspoon salt
¼ teaspoon white pepper
½ teaspoon grated ginger
¼ teaspoon sesame oil
¼ tablespoon corn flour
5 cups water
1 (3½-ounce) pack enoki mushrooms, 1 inch of the stem bottoms removed
1 piece of dried seaweed, soaked
Salt and white pepper, to taste

1. In a bowl, mix the ground pork with the salt, pepper, ginger, sesame oil, and corn flour. Leave to marinate while preparing the rice cooker for the soup.

2. Add the water to the rice cooker pot, cover, and set to Cook.

3. When the water boils, make little balls out of the marinated pork and add to the soup. Add the mushrooms, cover the rice cooker, and allow to boil for about 10 minutes.

4. When the soup is bubbling vigorously, switch to Warm, add the seaweed, and allow to cook for 20 minutes until pork cooks through. Add salt and pepper to taste. Serve warm.

Seaweed and Nutrition

Seaweed is nutritious, as it contains high amounts of B vitamins and minerals such as iodine. It is easy to incorporate seaweed in your cooking, since most dried seaweeds require only brief soaking and cooking.

Hot and Sour Soup

In Chinese supermarkets you can find black fungus in the dried goods section; hot bean paste with other bottled Chinese sauces; fresh bamboo shoots in the produce section; and canned bamboo shoots with other canned products. Or you can order all these ingredients online.

INGREDIENTS | SERVES 3 OR 4

½ cup thinly sliced or shredded lean pork
1 tablespoon Chinese cooking wine
½ teaspoon corn flour
¼ teaspoon salt
½ teaspoon white pepper
5 cups water (or half water and half chicken or vegetable stock)
4 to 6 fresh shiitake mushroom caps, thinly sliced
1 (3½-ounce) pack enoki mushrooms, 1 inch of the stem bottoms removed
½ cup soaked black fungus, julienned
½ (8-ounce) can of bamboo shoots, or ½ cup finely shredded fresh bamboo shoots
1 tablespoon hot bean paste
1 (10½-ounce) block soft tofu, cut into strips
Salt and white pepper, to taste
1 egg, lightly whisked
½ teaspoon black vinegar
1 green onion, finely chopped, for garnish

1. In a bowl, combine the pork, Chinese cooking wine, corn flour, salt, and pepper. Leave to marinate while preparing the rice cooker for the soup.

2. Add the water or mixed water and stock to the rice cooker pot, cover, and set to Cook.

3. When the liquid boils, add the marinated pork, mushrooms, black fungus, and bamboo shoots. Cover rice cooker and cook for about 5 minutes or until mixture returns to a boil.

4. Add the hot bean paste and stir lightly. Add the tofu, cover the rice cooker, and allow to boil for about 10 minutes.

5. When the soup is bubbling vigorously, switch to Warm and allow to cook for about 15 minutes. Add salt and pepper to taste.

6. About 5 minutes before serving, gently stir in egg and add a dash of black vinegar, then switch rice cooker off. Garnish with green onions and serve warm.

Chinese Fish Soup

This is a nutritious and healthy soup you can easily make at home. Some Chinese families like to use pomfret fish (the whole fish) for this soup. This recipe uses codfish, which is readily available in most supermarkets.

INGREDIENTS | SERVES 2 OR 3

2 codfish fillets, cut into about ¼-inch slices

¼ teaspoon salt

¼ teaspoon white pepper

1 teaspoon Chinese cooking wine

5 cups water

1 tomato, cut into 4 to 6 wedges

½-inch piece ginger, thinly sliced

1 green onion, finely chopped, for garnish

1 teaspoon Fried Golden Shallots (page 284), for garnish

1 teaspoon seeded and thinly sliced red chili pepper, for garnish

Ground white pepper, to taste

1. Season fish slices with salt, pepper, and Chinese cooking wine. Set aside while preparing the rice cooker for cooking the soup.

2. Add the water to the rice cooker pot, cover, and set to Cook. When the water boils, add the fish slices in small batches. Once the fish is cooked (turns opaque), in about 5 to 8 minutes, remove the slices from the simmering soup and set aside in a serving bowl. Do not overcook the fish.

3. Add tomatoes, ginger, and half the quantity of green onions. Cover the rice cooker and bring to a boil. When the water boils, switch to Warm and allow to simmer for about 10 minutes.

4. Ladle soup over cooked fish slices. Add white pepper to taste. Garnish with remaining green onions, fried shallots, and sliced red chili.

Cooking Tip

If you use whole fish, you can cut a few shallow slits on the fish so that it cooks more easily. Also make sure the fishmonger scales and cleans the fish thoroughly for you. It definitely is cleaner and easier to use fish slices cut from a fillet rather than using a whole fish. In addition, fillets cook more quickly.

Fishball (Dumpling) Soup

Store-bought fishballs are made of fish meat that has been finely pulverized. Homemade fishballs are usually handmade, either using ready-made fish paste or finely minced fresh fish (usually threadfin).

INGREDIENTS | SERVES 3 OR 4

6 peeled and deveined shrimp, minced

1 threadfin fillet (about ½ pound), minced with back of cleaver/chopper

½ whisked egg white (or ¼ tablespoon corn flour)

¼ teaspoon salt

¼ teaspoon white pepper

¼ teaspoon sesame oil

1 tablespoon finely chopped cilantro leaves and stems

4 cups water (or half water and half chicken stock)

6 lettuce leaves

1 green onion, finely chopped, for garnish

Cooking Tip

Do not try to chop the shrimp and fish in a food processor. Doing so will produce more moisture than will mincing the shrimp using a cleaver/chopper. Too much moisture is undesirable for making firmly shaped patties or balls.

1. Combine minced shrimp and fish with egg white. Season with salt, pepper, sesame oil, and cilantro. Form into small balls. Set aside while preparing rice cooker for soup.

2. Add water or water and stock to the rice cooker pot, cover, and set to Cook. When the liquid boils, add the fishballs, cover the rice cooker, and boil for about 10 minutes, switching to Warm if mixture boils too vigorously.

3. Once the fishballs are cooked (they will turn opaque and float to the top), remove them from the simmering soup and place into serving bowls lined with lettuce. Ladle some soup over the fishballs in the bowl before serving. Garnish with green onions.

Halibut and Asparagus Soup

Add cooked rice to the soup and make it a nutritious one-dish meal.

INGREDIENTS | SERVES 2 OR 3

1 tablespoon finely diced pancetta

4 ounces (¼ pound) fresh asparagus, cut into finger-length pieces

3 cups water (or mix half with chicken stock)

2 halibut or codfish fillets, cut into ½-inch slices

¼ teaspoon salt

¼ teaspoon white pepper

1 teaspoon Chinese cooking wine

1 green onion, finely chopped, for garnish

1 teaspoon Fried Golden Shallots (page 284), for garnish

1 teaspoon seeded, thinly sliced red chili pepper, for garnish

Salt and ground black pepper, to taste

Cooking Tip
As pancetta cooks it releases some oil, which can be used to fry the asparagus. It gives the entire soup mixture more flavor and makes it more robust. If you do not want to use pancetta, substitute 1 tablespoon of vegetable oil for frying the asparagus.

1. Cover the rice cooker and set to Cook. When the base of the cooker pot gets warm, add the pancetta and fry for 2 to 3 minutes until it begins to brown at edges and oil is released.

2. Add the asparagus and stir-fry with the pancetta until the asparagus is lightly colored and tender. Divide the asparagus and pancetta among the serving bowls.

3. Wipe out the oil in the rice cooker pot, add the water or water and stock, cover, and set to Cook. When the water boils, add the fish slices in small batches to cook. Once fish is cooked (turns opaque) in about 5 to 8 minutes, remove from the simmering soup and set aside in the serving bowls along with the asparagus and pancetta.

4. To serve, ladle soup into the serving bowls. Add salt and pepper. Garnish with green onion, Fried Golden Shallots, and red chili.

Coconut Chicken Soup

This spicy soup is known as Tom Ka Gai *in Thai cuisine. Kick up the spice level by adding paprika or cayenne pepper powder.*

INGREDIENTS | SERVES 2 OR 3

2 tablespoons vegetable oil
¼ pound boneless chicken thigh, cut into thin strips
1 small (6-ounce) can coconut milk
1 cup water
1 tablespoon grated ginger
1 tablespoon fish sauce
1 tablespoon lime juice
½ teaspoon red chili powder
¼ teaspoon turmeric
¼ cup finely chopped fresh cilantro, for garnish

1. Add the oil to the rice cooker, cover, and set to Cook. When the base of the cooker pot gets warm, add the chicken and fry for 2 to 3 minutes, stirring occasionally, until the chicken is slightly browned. Remove chicken and set aside.

2. Switch the rice cooker to Warm and add the coconut milk and water. Cover the rice cooker, set to Cook, and bring to a boil. Once boiling, switch to Warm again and add the ginger, fish sauce, lime juice, red chili powder, and turmeric. Stir well.

3. Add the chicken, cover the rice cooker, and set to Cook. Cook the mixture for about 15 minutes, or until the chicken cooks through, switching to Warm once the mixture begins to bubble. Garnish with cilantro and serve warm.

Chicken Herbal Soup

To cook this soup, you can buy pre-packed herbs from Chinese medicine shops, Chinese supermarkets, or on the Internet.

INGREDIENTS | SERVES 2 OR 3

1 herbal pack for chicken soup
5 cups water
2 chicken legs

Other Uses for Chinese Herbal Packs

Instead of boiling soup, you can also make herbal steamed chicken with the same herbal pack. Place the chicken on a piece of foil and sprinkle with the herbs. Make a sauce mixture of 1 teaspoon sesame oil, 1 teaspoon dark soy sauce, 1 tablespoon Chinese cooking wine, and 1 tablespoon oyster sauce; drizzle the sauce over the chicken and herbs. Fold the foil into a tight packet, place it into a steamer basket, and steam in the rice cooker for about 30 minutes until chicken cooks through.

1. Parboil chicken in boiling water for a few minutes as directed in the Cooking Tip for Chicken and Daikon Soup (page 42). Drain and set aside.

2. Add water to the rice cooker pot, cover, and set to Cook. When the water boils, add the parboiled chicken and the herbal pack.

3. After the water returns to a boil, switch the rice cooker to Warm and simmer for about 2 hours until the chicken cooks through.

Miso Soup

There are many varieties of miso. The most common are red miso (made from white rice, barley, or soybeans by natural fermentation) and white miso (made from a lot of rice and fewer soybeans). Any miso variety would work in this recipe.

INGREDIENTS | SERVES 4

4 cups water
½ pack (about 5 ounces) soft tofu, cut into ½-inch cubes
1 cup baby spinach
2 tablespoons miso
2 green onions, finely chopped

1. Add the water to the rice cooker pot, cover, and set to Cook. When the water boils, add the tofu and simmer, covered for 2 to 3 minutes. Stir in spinach and simmer for 30 seconds.

2. Ladle about 2 tablespoons soup liquid from the rice cooker into a small bowl. Add the miso to the bowl and stir to dissolve the miso; then stir the contents of the bowl back into the rice cooker pot, set it to Warm, and cover it. Let soup sit for about 5 minutes and garnish with green onions before serving.

Green Tea Miso Soup

Green tea is rich in catechin polyphenols and can be a powerful antioxidant. Green tea is not as strong or as bitter as black tea, which makes it easier to incorporate in cooking. Green tea makes an otherwise ordinary miso soup extraordinary in this recipe.

INGREDIENTS | SERVES 4

4 green tea bags
4 cups boiling water for brewing tea
2 tablespoons vegetable oil
1 shallot, peeled and thinly sliced
½ pack (about 5 ounces) soft tofu, cut into ½-inch cubes
1 cup spinach
1 tablespoon miso
1 green onion, finely chopped

Benefits of Miso

As miso is typically fermented with a vitamin B_{12}-synthesizing bacteria, it is commonly recommended as a B_{12} source for vegans. Miso contains trace minerals such as zinc, manganese, and copper, all of which your body requires daily. Miso therefore is considered a nutritious flavor enhancer.

1. Place tea bags in teapot with boiling water and allow to sit for 5 minutes. Remove the tea bags and reserve the tea for use in soup.

2. Add the oil to the rice cooker, cover, and set to Cook. When the base of the cooker pot gets warm, add the shallots and fry for 2 to 3 minutes until soft.

3. Add the brewed tea, cover the rice cooker, and bring the mixture to a boil. Once boiling, switch the rice cooker to Warm and simmer, covered, about 10 minutes.

4. Add the tofu and simmer, covered, for 2 to 3 minutes. Stir in spinach and simmer for 30 seconds.

5. Ladle 2 tablespoons of soup liquid into a small bowl. Add the miso to the bowl and stir to dissolve the miso; then stir the contents of the bowl back into the rice cooker and set it to Warm. Let soup sit for about 5 minutes and garnish with green onions before serving.

Tom Yum Soup

Usually known as Tom Yum Goong in Thai cuisine, there are two versions—the clear version and the "milky" version. The addition of milk in this recipe gives the soup a better balance of spice.

INGREDIENTS | SERVES 2 OR 3

- 2 tablespoons vegetable oil
- 1 tablespoon Tom Yum paste
- 1 stalk lemongrass (bruise the bottom part)
- 2 cups water, divided use
- 4 fresh shiitake mushroom caps, cut into halves
- 10 French beans, ends trimmed, cut in half lengthwise
- 6 to 8 medium-sized shrimp, peeled and deveined
- 6 to 8 clams
- 2 tablespoons whole milk
- 1 fresh red chili pepper, seeded and thinly sliced, as garnish

Cooking Tip

Choose clams with tightly closed shells for cooking. These are fresh clams. Dead clams are those that are open prior to cooking. You should discard these clams and not use them in cooking.

1. Add the oil to the rice cooker, cover, and set to Cook. When the base of the cooker pot gets warm, add the Tom Yum paste and lemongrass, and fry for about 1 to 2 minutes.

2. Stir in 1 cup of the water, cover the rice cooker, and cook for 2 to 3 minutes.

3. When the mixture boils, switch to Warm and add the mushrooms, green beans, and remaining water. Cover the rice cooker and set to Cook for 2 minutes or until the soup returns to a boil; then switch the rice cooker to Warm.

4. Add the shrimp and clams, stir well, cover the rice cooker, and set to Cook. Cook for about 12 to 15 minutes until shrimp turn pink and clams open.

5. Remove the shrimp, clams, mushrooms, and green beans and divide among the serving bowls.

6. Make sure the rice cooker is set to Warm and then gently stir in milk. Simmer at Warm for about 1 minute with the rice cooker covered. Ladle soup over serving bowls and garnish with red chili.

Kimchi Tofu Soup

Kimchi, which is served as a side dish or condiment, is no longer solely found in Korean cuisine. It is also popular in many countries throughout Asia, Europe, and North America. You can use kimchi as a flavor enhancer in stir-fries and soups.

INGREDIENTS | SERVES 3 OR 4

4 cups water

1 (10½-ounce) block soft tofu, cut into cubes

½ cup kimchi, finely chopped into thin shreds

2 green onions, finely chopped, for garnish

1. Add the water into the rice cooker pot, cover, and set to Cook.
2. When the water boils, add the tofu, cover the rice cooker, and allow it to return to a simmer.
3. Switch the rice cooker to Warm, stir in kimchi, and simmer, covered, for another 5 minutes.
4. Garnish with green onions before serving.

Minestrone

The common ingredients in Minestrone include onions, celery, carrots, beans, and tomatoes. You can make your soup chunky or less chunky by varying the amount of water and the way you cut the vegetables.

INGREDIENTS | SERVES 4

2 tablespoons extra-virgin olive oil

2 cloves garlic, finely minced

1 medium-sized onion, finely sliced

1 medium-sized potato, peeled and diced

1 small carrot, diced

2 stalks celery, diced

6 to 8 cherry tomatoes, cut into halves

6 cups water (or half water and half chicken or vegetable stock)

½ cup uncooked shell pasta

Salt and freshly ground black pepper, to taste

½ teaspoon dried basil, for garnish

1. Add the oil to the rice cooker, cover, and set to Cook. When the base of the cooker pot gets warm, add the garlic and onion and fry for 2 to 3 minutes.
2. Add potatoes, carrots, celery, and tomatoes and fry for another 2 to 3 minutes.
3. Add the water or water and broth, cover the rice cooker, and bring to a boil. Continue boiling until vegetables turn slightly tender.
4. Add the shell pasta and boil for another 5 to 6 minutes until pasta cooks through.
5. Switch to Warm and simmer, covered, for about 15 minutes. Add salt and pepper to taste. Garnish with basil and serve with toasted bread.

Cream of Mushroom Soup

There are many ways of cooking this classic soup, up to the point of being luxurious and adding truffle oil as a finishing touch. This is a simple homemade version.

INGREDIENTS | SERVES 3 OR 4

½ pound white or brown cremini mushrooms
2 tablespoons butter, divided use
½ medium-sized onion, finely chopped
3 cups vegetable stock
Salt and freshly ground black pepper to taste
1 cup heavy cream
1 teaspoon flour to thicken soup (optional)

1. Coarsely chop mushrooms in a food processor or with a sharp knife.

2. Add 1 tablespoon of the butter into the rice cooker, cover, and set to Cook. When the base of the cooker pot gets warm and the butter melts, add the onions and fry for 5 minutes until onions become soft.

3. Add the mushrooms and remaining butter and continue to fry, covered, for about 5 to 8 minutes, checking occasionally for the mushrooms and onions to be properly cooked (turn tender) in the process of frying.

4. Slowly stir in the stock, salt, and pepper, cover the rice cooker, and bring to a boil.

5. Once the mixture is boiling, switch the rice cooker to Warm, gently stir in the heavy cream, and allow to simmer, covered, for about 5 minutes.

6. About 5 minutes before serving the soup, stir in the flour to thicken the soup if desired, and simmer for the remaining 5 minutes. Serve warm.

Curried Carrot and Ginger Soup

The addition of a little curry powder makes this a mildly spicy soup, comforting on cold winter days.

INGREDIENTS | SERVES 2 OR 3

1 tablespoon extra-virgin olive oil
½ medium-sized onion, finely chopped
2 cloves garlic, finely minced
1 carrot, thinly sliced into shreds
1 teaspoon grated ginger
½ teaspoon curry powder
2 cups water
Salt and pepper, to taste
½-inch piece fresh ginger, sliced into fine shreds
1 cup coconut milk

1. Add the oil to the rice cooker, cover, and set to Cook. When the base of the cooker pot gets warm, add the onions and garlic and fry for about 5 minutes until onions become soft.

2. Add the carrots, grated ginger, and curry powder, and continue to cook for about 2 to 3 minutes.

3. Add the water, cover the rice cooker, and bring to a boil.

4. Once the mixture is boiling, switch the rice cooker to Warm, add salt, pepper, and ginger shreds, and gently stir in coconut milk. Simmer, covered, for 15 minutes. Serve warm.

Storing Ginger

Put unpeeled fresh ginger in a small paper bag and store in the fridge for about one to two weeks. You can also wrap the ginger in newspaper and store in a cool, dry place.

Potato, Cabbage, and Spicy Sausage Soup

Compared to soups such as Minestrone (page 52) and Curried Carrot and Ginger Soup (page 54), this soup is heartier due to the addition of the potato and meat. Substitute the sausages with chorizo sausage or salami as a variation and to suit your preference.

INGREDIENTS | SERVES 2 OR 3

1 tablespoon extra-virgin olive oil
2 shallots, thinly sliced
2 cloves garlic, finely minced
2 spicy Italian sausages, cut to ½-inch cubes
1 potato, peeled and cut into ½-inch cubes
3 cups tightly packed, finely shredded cabbage
4 cups water or chicken stock
¼ teaspoon paprika, for garnish

1. Add the oil to the rice cooker, cover, and set to Cook. When the base of the cooker pot gets warm, add the shallots, garlic, and Italian sausage. Fry for about 8 minutes until the onions turn soft and the sausage is browned at the edges, covering rice cooker occasionally in the process of frying.

2. Add the potatoes and cabbage and continue to fry about 8 minutes until cabbage turns slightly tender, covering rice cooker occasionally in the process of frying.

3. Add water or stock to the pot, cover the rice cooker, and bring to a boil.

4. When the mixture is boiling, switch the rice cooker to Warm and simmer for 20 to 25 minutes until potatoes cook through. Sprinkle with paprika for added spice.

CHAPTER 4 **SOUP DU JOUR**

CHAPTER 5

The Mighty Rice

Seafood Tom Yum Rice
57

Japanese Chicken Donburi
58

Korean Bibimbap
59

Fragrant Coconut Rice
60

Indian Vegetable Biryani
61

Tomato Rice
62

Yellow Rice
63

Chicken Rice
64

Chinese "Clay-Pot" Rice
65

Asian "Risotto"
66

Pumpkin Rice
67

Savory Cabbage Rice
68

Seafood Fried Rice
69

Savory Taro Rice
70

Beef Fried Rice
71

Egg and Shrimp Fried Rice
72

Beans and Rice
73

Shrimp Pilaf
74

Rice Salad
75

Asian "Paella"
76

Easy Lemon Buttered Rice
77

Easy Spiced Rice with Peppers and Pine Nuts
78

Ground Beef and Rice Soup
79

Fish Kedgeree
80

Seafood Tom Yum Rice

This easy fried-rice recipe, characterized by the distinct, mildly spicy, and tangy flavors of fragrant Thai herbs, makes use of ready-made Tom Yum paste, which is available in the ethnic sections of many supermarkets. This bottled paste boosts the flavor of dishes almost instantly.

INGREDIENTS | SERVES 2

- 2 tablespoons vegetable oil
- 12 medium-sized peeled shrimps, deveined and diced
- 1 stalk lemongrass, bottom white part bruised
- 2 teaspoons Tom Yum paste
- 1 cup diced string beans
- ½ cup frozen corn
- ½ cup frozen green peas
- ½ cup diced green and red bell peppers
- 2 fresh red chili peppers, sliced thinly
- 3 tablespoons water, for frying with Tom Yum paste mixture
- 4 cups warm cooked rice

1. Add the oil to the rice cooker pot, cover, and set to Cook. When the base of the cooker pot gets warm, add the shrimp and fry for 2 to 3 minutes until cooked (turns pink). Dish out and set aside. Leave the remaining oil in the pot.

2. Add the lemongrass to the pot and fry for about 3 minutes until fragrant.

3. Add the Tom Yum paste, long beans, corn, peas, bell peppers, and red chilies. Fry for about 5 minutes.

4. Stir in the water gradually, cover the rice cooker, and allow to reach a simmer. Once the mixture is simmering, lift up the rice cooker lid and continue cooking until the vegetables become tender.

5. Return the shrimp to the pot and mix well. Make sure there is some gravy, but not too much, since you do not want the rice to become too soggy. Dish out mixture and set aside.

6. Add the cooked rice to the rice cooker. Return the Tom Yum mixture to the rice cooker and toss it with the rice, mixing thoroughly. Keep in the rice cooker on Warm until ready to serve.

Do You Know?
Lemongrass is also known as citronella grass or fever grass. The oil of citronella is commonly used as a mosquito repellent.

Japanese Chicken Donburi

Donburi and *Don* *have been used interchangeably to mean "bowl" or "bowl of a meal of rice." The common Donburi are Katsudon (Pork Cutlet Donburi), Gyudon (Beef Donburi), Oyakodon (Chicken Donburi), and Unadon (Eel Donburi).*

INGREDIENTS | SERVES 2

½ cup dashi stock
1 teaspoon mirin
1 teaspoon Japanese soy sauce (shoyu)
Salt, to taste
1 medium-sized onion, thinly sliced
1 boneless chicken thigh, cut into bite-sized pieces
2 eggs, lightly whisked
4 cups warm cooked Sushi Rice (page 13) without the vinegar, divided in 2 serving bowls

1. In a bowl, mix dashi stock, mirin, Japanese soy sauce, and salt. Add half the stock mixture to the rice cooker, cover, set to Cook, and bring mixture to a slight simmer.

2. When simmering, add half the onions, cover the rice cooker, and cook for about 3 minutes until onions turn soft, switching to Warm if mixture boils vigorously.

3. Add half of the chicken, set the rice cooker to Cook, and cook for about 5 minutes or until chicken cooks through, switching to Warm if the mixture boils too vigorously.

4. Switch the rice cooker to Warm. Gradually pour in half the eggs and allow to simmer until the egg almost sets. Gently slide the chicken, onions, and egg mixture into a serving bowl, on top of the cooked rice.

5. Repeat with remaining half of stock mixture, onions, chicken, and eggs.

What Is Dashi Stock?

The essential two ingredients to dashi stock are kombu seaweed and bonito flakes. Dashi stock is the base of many soups and noodle dishes in Japan such as miso, ramen, and soba.

Korean Bibimbap

Bibimbap (which literally means "mixed rice") is a bowl of warm white rice topped with seasoned vegetables, thinly sliced beef, fried egg (sometimes raw egg if a stone pot is used instead of a bowl) and gochujang (Korean chili pepper paste). Before serving, all these ingredients are stirred together with the rice.

INGREDIENTS | SERVES 3 OR 4

1 (8-ounce) salmon fillet, lightly seasoned with salt and black pepper
½ pound fresh baby spinach
3 tablespoons vegetable oil
2 eggs, lightly whisked
5 cups warm cooked rice
½ green bell pepper, seeded and diced
½ cup finely chopped kimchi
1 tablespoon Korean gochujang
¼ cup finely chopped green onions, for garnish
½ teaspoon sesame oil, for garnish

1. Fill the rice cooker pot with water to about the 4-cup mark. Cover the rice cooker and set to Cook. Place the salmon on a plate that will fit into the steamer insert or basket. When the water in the rice cooker boils, place the steamer insert or basket that holds the plate of salmon into the rice cooker and steam, with the rice cooker covered, for about 6 minutes until the salmon cooks through. Remove the salmon from the plate and with the help of two forks, break the fish into bite-sized pieces.

2. Place the spinach on the plate in the steamer insert or basket and steam for 1 to 2 minutes until the spinach becomes tender. Remove the plate of spinach and drain off excess liquid. When cooled, julienne the spinach (cut into strips).

3. Clean out the rice cooker and wipe dry. Add the oil to the rice cooker, cover, and set to Cook. When the base of the cooker pot gets warm, add the eggs and fry into an omelet. Remove eggs from the cooker and set aside. When cooled, slice into thin strips.

4. Add the cooked rice into the rice cooker and set to Cook. Add bell peppers and kimchi, and mix well with rice.

5. Smooth the top of the rice in the rice cooker, then arrange the salmon, eggs, and spinach over the rice. Cover the rice cooker and switch to Warm.

6. Before serving, add the gochujang on top of the rice, and garnish with green onions and a drizzle of sesame oil. When served, fluff up the rice, mixing with all the ingredients. Garnish with green onions and a drizzle of sesame oil.

Fragrant Coconut Rice

This is also popularly known as Nasi Lemak *in Singapore and Malaysia.* Nasi *means "rice" and* lemak *means "cream." Because the cream used in Nasi Lemak is coconut cream or thick coconut milk, Nasi Lemak is also known as coconut rice. It usually is served with cucumber, hard-boiled egg, and sambal chili.*

INGREDIENTS | SERVES 3 OR 4

2 cups long-grain rice
1 cup water
1½ cups thick coconut milk
4 screwpine leaves, cleaned and knotted together
½ teaspoon salt

Do You Know?
Screwpine leaves are also known as pandan leaves. An Asian ingredient used commonly in Southeast Asian cooking, these long leaves can sometimes be found in the frozen section of Asian supermarkets and can be used when cooking savory dishes and sweet desserts.

1. Rinse rice well by gently swirling the rice in the cooker pot with 2 or 3 changes of cold water until the water is not "cloudy" anymore. Drain rice and return to the rice cooker pot.

2. Add water, coconut milk, screwpine leaves, and salt to the rice in the pot, cover the rice cooker, and set to Cook. (Cooking time varies with the type of rice cooker used. Most automatic rice cookers will switch to Warm when the rice is cooked.)

3. After rice is cooked, do not open the cover immediately. Let it sit for 5 to 10 minutes to vent off the remaining steam. Fluff up the rice before serving.

Indian Vegetable Biryani

In Hyderabad, India, this dish is usually named Dum Biryani *due to the method of slow cooking (Dum Pukht), whereby the meat (usually chicken, mutton, or lamb) is layered with the rice and cooked under low flame in a sealed container.*

INGREDIENTS | SERVES 3 OR 4

- 2 cups basmati rice
- 3 tablespoons butter, divided use
- 3 shallots, thinly sliced
- ¼ cup cashews
- ¼ cup raisins
- 1 (2-inch) cinnamon stick
- 6 cloves
- 6 cardamom pods
- ½ teaspoon turmeric
- ½ cup diced tomatoes with juice
- 2 cups water, for cooking rice
- ½ teaspoon salt

1. Rinse rice well by gently swirling the rice in the cooker pot with 2 or 3 changes of cold water until the water is not "cloudy" anymore. Drain rice and set aside in a separate bowl.

2. Clean out the rice cooker pot and wipe dry. Add 2 tablespoons of the butter to the rice cooker pot, cover, and set to Cook. When the base of the cooker pot gets warm, add the shallots and fry about 5 minutes until shallots turn soft. Remove and set aside.

3. Add the cashews and raisins and fry for about 2 minutes, covering rice cooker occasionally in the process of frying. Remove and set aside.

4. Add remaining butter to the pot. Add the cinnamon, cloves, cardamom pods, turmeric, and diced tomatoes, and fry for about 2 to 3 minutes.

5. Stir in the rice and mix well with the spices.

6. Return the shallots to the pot, add the water and salt to the pot, cover the rice cooker, and cook the rice until done. (Cooking time varies with the kind of rice cooker used. Most automatic rice cookers will switch to Warm when the rice is cooked.)

7. After the rice is cooked, do not open the cover immediately. Let it sit for 5 to 10 minutes to vent off the remaining steam. Fluff up the rice and top with cashew nuts and raisins before serving.

Tomato Rice

This easy recipe uses tomatoes to flavor up rice. If desired, serve with curry and cucumber raita (a yogurt condiment).

INGREDIENTS | SERVES 3 OR 4

2 cups basmati rice
2 tablespoons butter
1 (2-inch) cinnamon stick
½ cup diced tomatoes with juice
2 cups water or Vegetable Stock (page 18)
½ teaspoon salt

Make Your Own Cucumber Raita

This condiment, which is popular in Indian cuisine, is easy to prepare. Drain 1 cup peeled and thinly sliced cucumber on paper towel. While the cucumber is draining, stir ½ teaspoon cumin and ½ teaspoon salt into ½ cup plain yogurt. Add sliced cucumbers to the yogurt mixture and mix well. Serve as a good cooling partner with spicy curries.

1. Rinse rice well by gently swirling the rice in the cooker pot with 2 or 3 changes of cold water. Drain rice and set aside.

2. Clean out the rice cooker pot and wipe dry. Add the butter to the rice cooker pot, cover, and set to Cook. When the base of the cooker pot gets warm, add the cinnamon and fry for about 2 minutes, covering rice cooker occasionally in the process of frying.

3. Stir in diced tomatoes, water or vegetable stock, salt, and rice; mix well. Cover rice cooker and cook the rice until done, about 30 minutes. (Cooking time varies with the kind of rice cooker used. Most automatic rice cookers will switch to Warm when the rice is cooked.)

4. After rice is cooked, do not open the cover immediately. Let it sit for 5 to 10 minutes to vent off the remaining steam. Fluff up the rice before serving.

Yellow Rice

This dish is also known as Nasi Kunyit. Kunyit is a Malay word for turmeric, which is the ingredient that gives this rice its yellow color. Traditionally, sticky glutinous rice is used when making Nasi Kunyit. This recipe uses regular long-grain rice instead, as that variety is most common and popular in many homes.

INGREDIENTS | SERVES 3 OR 4

2 cups long-grain rice
1 tablespoon vegetable oil
1 (2-inch) cinnamon stick
3 cardamom pods
1 star anise pod
1 teaspoon turmeric
1 teaspoon ground cumin
½ teaspoon salt
2½ cups water

1. Rinse rice well by gently swirling the rice in the cooker pot with 2 or 3 changes of cold water. Drain rice and set aside in a separate bowl.

2. Clean out the rice cooker pot and wipe dry. Add the oil to the rice cooker pot, cover, and set to Cook. When the base of the cooker pot gets warm, add the cinnamon, cardamom, and star anise and fry for about 5 minutes until fragrant, covering rice cooker occasionally in the process of frying.

3. Add the rice, turmeric, cumin, and salt to the pot and mix well.

4. Add the water and cover. Cook until rice is done. (Cooking time varies with the kind of rice cooker used. Most automatic rice cookers will switch to Warm when the rice is cooked.)

5. After rice is cooked, do not open the cover immediately. Let it sit for 5 to 10 minutes to vent off the remaining steam. Fluff up the rice before serving.

Chicken Rice

This is sometimes touted as the national dish in Singapore, initially brought in by the immigrants from Hainan, China. Because its roots are in Hainan, this dish is also known as Hainanese Chicken Rice.

INGREDIENTS | SERVES 3 OR 4

4 cups cold water, or more as needed to immerse the chicken
½-inch piece fresh ginger, sliced for use in stock
3 green onions, cut into finger-length pieces, divided use
1 pound chicken (thighs and drumsticks, or half a whole chicken)
2 cups long-grain rice
2 tablespoons vegetable oil
3 cloves garlic, crushed
1 teaspoon grated ginger, for rice
3 screwpine leaves, cleaned and knotted together
3 cups reserved chicken stock
Salt, to taste

Cooking Tip

There are two essential tips for moist and tender chicken in Chicken Rice. First, never allow the chicken to boil for a long time. Instead, simmer at low heat to cook the chicken. Second, bathe the chicken in an ice-water bath until chicken is cold to create a springy and moist texture in the chicken.

1. Add the water to the pot, cover, and set to Cook. When the water boils, add the sliced ginger and half the green onions. Completely immerse the chicken in the pot; cover and return to a boil.

2. Switch the rice cooker to Warm and allow to simmer, covered, for about 45 minutes. After 45 minutes, lift up the rice cooker lid and skim the top of the stock.

3. Switch the rice cooker to Cook and again return to a boil (this should take about 6 to 8 minutes). Then switch to Warm again, and allow the chicken to simmer, covered, for another 30 minutes.

4. Strain the contents of the rice cooker over a large bowl. Reserve the chicken stock; chop the chicken to bite-sized pieces and set aside.

5. Rinse rice well by gently swirling the rice with 2 or 3 changes of water. Drain rice and set aside in a separate bowl.

6. Clean out rice cooker and wipe dry. Add the oil to the rice cooker, cover, and set to Cook. When the base of the cooker pot gets warm, add the minced garlic, grated ginger, screwpine leaves, remaining green onions, and the rinsed rice. Fry the mixture for about 2 minutes, until fragrant, covering rice cooker occasionally in the process of frying. Stir in 3 cups reserved chicken stock gradually and add salt to taste. Cover the rice cooker, set to Cook, and cook the rice until completely done.

7. After the rice is cooked, do not open the cover immediately. Let it sit for 5 minutes to vent off the remaining steam. Fluff up the rice before serving. Serve with the chopped chicken.

Chinese "Clay-Pot" Rice

In traditional clay-pot cooking, the food inside an unglazed clay pot is cooked over a charcoal fire, giving the finished dish a distinctive aromatic flavor. This recipe adapts clay-pot cooking and makes it easier to cook at home using a rice cooker.

INGREDIENTS | SERVES 3 OR 4

½ pound chicken (thighs, breasts, or drumsticks), chopped into bite-sized pieces

2 tablespoons oyster sauce

1 tablespoon dark soy sauce

½ teaspoon sesame oil

½ teaspoon ground white pepper

¼ teaspoon brown sugar

1 tablespoon Chinese cooking wine

½ teaspoon corn flour

2 cups long-grain rice

3 tablespoons vegetable oil

1 teaspoon grated ginger

6 fresh shiitake mushroom caps, thinly sliced

3 cups water

2 green onions, finely chopped

1. Combine the chicken with the oyster sauce, soy sauce, sesame oil, white pepper, brown sugar, Chinese cooking wine, and corn flour. Let the chicken marinate in the fridge for 1 to 2 hours.

2. Rinse rice well by gently swirling the rice in the cooker pot with 2 or 3 changes of cold water. Drain the rice and set aside in a separate bowl.

3. Add the vegetable oil to the rice cooker, cover, and set to Cook. When the base of the cooker pot gets warm, add the chicken, the marinade, ginger, and shiitake mushrooms. Fry the chicken for 3 to 5 minutes until partially cooked, covering rice cooker occasionally in the process of frying. Dish out the chicken mixture and set aside in a bowl; dish out half of the sauce mixture into the same bowl. Leave the remaining half of the sauce mixture in the rice cooker.

4. With the rice cooker at Warm, add the rinsed rice and the water; mix well with the sauce mixture. Cover the rice cooker and set to Cook. (Cooking time varies with the type of rice cooker used. Most automatic rice cookers will switch to warm when the rice is cooked.) About 6 to 8 minutes before the rice is completely cooked (when the rice is almost dry), return the chicken and reserved sauce into the rice cooker and continue to cook until rice is completely done.

5. Switch the rice cooker to Warm for about 15 minutes before serving. Garnish with green onions.

Asian "Risotto"

In some parts of Asia, such as Hong Kong, Singapore, and Malaysia, rice is served soaked in thick gravy. The Cantonese call this dish Mui Fun. It is similar to risotto, which is also often served wet.

INGREDIENTS | SERVES 3 OR 4

2 tablespoons vegetable oil
3 cloves garlic, finely minced
1 teaspoon grated ginger
12 shrimp, peeled, deveined, and diced
½ cup baby scallops
4 fresh shiitake mushrooms caps, diced
2 cups broccoli florets, blanched
1 tablespoon oyster sauce
2 cups hot water
Salt and ground white pepper, to taste
2 eggs, lightly whisked
4 cups warm cooked rice, set aside on a plate

Cooking Tip

Instead of preparing different seafood items use a frozen seafood pack, which often contains a mix of items such as shrimp, baby scallops, and calamari. It will greatly reduce preparation time as well as shopping time.

1. Add the oil to the rice cooker, cover, and set to Cook. When the base of the cooker pot gets warm, add the garlic, ginger, shrimp, and baby scallops and fry for about 5 to 8 minutes until almost cooked (when shrimp turn pink). Dish out the seafood with half of the gravy and set aside. Leave the remaining seafood gravy in the pot.

2. Add the mushrooms, broccoli, oyster sauce, and hot water; stir well. Cover the rice cooker and bring mixture to a simmer. This will take 1 to 2 minutes.

3. Once simmering, return the cooked seafood to the pot. Add salt and pepper to taste. Cover the rice cooker and continue to cook the seafood mixture, stirring occasionally, until mixture starts to boil again and the seafood gravy starts to reduce.

4. Switch the rice cooker to Warm and slowly add the whisked eggs. Swirl the eggs gently in one direction using a chopstick. The warmth of the cooked ingredients will set the egg to a runny and creamy texture.

5. Pour the seafood and egg gravy on top of the cooked rice and serve immediately. It needs to be eaten wet!

Pumpkin Rice

Raisins and gojiberries can be natural sweeteners and optional ingredients. Add them (about 1 teaspoon, each) when the rice is almost done.

INGREDIENTS | SERVES 3 OR 4

2 cups long-grain rice
2 tablespoons vegetable oil
2 cloves garlic, finely minced
3 shallots, thinly sliced
½ pound lean pork, thinly sliced, less than ¼-inch thick
6 fresh shiitake mushrooms caps, diced
1 cup diced fresh pumpkin
¼ teaspoon salt
Ground white pepper, to taste
3 cups water

1. Rinse rice well by gently swirling the rice in the cooker pot with 2 or 3 changes of cold water. Drain rice and set aside in a separate bowl.

2. Add the oil to the rice cooker, cover, and set to Cook. When the base of the cooker pot gets warm, add the garlic, shallots, pork, and mushrooms and fry for 3 to 5 minutes until pork is partially cooked (or turns brown at the surface). Dish out and set aside.

3. With rice cooker still on Cook setting, add diced pumpkin and salt to the remaining oil in the pot and fry for about 3 minutes, covering rice cooker occasionally in the process of frying. Add white pepper to taste.

4. Add the rinsed rice and 3 cups water to the pot. Return the pork mixture to the pot. Stir and mix well with the pumpkin. Cover the rice cooker and cook the rice until completely done. (Cooking time varies with the type of rice cooker used. Most automatic rice cookers will switch to Warm when the rice is cooked.)

5. Let rice sit in the rice cooker for 5 to 10 minutes at Warm to vent off the remaining steam before serving.

Savory Cabbage Rice

When simmered and cooked until soft and tender, round cabbage becomes naturally sweet. It complements the savory meat in this rice dish very well.

INGREDIENTS | SERVES 3 OR 4

1 teaspoon oyster sauce
1 teaspoon dark soy sauce
½ cup hot water
2 cups long-grain rice
2 tablespoons vegetable oil
2 cloves garlic, finely minced
3 shallots, thinly sliced
½ pound lean pork, thinly sliced, to less than ¼-inch thick
6 fresh shiitake mushrooms caps, diced
½ pound round cabbage, thinly sliced
3 cups water, for cooking rice
Ground white pepper, to taste

Cooking Tip

Instead of using fresh meat, use leftover meat such as leftover barbecued roast. Chop the leftover roast into bite-sized pieces and fry them with the cabbage, then set aside to be added to the rice when rice is partially done in the cooker. Using leftovers will save time and flavor up this rice dish very well.

1. Mix oyster sauce, soy sauce, and hot water in a bowl. Set aside.

2. Rinse rice well by gently swirling the rice in the cooker pot with 2 or 3 changes of cold water. Drain rice and set aside in a separate bowl.

3. Add the oil to the rice cooker, cover, and set to Cook. When the base of the cooker pot gets warm, add the garlic, shallots, pork, and mushrooms and fry for 3 to 5 minutes until pork is partially cooked (or turns brown at the surface), covering rice cooker occasionally in the process of frying. Dish out and set aside.

4. With rice cooker still on Cook, add the cabbage to the pot and fry for about 3 minutes until cabbage turns slightly tender (yet not limp).

5. Add the sauce mixture to the pot and mix well with the cabbage and pork. Cook for 1 minute. Dish out and set aside.

6. Add the rinsed rice and 3 cups water to the pot. Cover the rice cooker and set to Cook. (Cooking time varies with the type of rice cooker used.) About 10 minutes before the rice completely cooks in the rice cooker (when the rice is almost dry), return the pork and cabbage mixture to the rice cooker and continue to cook until rice is completely done.

7. Set the rice cooker to Warm for about 15 minutes before serving.

Seafood Fried Rice

If you prefer a spicier dish, substitute 1 teaspoon of ready-made chili paste or curry paste for the oyster sauce. The spicy version of this fried rice is sometimes known as Nasi Goreng in Indonesia, Malaysia, and Singapore. Goreng means "fried" in Malay.

INGREDIENTS | SERVES 2 OR 3

3 tablespoons vegetable oil
2 cloves garlic, finely minced
3 shallots, thinly sliced
12 shrimp, peeled, deveined, and diced
½ cup baby scallops
1 cup diced string beans
½ cup frozen corn, thawed
½ cup frozen green peas, thawed
1 teaspoon oyster sauce
1 tablespoon warm water
3 cups of warm cooked rice
1 fresh red chili pepper, thinly sliced, for garnish

1. Add the oil to the rice cooker, cover, and set to Cook. When the base of the cooker pot gets warm, add the garlic, shallots, shrimp, and baby scallops and fry for about 5 to 8 minutes until shrimp and scallops are cooked (when shrimp turn pink, and scallops turn white). Dish out seafood and set aside.

2. Add the long beans, corn, and peas to the rice cooker and fry for about 3 to 5 minutes until vegetables become tender (yet not limp).

3. Return the seafood to the pot, add the oyster sauce and warm water, and mix well. Make sure there is 2 to 3 tablespoons of gravy but not too much, since you do not want the rice to be too soggy.

4. Add the cooked rice to the rice cooker and mix with seafood and vegetables thoroughly by fluffing up the rice with the mixture. Cover rice cooker. The rice cooker will automatically switch to Warm in a few minutes, when there is not much moisture left in the cooking mixture.

5. Keep the rice cooker at Warm for about 15 minutes before serving. Garnish with red chili.

Savory Taro Rice

Chinese dried shrimp are usually added when cooking savory taro rice. If using dried shrimp, omit the oyster sauce and reduce dark soy sauce to half, as dried shrimp are salty enough to add flavor to the rice. Fry the dried shrimp together with the taro cubes in this recipe.

INGREDIENTS | SERVES 3 OR 4

2 cups long-grain rice
2 tablespoons vegetable oil
2 cloves garlic, finely minced
3 shallots, thinly sliced
½ pound lean pork, cut into ½-inch cubes
4 fresh shiitake mushrooms caps, diced
2 cups diced taro (½-inch cubes)
½ teaspoon ground white pepper
Salt, to taste
3 cups water
1 teaspoon oyster sauce
1 teaspoon dark soy sauce
1 green onion, thinly sliced, for garnish

1. Rinse rice well by gently swirling the rice in the cooker pot with 2 or 3 changes of cold water. Drain rice and set aside in a separate bowl.

2. Add the oil to the rice cooker, cover, and set to Cook. When the base of the cooker pot gets warm, add the garlic, shallots, pork, and mushrooms and fry, stirring occasionally for about 3 minutes until pork is partially cooked (or turns brown at the surface). Dish out and set aside.

3. With the rice cooker still on Cook, add the taro cubes, white pepper, and salt to the pot and fry for about 3 minutes.

4. Add the rinsed rice, 3 cups water, oyster sauce, and soy sauce to the pot; mix well.

5. Return the pork mixture to the pot. Stir and mix well with the rice and taro cubes. Cover the rice cooker and cook the rice until completely done. (Cooking time varies with the type of rice cooker used. Most automatic rice cookers will switch to Warm when the rice is cooked.)

6. Let rice sit in the rice cooker for 5 to 10 minutes at Warm to vent off the remaining steam. Fluff up the rice before serving.

Taro and Potato

Taro is starchy, similar to potatoes. However, this tuber, when cooked, tastes more nutty than potatoes. The storage of taro is similar to potatoes. Store taro in a cool and dry location, for up to one week.

Beef Fried Rice

Ground beef cooks easily, but do not overcook it, as it will turn out rubbery and dry.

INGREDIENTS | SERVES 2 OR 3

3 tablespoons oil
3 shallots, thinly sliced
½ pound ground beef
¼ cup warm water
4 cups warm cooked rice
Salt and ground black pepper, to taste
1 green onion, finely chopped, for garnish

1. Add the oil to the rice cooker, cover, and set to Cook. When the base of the cooker pot gets warm, add the shallots and fry for about 8 minutes until slightly soft and caramelized.

2. Add the ground beef and fry briskly for about 8 to 10 minutes until beef turns brown on the surface and partially cooks through, being sure to cover the rice cooker occasionally in the processing of cooking.

3. Stir in the water, cover the rice cooker, and cook for 1 to 2 minutes, then switch to Warm and simmer the beef for about 8 to 10 minutes until completely cooked through.

4. Add the cooked rice into the rice cooker and mix well with the beef and shallots. Add salt and pepper to taste while fluffing up the rice.

5. Keep the rice cooker at Warm for about 15 minutes before serving. Garnish with green onions.

Egg and Shrimp Fried Rice

Substitute broccoli stems for the peas to add similar color and a hint of sweetness to the rice. Thinly slice the broccoli stems and then dice to smaller bits. Prepared in this way, they can be such a wonderful addition to many rice dishes.

INGREDIENTS | SERVES 2

- 3 tablespoons oil, divided use
- 2 cloves garlic, finely minced
- ½ cup frozen peas, thawed
- 2 eggs, lightly whisked
- 10 to 12 shrimp, peeled, deveined, and diced
- 4 cups warm cooked rice
- 1 teaspoon dark soy sauce
- Salt and ground white pepper, to taste
- 1 green onion, finely chopped, for garnish
- 1 fresh red chili pepper, seeded and thinly sliced, for garnish

Cooking Tip

When cooking fried rice over the stovetop, leftover cooked rice is typically used because it has become drier during storage in the fridge. Rice with less moisture is easier to fry in a pan or wok since it does not stick to the pan or wok surface under heat. In addition, the rice grains tend not to stick to one another and so will not result in clumpy fried rice! One benefit of using a rice cooker to make fried rice is that you do not have to worry about the rice sticking to itself or to pan and wok surfaces.

1. Add 1½ tablespoons of the oil to the rice cooker, cover, and set to Cook. When the base of the cooker pot gets warm, add the garlic and peas and sauté for about 5 minutes until the peas turn tender and cook through. Dish out and set aside.

2. With the rice cooker still on Cook, add the remaining 1½ tablespoons of oil. When the base of the pot gets warm, add the eggs. Scramble the eggs gently in the pot.

3. Add the shrimp and fry for about 8 minutes until shrimp cook through (turn pink) and egg is cooked.

4. Add the cooked rice, soy sauce, and pea mixture to the pot and mix well with the eggs and shrimp.

5. Keep the rice cooker at Warm for about 15 minutes before serving. Sprinkle with salt and pepper to taste. Garnish with green onion and red chili.

Beans and Rice

To vary this recipe, substitute curry powder for the garam masala powder. You also can try different kinds of beans, such as lentils and black beans, based on your personal preferences.

INGREDIENTS | SERVES 3 OR 4

2 cups long-grain rice
2 tablespoons butter
3 shallots, thinly sliced
1 cup diced tomatoes, with juice
1 cup canned garbanzo beans, drained
2 cups water or stock
¼ teaspoon garam masala
Salt, to taste

1. Rinse rice well by gently swirling the rice in the cooker pot with 2 or 3 changes of cold water. Drain the rice and set it aside in a separate bowl.

2. Clean out the rice cooker pot and wipe dry. Add the butter to the rice cooker pot, cover, and set to Cook. When the base of the cooker pot gets warm, add the shallots and fry for about 5 minutes until shallots turn soft.

3. Add the tomatoes and fry for 1 to 2 minutes.

4. Stir in the rice, beans, and the 2 cups water or stock and mix well with the shallots and tomatoes.

5. Add the garam masala and salt, and mix well with rice. Cover rice cooker and cook the rice until done. (Cooking time varies with the type of rice cooker used. Most automatic rice cookers will switch to Warm when the rice is cooked.)

6. After rice is cooked, do not open the cover immediately. Let it sit for 5 minutes to vent off the remaining steam. Fluff up the rice before serving.

Shrimp Pilaf

By definition, "pilaf" means rice cooked in seasoned broth with poultry or seafood and sometimes tomatoes. In the United States, pilaf is usually served as a side dish accompanying a main course such as grilled fish. Essentially, Indian Vegetable Biryani (page 61) is also considered a kind of pilaf.

INGREDIENTS | **SERVES 3 OR 4**

2 cups basmati rice
2 tablespoons butter, divided use
6 shallots, thinly sliced
1½ cups diced tomatoes, with juice
½ teaspoon red chili powder
1 teaspoon grated ginger
½ teaspoon garam masala
½ teaspoon salt
½ cup water
2 pounds shrimp, peeled and deveined
1 (2-inch) cinnamon stick
4 cardamom pods
6 whole cloves
2½ cups Shrimp Stock (page 17)
½ cup finely chopped cilantro leaves, for garnish

Basmati Rice
This long-grain variety is typically used in Indian cooking and is characterized by the thinness of the grain and its fragrance. Basmati rice grains tend to stay whole and separate when cooked with oil and spices.

1. Rinse rice well by gently swirling the rice in the cooker pot with 2 or 3 changes of cold water. Drain the rice and set aside in a separate bowl.

2. Clean out the rice cooker pot and wipe dry. Add 1 tablespoon of the butter to the rice cooker pot, cover, and set to Cook. When the base of the cooker pot gets warm, add the shallots and fry until shallots turn soft.

3. Add the tomatoes and chili powder and fry for about 2 minutes. Add the grated ginger, garam masala, salt, and water. Mix well. Stir in the shrimp and cook for about 8 minutes until the shrimp cook through (turn pink) and the gravy slightly reduces, being sure to cover the rice cooker occasionally in the process of cooking. Dish out the shrimp mixture and set aside.

4. Add the remaining 1 tablespoon of butter to the rice cooker pot. When base of cooker pot gets warm, add the cinnamon, cardamom, and cloves and fry until fragrant.

5. Add the rinsed rice and Shrimp Stock to the pot and mix well with the spices. Cover the rice cooker, switch to Cook and cook the rice until done. (Cooking time varies with the type of rice cooker used. Most automatic rice cookers will switch to Warm when the rice is cooked.)

6. After rice is cooked, do not open the cover immediately. Let it sit for 5 to 10 minutes to vent off the remaining steam. Fluff up the rice and gently slide the shrimp mixture back over the top of the rice before serving. Garnish with cilantro.

Rice Salad

Popularly known as Nasi Ulam in Malaysia, this is an herb-based rice dish or simply a rice salad with a variety of herbs and vegetables.

INGREDIENTS | SERVES 3 OR 4

6 whole round cabbage leaves
4 long beans, cut into halves
2 shallots (or small red onions), thinly sliced
2 tablespoons lime juice
4 cups warm cooked rice
½ cup finely chopped herb medley (mint leaves, kaffir lime leaves, basil leaves, cilantro leaves)

1. Fill the rice cooker pot with water to about the 4-cup mark. Cover the rice cooker and set to Cook. Place the cabbage and long beans on a plate that will fit into the steamer insert or basket. When the water in the rice cooker boils, place the steamer insert or basket that holds the plate of vegetables into the rice cooker and steam for 6 to 8 minutes, with the cooker covered, until the vegetables become tender. Set aside to cool. When cooled, finely slice the cabbage and dice the long beans. Drain excess moisture from the vegetables.

2. While waiting for vegetables to cool, prepare salad dressing by combining the shallots and lime juice in a bowl. Set aside.

3. Mix the vegetables and the dressing in a deep mixing bowl. Add the cooked rice and mix with medley of herbs. Serve rice salad as a side dish.

Asian "Paella"

Paella, which is another form of pilaf, is a traditional Spanish dish. This recipe makes use of mainly Chinese ingredients but layers up the rice similarly to how paella is cooked.

INGREDIENTS | SERVES 4

2 cups long-grain rice
2 tablespoons vegetable oil
½ pound boneless chicken pieces (thighs and breasts), chopped into bite-sized pieces
½ cup finely chopped onions
3 cloves garlic, finely minced
1 teaspoon grated ginger
1 tablespoon Chinese cooking wine
3 cups water or stock
10 shrimp, peeled, deveined, and diced into bite-sized pieces
½ cup thinly sliced green bell pepper
½ cup thinly sliced red bell pepper

1. Rinse rice well by gently swirling the rice in the cooker pot with 2 or 3 changes of cold water. Drain rice and set aside in a separate bowl.

2. Add the oil to the rice cooker, cover, and set to Cook. When the base of the cooker pot gets warm, add the chicken, onions, garlic, and ginger, and fry for about 3 minutes.

3. Add the Chinese cooking wine and continue to fry for 1 minute longer, or until chicken is partially cooked (chicken turns brown on the surface).

4. Stir in the rice and the 3 cups water or stock and mix well with the chicken. Cover rice cooker and cook rice. (Time to cook the rice varies with the type of rice cooker used. Most automatic rice cookers will switch to Warm when the rice is cooked.)

5. About 10 to 12 minutes before the rice is completely cooked (when the rice is almost dry), add the shrimp and bell peppers on top of the rice and continue to cook until the rice is completely done. During this time, the steam generated by the cooking process will cook the shrimp (shrimp turns pink when cooked).

6. Set the rice cooker on Warm for about 15 minutes before serving.

Do You Know?

Red onions are typically used raw or minimally cooked, while white and yellow onions are usually used for longer cooking. Typically, a darker-fleshed onion is milder and sweeter than others. However, that is not always true. A shallot is also a member of the onion family, but is formed in bulbs like garlic rather than like onions. Shallots are milder in flavor, and thus sometimes are used interchangeably with small red onions.

Easy Lemon Buttered Rice

This is best served as a side dish with grilled fish and roasted vegetables.

INGREDIENTS | SERVES 3 OR 4

2 cups long-grain rice
2 tablespoons butter
2 shallots, thinly sliced
3 cups water or Chicken Stock (page 16)
Zest of half a lemon
2 tablespoons lemon juice
Salt and black pepper, to taste

1. Rinse rice well by gently swirling the rice in the cooker pot with 2 or 3 changes of cold water until the water is not "cloudy" anymore. Drain rice and set aside in a separate bowl.

2. Add the butter to the rice cooker, cover, and set to Cook. When the base of the cooker pot gets warm, add the shallots and fry about 5 minutes until shallots are soft.

3. Add the rinsed rice and stir to coat the rice well with butter and shallots. Add the water or chicken stock to the rice, cover the rice cooker, and cook until the rice is done. (Cooking time varies with the type of rice cooker used. Most automatic rice cookers will switch to Warm when the rice is cooked.)

4. When the rice is done, add the lemon zest and drizzle lemon juice into the rice. Mix well by fluffing up the rice.

5. Sprinkle salt and black pepper on the rice to taste. Keep the rice cooker at Warm for about 5 minutes before serving.

Easy Spiced Rice with Peppers and Pine Nuts

You can try a different variety of nuts in this recipe, but remember to finely chop nuts that are bigger in size to get a balanced bite and texture in the rice. You want to have a consistent bite in every spoonful of rice.

INGREDIENTS | SERVES 3 OR 4

2 cups uncooked long-grain rice
3 cups Chicken Stock (page 16)
½ teaspoon turmeric
1 star anise pod
3 or 4 cardamom pods
3 or 4 whole cloves
½ cup diced green bell peppers
½ cup diced red bell peppers
½ cup pine nuts
Salt and black pepper, to taste

1. Rinse rice well by gently swirling the rice in the cooker pot with 2 or 3 changes of cold water. Drain rice and leave it in the pot.

2. Add enough Chicken Stock to cover the rice by about ½ inch. Add the turmeric, star anise, cardamon, and cloves and mix well. Cover the pot, set to Cook, and cook until the rice is done. (Cooking time varies with the type of rice cooker used. Most automatic rice cookers will switch to Warm when the rice is cooked.)

3. When the rice is cooked, top with the green and red bell peppers and pine nuts.

4. Turn the rice cooker to Warm for about 15 minutes, and add salt and pepper, then fluff up the rice before serving.

Do You Know?

Cardamom comes in several forms. The pod, which is the preferred form and retains aroma and flavor well and for a long period; the seed, which is generally crushed or ground prior to use; and ground cardamom, which is usually used because it's the most convenient but compromises slightly on freshness and full flavor.

Ground Beef and Rice Soup

To make a more robust rice soup, you can substitute leeks for the shallots or use a mixture of both to increase the depth and flavor.

INGREDIENTS | SERVES 3 OR 4

2 tablespoons butter
3 shallots, thinly sliced
2 cloves garlic, finely minced
½ pound ground beef
1 teaspoon dark soy sauce
½ teaspoon ground white pepper
1 teaspoon Chinese cooking wine
8 cups water
3 cups warm cooked rice, divided among 4 serving bowls
3 green onions, thinly sliced, for garnish

1. Add the butter to the rice cooker, cover, and set to Cook. When the base of the cooker pot gets warm, add the shallots and fry for about 5 minutes until shallots are soft.

2. Add the garlic and continue to fry for about 1 minute.

3. Add the ground beef, soy sauce, and white pepper. Fry for about 2 to 3 minutes, covering the rice cooker occasionally in the process of frying.

4. Add the Chinese cooking wine and fry for 1 minute.

5. Add the water. When soup mixture in the rice cooker boils, switch the rice cooker to Warm and simmer for about 15 minutes, until beef cooks through.

6. Before serving, ladle soup over cooked rice in serving bowls. Garnish with green onions.

Fish Kedgeree

Traditionally, kedgeree is a dish of flaked fish, cooked rice, hard-boiled eggs, and butter. Make it flexible, your way, by using leftover cooked fish (preferably grilled), fresh fish cooked on the same day, or canned fish.

INGREDIENTS | SERVES 3 OR 4

½ pound salmon
2 tablespoons butter
3 shallots, thinly sliced
2 cloves garlic, finely minced
5 cups warm cooked rice
2 hard-boiled eggs, peeled and chopped
2 green onions, finely chopped
¼ cup finely chopped cilantro leaves
Salt and black pepper, to taste

Cooking Tip

In addition to using leftover cooked fish, you also can whip up kedgeree easily when you have leftover hard-boiled eggs. If you will cook the hard-boiled eggs on the same day that you try this recipe, you can save time by boiling the eggs in the rice cooker before you steam the salmon. Place room-temperature eggs in the rice cooker, with enough cold water to cover them. Turn the rice cooker to Cook. Bring the water to a boil; continue boiling the eggs for 8 minutes with the rice cooker covered. Remove the eggs (leaving the boiling water in the pot) and run cold water over them. While the water in the rice cooker is still boiling, place the steamer insert or basket that holds the plate of salmon into the rice cooker, cover the cooker, and steam the salmon as directed in this recipe.

1. Fill the rice cooker pot with water to about the 4-cup mark. Cover the rice cooker and set to Cook. While the water is coming to a boil, place the salmon on a plate that will fit in the steamer insert or basket. When the water boils, place the plate that holds the salmon into the steamer insert or basket. Cover the rice cooker and steam for about 6 to 8 minutes or until the salmon cooks through (turns to light pinkish orange). Set aside the salmon and break into bite-sized flakes.

2. Clean out the rice cooker and wipe dry. Add the butter to the rice cooker, cover, and set to Cook. When the base of the cooker pot gets warm, add the shallots and fry about 5 minutes until shallots are soft, covering the rice cooker occasionally.

3. Add the garlic and continue to fry for about 1 minute, covering the rice cooker occasionally.

4. Add the cooked rice and flaked salmon and mix well to incorporate all the flavors.

5. Top with hard-boiled eggs, green onions, cilantro, black pepper, and salt. Switch rice cooker to Warm and allow it to sit for 5 to 10 minutes before serving.

CHAPTER 6

Comfort Congee (Rice Porridge) and Grains

Fish Congee
82

Seafood Congee
83

Chicken Congee
84

Tuna and Corn Congee
84

Pork Congee
85

Pumpkin Congee
86

Sweet Potato Congee
87

Gojiberry Congee
87

Taro and Spinach Congee
88

Corn, Carrot, and Pea Congee
89

Fish Congee

There are two common types of fish congee in Asia. In one of them (this recipe) the fish is cooked together with the rice porridge, and the finished dish has a "gluey" consistency. The other is a fish soup ladled over fish slices and rice (similar to Halibut and Asparagus Soup, page 47).

INGREDIENTS | **SERVES 2**

1 cup long-grain rice

2 fish fillets (snapper, cod, sea bass), cut into about ¼-inch-thick slices

¼ teaspoon salt

¼ teaspoon ground white pepper

½ teaspoon sesame oil

1 teaspoon Chinese cooking wine

4 to 6 cups water, less water for thicker consistency

1-inch piece fresh ginger, thinly sliced

½ teaspoon sesame oil, to be drizzled

Ground white pepper, to taste

¼ cup finely chopped green onions, for garnish

¼ cup Fried Ginger Strips (page 284), for garnish

Rice Storage Tips

Place the opened rice package in an airtight container to help keep out moisture and rice weevils. Store the container in a dry, cool place.

1. Rinse rice well by gently swirling the rice in the cooker pot with 2 or 3 changes of cold water. Drain rice.

2. Combine the fish slices with salt, pepper, sesame oil, and Chinese cooking wine. Set in the fridge to marinate.

3. Add the rinsed rice and the water to the rice cooker, cover, and set to Cook. When you hear the rice cooker making noises and see some over-bubbling of fluid at the lid, lift up the rice cooker cover. Add the ginger slices, stir the congee, and continue to cook for 30 to 45 minutes with the cover tilted slightly to vent the steam pressure, stirring occasionally. During this process, adjust the amount of water depending on whether you like soupy or thick rice congee.

4. Add the marinated fish slices to the congee, partially cover the rice cooker, and bring to a boil again. The fish slices should be cooked (turns opaque) in about 5 minutes. (Do not overcook the fish by boiling the congee for too long.)

5. Dish out congee into serving bowls and drizzle each with two drops of sesame oil. Add a dash of pepper and garnish with green onions and Fried Ginger Strips before serving.

Seafood Congee

To add variety, you can also add fishballs to your seafood congee. You can buy them already made or make your own as directed in Fishball (Dumpling) Soup, page 46.

INGREDIENTS | SERVES 2 OR 3

1 cup long-grain rice, rinsed and drained

4 to 5 cups water, less water for thicker consistency

1-inch piece fresh ginger, thinly sliced

½ cup shrimp, peeled, deveined, and diced

½ cup fresh baby scallops

1 fish fillet (cod), thinly sliced

Ground white pepper, to taste

2 green onions, finely chopped, for garnish

1. Add rinsed rice and the water to rice cooker, cover, and set to Cook. When you hear the rice cooker making noises and see some over-bubbling of fluid at the lid, lift up the rice cooker cover. Add the ginger, stir well, and continue to simmer for 30 to 45 minutes with the cover tilted slightly to vent the steam pressure, stirring occasionally, until the rice turns into a soft pulp.

2. Stir in shrimp, scallops, fish slices, and pepper. Partially cover rice cooker and simmer for 15 to 20 minutes until seafood cooks through.

3. During this process, adjust the amount of water depending on whether you like soupy or thick rice congee. Garnish with green onions.

Chicken Congee

Leftover Thanksgiving turkey? Shred the turkey and substitute it for the chicken in this recipe.

INGREDIENTS | SERVES 2 OR 3

1 cup long-grain rice, rinsed and drained

4 to 5 cups Chicken Stock (page 16), less stock for thicker consistency

½ pound boneless chicken (thighs and breasts), cut into thin strips

½-inch piece fresh ginger, finely shredded

Salt and ground white pepper, to taste

¼ teaspoon sesame oil, for drizzling

1 green onion, finely chopped, for garnish

1. Add the rinsed rice and chicken stock to rice cooker, cover, and set to Cook. When you hear the rice cooker making noises and see some over-bubbling of fluid at the lid, lift up the rice cooker cover. Continue to simmer for 30 to 45 minutes with the cover tilted slightly to vent the steam pressure, stirring occasionally, until the rice turns into a soft pulp.

2. Stir in the chicken, ginger, salt, and pepper. Simmer and cook, partially covered, for 15 to 20 minutes until chicken cooks through. Continue cooking and adjust the amount of water, depending on whether you like soupy or thick rice congee. Before serving, drizzle with sesame oil and garnish with green onions.

Tuna and Corn Congee

Tuna or salmon flakes can make this congee a nutritious and comforting breakfast meal.

INGREDIENTS | SERVES 2 OR 3

1 cup long-grain rice, rinsed and drained

4 to 5 cups water, less water for thicker consistency

1 cup flaked tuna from a can

1 cup corn kernels, drained

Ground white pepper, to taste

1. Add the rinsed rice and water to the rice cooker, cover, and set to Cook. When you hear the rice cooker making noises and see some over-bubbling of fluid at the lid, lift up the rice cooker cover, stir the congee, and continue to cook for 30 to 45 minutes with the cover tilted slightly to vent the steam pressure. Stir occasionally.

2. Add flaked tuna, corn, and pepper, and continue cooking for 15 to 20 minutes, stirring occasionally. Adjust the amount of water, depending on whether you like soupy or thick rice congee.

Pork Congee

Make pork meatballs (as in the Meatballs and Napa Cabbage Soup recipe, page 41) and add them to the pork congee.

INGREDIENTS | SERVES 2 OR 3

2 tablespoons vegetable oil
½ pound lean pork strips (about ¼-inch thick each strip)
2 cloves garlic, thinly sliced
4 fresh shiitake mushroom caps, thinly sliced
½ teaspoon dark soy sauce
¼ teaspoon salt
¼ teaspoon pepper
1 cup long-grain rice, rinsed and drained
4 to 5 cups water, less water for thicker consistency
Ground white pepper, to taste
2 green onions, finely chopped, for garnish

1. Add the oil to the rice cooker, cover, and set to Cook. When the base of the cooker pot gets warm, add the pork, garlic, mushrooms, soy sauce, salt, and pepper. Fry for about 5 to 8 minutes until fragrant, covering the rice cooker occasionally in the process of frying.

2. When fragrant, dish out half of the pork mixture and set aside in a bowl.

3. Add the rinsed rice to the remaining pork mixture; stir to mix well.

4. Slowly add the water, cover the rice cooker, and allow the mixture to come to a boil. When you hear the rice cooker making noises and see some over-bubbling of fluid at the lid, lift up the rice cooker cover.

5. Add the reserved pork mixture, stir gently, and continue to simmer for 30 to 45 minutes with the cover tilted slightly to vent the steam pressure. Stir occasionally, until the rice turns into a soft pulp. During this process you can adjust the amount of water, depending on whether you like soupy or thick rice congee.

6. Season with white pepper and garnish with green onions before serving.

Pumpkin Congee

Pumpkin adds a mild sweetness to this dish, and complements the savory flavor of the pork.

INGREDIENTS | SERVES 2 OR 3

2 tablespoons vegetable oil
½ pound ground pork
2 cloves garlic, finely minced
2 fresh shiitake mushroom caps, finely diced
1 cup finely diced pumpkin (½-inch cubes)
½ teaspoon dark soy sauce
¼ teaspoon salt
¼ teaspoon pepper
1 cup long-grain rice, rinsed and drained
4 to 5 cups water, less water for thicker consistency
Ground white pepper, to taste
2 green onions, finely chopped, for garnish

Cooking Tip

In many Chinese restaurants, the rice congee served is so smooth that you cannot even see the whole grains anymore. A lot of chefs use a mixture of rice grains (broken grains, pearl rice grains, and others) to achieve the smooth "gluey" consistency. If you are using only long-grain or short-grain rice at home, you can stir the rice mixture at intervals during cooking and simmering. This will break up the whole grains and allow the final consistency to be smooth.

1. Add the oil to the rice cooker, cover, and set to Cook. When the base of the cooker pot gets warm, add the pork, garlic, mushrooms, pumpkin, soy sauce, salt, and pepper. Fry for about 5 to 8 minutes until fragrant, covering the rice cooker occasionally in the process of frying.

2. When fragrant, dish out half of the pork mixture and set aside in a bowl.

3. Add the rinsed rice to the remaining pork mixture; stir to mix well.

4. Slowly add the water, cover the rice cooker, and allow the mixture to come to a boil. When you hear the rice cooker making noises and see some over-bubbling of fluid at the lid, lift up the rice cooker cover. Add the reserved pork mixture, stir gently, and continue to simmer for 30 to 45 minutes with the cover tilted slightly to vent the steam pressure. Stir occasionally, until the rice turns into a soft pulp. During this process you can adjust the amount of water, depending on whether you like soupy or thick rice congee.

5. Season with pepper and garnish with green onions before serving.

Sweet Potato Congee

Adding sweet potatoes to rice porridge seems to have originated during wartime, when rice was considered expensive and sweet potatoes were in abundance. The sweet potatoes were added to rice congee to give it more bulk and substance.

INGREDIENTS | SERVES 4

1 cup long-grain rice, rinsed and drained

4 to 5 cups water, less water for thicker consistency

1 peeled sweet potato, cut into 1-inch chunks

Salt, to taste

1. Add the rinsed rice and water to the rice cooker, cover, and set to Cook. When you hear the rice cooker making noises and see some over-bubbling of fluid at the lid, lift up the rice cooker cover.

2. Add the sweet potatoes and salt, stir the congee, and continue to cook for 30 to 45 minutes with the cover tilted slightly to vent the steam pressure. Stir occasionally. During this process you can adjust the amount of water, depending on whether you like soupy or thick rice congee.

Gojiberry Congee

Presoak the dried gojiberries in water to soften them slightly prior to cooking. Do not add them until about 5 minutes before serving the congee, because the gojiberries become bitter when they are cooked too long.

INGREDIENTS | SERVES 2 OR 3

1 cup long-grain rice, rinsed and drained

4 to 5 cups water, less water for thicker consistency

½ cup dried gojiberries, soaked in warm water

1. Add the rinsed rice and water to the rice cooker, cover, and set to Cook. When you hear the rice cooker making noises and see some over-bubbling of fluid at the lid, lift up the rice cooker cover, stir the congee, and continue to cook for 30 to 45 minutes with the cover tilted slightly to vent the steam pressure. Stir occasionally. During this process you can adjust the amount of water, depending on whether you like soupy or thick rice congee.

2. About 5 minutes before serving the congee, stir in gojiberries.

Do You Know?

Gojiberry is also known as Chinese wolfberry and has been touted as one of the superfoods in recent years due to the amount of antioxidants, nutrients, and fiber the berries contain. Specifically, gojiberry has high amounts of beta carotene, essential minerals, and vitamins B and C. In traditional Chinese medicine, gojiberry is also a natural supplement known to relieve eye strain.

CHAPTER 6 **COMFORT CONGEE (RICE PORRIDGE) AND GRAINS**

Taro and Spinach Congee

Substitute chicken or beef for the pork if preferred.

INGREDIENTS | SERVES 2 OR 3

2 tablespoons vegetable oil

½ pound lean pork strips (about ¼-inch thick each strip)

1 cup peeled and cubed taro (½-inch cubes)

½ teaspoon dark soy sauce

¼ teaspoon salt

¼ teaspoon pepper

1 cup long-grain rice, rinsed and drained

4 to 5 cups water, less water for thicker consistency

3 cups tightly packed fresh baby spinach

Do You Know?

Congee is one of the common Chinese home remedies for the symptoms of colds and flu. It is believed that the cooking liquid in which the congee is simmered contains a lot of vitamin B (due to the rice grains breaking down) and can boost both the immune system and energy level. The liquid also prevents the dehydration that can occur with a cold or the flu.

1. Add the oil to the rice cooker, cover, and set to Cook. When the base of the cooker pot gets warm, add the pork, taro cubes, soy sauce, salt, and pepper. Fry for about 5 to 8 minutes until fragrant, covering the rice cooker occasionally in the process of frying. When fragrant, dish out the pork and taro mixture and set aside in a bowl.

2. Add the rinsed rice and water to the rice cooker, and cover. When you hear the rice cooker making noises and see some over-bubbling of fluid at the lid, lift up the rice cooker cover.

3. Add the pork and taro mixture, stir the congee, and continue to cook for about 30 minutes with the cover tilted slightly to vent the steam pressure, stirring occasionally. During this process you can adjust the amount of water, depending on whether you like soupy or thick rice congee.

4. About 5 minutes before serving, stir in the spinach.

Corn, Carrot, and Pea Congee

This is an easy recipe when frozen vegetables are used.

INGREDIENTS | SERVES 2 OR 3

4 to 5 cups Chicken Stock (page 16), less stock for thicker consistency

1 cup long-grain rice, rinsed and drained

1½ to 2 cups frozen mixed vegetables (corn, carrots, and peas)

½ teaspoon salt

Ground white pepper, to taste

2 green onions, finely chopped, for garnish

1. Add the rinsed rice and chicken stock to rice cooker, cover, and set to Cook. When you hear the rice cooker making noises and see some over-bubbling of fluid at the lid, lift up the rice cooker cover and continue to simmer for 30 to 45 minutes with the cover tilted slightly to vent the steam pressure. Stir occasionally, until the rice turns into a soft pulp.

2. Add the vegetables, salt, and pepper and continue cooking for 15 to 20 minutes. Adjust the amount of water, depending on whether you like soupy or thick rice congee.

3. Garnish with green onions and serve.

CHAPTER 7

Pasta Fusion

Fish Pasta
91

Beef and Shiitake Pasta
92

Chicken and Shrimp Pasta
93

Chicken Macaroni
94

Tomato and Shrimp Pasta
95

Creamy Mushroom Pasta
96

Pasta and Leek Stir-Fry
97

Pasta Arrabiata
97

Easy Shrimp and Celery Pasta Salad
98

Lentil Soup with Pasta
99

Spicy Italian Sausage Pasta
100

Lemon Pasta
101

Mushroom Pasta
101

Macaroni with Chinese Meat Sauce
102

Spinach and Pine Nut Pasta
103

Pasta and Tuna Salad
103

Fish Pasta

Adding blanched vegetables, such as broccoli or Chinese vegetables like bok choy, will make your pasta more colorful and nutritious.

INGREDIENTS | SERVES 2

1 (6 ounce) snapper fillet, cut into ¼-inch thick slices
¼ teaspoon salt
¼ teaspoon freshly ground black pepper
3 tablespoons extra-virgin olive oil
1 large size onion, thinly sliced
3 cloves garlic, finely minced
1 (14½-ounce) can diced tomatoes, with juice
½ cup water or stock
Salt and freshly ground black pepper, to taste
½ pound fusilli, cooked (see Pasta, page 15)
½ teaspoon dried oregano
½ teaspoon dried basil

Cooking Tip

Bottled pasta sauces usually contain high amounts of sodium. Make your own Marinara Sauce (page 15) and you can control your sodium intake. It is worthwhile to make this effort.

1. Season the fish with salt and pepper. Set aside.

2. Add the oil to the rice cooker, cover, and set to Cook. When the base of the cooker pot gets warm, add the fish slices, cover the rice cooker, and cook the fish for about 3 minutes per side, until the fish cooks through. Dish out and set aside.

3. Using the remaining oil in the pot, add the onions and fry for about 8 minutes until they are soft and slightly caramelized.

4. Add the garlic and fry for about 1 to 2 minutes. Cover the rice cooker occasionally in the process of frying.

5. Stir in tomatoes and water or stock. Cover the rice cooker. When sauce starts to boil, lift rice cooker lid and continue to simmer for about 2 to 3 minutes until sauce reduces slightly. Add salt and pepper to taste. Switch rice cooker to Warm.

6. Add the cooked pasta and mix with sauce. Add dried basil and oregano and mix well. Dish out pasta into serving bowls, top with fish slices, and serve.

Beef and Shiitake Pasta

Use a mixture of fresh white, brown, or shiitake mushrooms for a different depth and flavor in this recipe.

INGREDIENTS | SERVES 2 OR 3

2 tablespoons extra-virgin olive oil
1 medium-size onion, thinly sliced
½ tablespoon butter
3 cloves garlic, finely minced
½ pound ground beef
6 fresh shiitake mushroom caps, thinly sliced
1 (14½-ounce) can diced tomatoes, with juice
1 cup water or stock
Salt and freshly ground black pepper, to taste
½ pound fusilli, cooked (see Pasta, page 15)
½ teaspoon dried basil, for garnish

1. Add the oil to the rice cooker, cover, and set to Cook. When the base of the cooker pot gets warm, add the onions and fry until slightly soft.

2. Add the butter and garlic and fry for about 2 minutes, covering the rice cooker occasionally in the process of frying.

3. Add the ground beef and mix well with the other ingredients. Fry for about 3 to 4 minutes until beef turns brown on the surface. Dish out and set aside.

4. Add the mushrooms, tomatoes, and water or stock to the pot and mix well. Cover the rice cooker. When the sauce mixture starts to boil, return the beef mixture to the rice cooker and allow mixture to come to a slight simmer. Then lift up rice cooker lid and simmer for about 10 to 12 minutes until sauce reduces slightly and beef cooks through.

5. Add salt and pepper to taste. Switch rice cooker to Warm.

6. Add the cooked pasta and mix thoroughly with the sauce. Garnish with basil and serve.

Chicken and Shrimp Pasta

Shell-shaped pasta is preferred for this recipe as it is easier to toss with the chicken and shrimp.

INGREDIENTS | SERVES 2 OR 3

2 tablespoons vegetable oil

3 cloves garlic, finely minced

¼ pound boneless chicken (thigh and breast), chopped into bite-sized pieces

8 to 10 shrimp, peeled, deveined, and diced

1 teaspoon oyster sauce

1 cup water or stock

Salt and ground white pepper, to taste

½ pound pasta, cooked (see Pasta, page 15)

1 cup blanched broccoli florets

1 fresh red chili pepper, seeded and thinly sliced, for garnish

Cooking Tip

Blanch the broccoli florets by plunging them into boiling water and cooking for 30 seconds or more, until the florets are slightly tender. Then remove the florets immediately and plunge them into an ice-water bath (also called "shocking"). The process of shocking stops further cooking in the broccoli and helps to retain a nice green color.

1. Add the oil to the rice cooker, cover, and set to Cook. When the base of the cooker pot gets warm, add the garlic and fry for about 1 minute.

2. Add the chicken and fry for about 5 minutes, until the chicken almost cooks through, covering the rice cooker occasionally in the processing of cooking.

3. Add the shrimp and fry for about 3 to 4 minutes, until the shrimp turn pink and cook through, covering the rice cooker occasionally in the process of cooking. The chicken will finish cooking during this time as well.

4. Add the oyster sauce and water or stock, cover the rice cooker, and allow the mixture to come to a boil. When mixture starts to boil, switch the rice cooker to Warm and continue to simmer for about 8 minutes until sauce slightly reduces.

5. Add salt and pepper, cooked pasta, and broccoli, and mix well. When the gravy gets mostly absorbed into the pasta, dish out and serve immediately. Garnish with sliced red chili.

Chicken Macaroni

Macaroni, a type of short, curved, hollow pasta, is also known as elbow pasta. Most commonly used in macaroni and cheese, macaroni is also perfect for soups, salads, and casseroles.

INGREDIENTS | SERVES 2

6 cups water, or enough to immerse the chicken
3 to 4 stalks celery, cut into bite-sized pieces
1 carrot, cut into bite-sized pieces
½ pound chicken (thighs and breasts)
½ pound macaroni, cooked (see Pasta, page 15)
1 green onion, finely chopped
Salt and ground white pepper, to taste

1. Add the water to the pot, cover, and set to Cook.

2. When the water boils, lift up the rice cooker lid, add the celery and carrots, and completely immerse the chicken into the pot. Cover the rice cooker and bring the soup to a boil.

3. When the soup starts boiling, switch the rice cooker to Warm and continue to simmer for about 45 minutes or until the chicken cooks through.

4. Dish out the chicken and thinly shred it. Set aside.

5. Divide the macaroni among the serving bowls, top with shredded chicken, and ladle soup, celery, and carrots over the macaroni.

6. Top with green onions, salt, and a dash of white pepper to taste.

Cooking Tip

When not serving this dish immediately, remove the celery and carrots once they are cooked. If they are kept warm in the rice cooker for too long, they will turn limp and become discolored. When ready to serve, spoon the chicken, celery, and carrots on top of the macaroni in the serving bowls, and ladle warm soup over the macaroni.

Tomato and Shrimp Pasta

Serve this pasta on an open omelet. It makes an entirely new presentation.

INGREDIENTS | SERVES 2 OR 3

2 tablespoons extra-virgin olive oil

3 shallots, thinly sliced

12 to 16 shrimp, peeled, deveined, and diced

1 (14½-ounce) can diced tomatoes, with juice

¼ teaspoon salt

¼ teaspoon freshly ground black pepper

½ pound fusilli, cooked (see Pasta, page 15)

¼ teaspoon dried oregano, for garnish

1. Add the oil to the rice cooker pot, cover, and set to Cook. When the base of the cooker pot gets warm, add the shallots and fry until shallots turn slightly soft.

2. Add the shrimp and fry for about 3 to 4 minutes or until shrimp cook through (turn pink), covering the rice cooker occasionally in the process of cooking.

3. Add the tomatoes, mix well, cover the rice cooker, and allow to come to a slight simmer.

4. Once simmering, lift up the rice cooker lid, add salt and black pepper to taste, and simmer until sauce reduces slightly.

5. Add the cooked pasta and mix well. Garnish with oregano before serving.

Creamy Mushroom Pasta

They are many types of pasta shapes, such as shell, tubular, and strand. Choosing the correct pasta shape for the sauce is important since different pasta shapes carry light or heavy sauces in different ways. The spiral shape of fusilli is perfect for this recipe.

INGREDIENTS | SERVES 2

2 tablespoons extra-virgin olive oil
½ tablespoon butter
3 shallots, thinly sliced
2 cups thinly sliced white or brown mushrooms
¼ teaspoon salt
¼ teaspoon freshly ground black pepper
1 cup whole milk
½ pound fusilli, cooked (see Pasta, page 15)
¼ cup grated Cheddar cheese
¼ cup grated Parmesan cheese

Cooking Tip
To make a thicker sauce, use 1 cup heavy cream instead of milk, or ½ cup heavy cream and ½ cup milk.

1. Add the oil and butter to the rice cooker pot, cover, and set to Cook. When the base of the cooker pot gets warm, add the shallots and fry for about 5 minutes until shallots turn slightly soft.

2. Add the mushrooms and fry for about 5 to 8 minutes until mushrooms become soft and moist, covering rice cooker occasionally in the process of frying.

3. Add the salt and freshly ground black pepper. Slowly stir the milk into the pot, cover the rice cooker, and bring to a slight simmer. When simmering, lift the rice cooker lid and stir the milk sauce constantly for about 5 minutes until it reduces slightly.

4. Add the cooked pasta to the sauce and stir until the sauce reduces further.

5. Top with Cheddar cheese and Parmesan cheese. Serve immediately.

Pasta and Leek Stir-Fry

Replace the leeks with thinly sliced onions as a variation.

INGREDIENTS | SERVES 2

2 tablespoons extra-virgin olive oil
½ pound leeks, thinly sliced
2 cups frozen corn, or canned corn kernels, drained
3 green onions, thinly sliced
Salt and freshly black pepper, to taste
½ pound fusilli, cooked (see Pasta, page 15)

1. Add the oil to the rice cooker pot, cover, and set to Cook. When the base of the cooker pot gets warm, add the leeks and corn and fry for about 5 minutes or more, until leeks turn slightly soft, covering rice cooker occasionally in the process of cooking. Add the green onions and continue to fry for about 1 minute.

2. Add the salt and pepper to taste, followed by the cooked pasta, switching to Warm when moisture starts to dry off from the pasta, stirring occasionally in the process of frying, with the rice cooker uncovered.

3. Stir the mixture well before serving.

Pasta Arrabiata

Arrabiata is traditionally a sauce made from garlic, tomatoes, basil, and red chili cooked in olive oil. The dish is usually served with pasta and chopped fresh parsley.

INGREDIENTS | SERVES 2

1 tablespoon butter
12 shrimp, peeled and deveined
2 cups Marinara Sauce (page 15)
4 whole red dried chili peppers
½ pound fusilli, cooked (see Pasta, page 15)
½ teaspoon dried oregano, for garnish

1. Add the butter to the rice cooker pot, cover, and set to Cook. When the base of the cooker pot gets warm, add the shrimp and fry 3 to 4 minutes until the shrimp cook through (turn pink), covering the rice cooker occasionally in the process of cooking. Dish out and set aside.

2. Stir the marinara sauce into the pot and cover. When the mixture starts to boil, lift up the rice cooker lid, add the red chili, stir well, and allow to simmer until sauce slightly reduces, stirring occasionally.

3. Switch to Warm, add the cooked pasta, and mix well.

4. Before serving, dish out the pasta onto serving plates and top it with cooked shrimp. Garnish with oregano.

Easy Shrimp and Celery Pasta Salad

Fresh large tomatoes can be substituted for the cherry tomatoes in this recipe. Slice large tomatoes into smaller wedges so they can be tossed easily in the salad.

INGREDIENTS | SERVES 2

- 12 to 16 shrimp, peeled and deveined
- 2 teaspoons grated ginger
- ½ pound fusilli, cooked (see Pasta, page 15)
- 1 stalk celery, finely shredded
- 4 cherry tomatoes, cut into quarters
- ½ teaspoon sesame oil
- Ground black and white pepper, to taste
- 1 green onion, finely chopped, for garnish

1. Season the shrimp with ginger and set aside on a plate that will fit into the steamer insert or basket.

2. Fill the rice cooker pot with water to about the 4-cup mark. Cover the rice cooker and set to Cook.

3. When the water in the rice cooker boils, place the steamer insert or basket that holds the plate of shrimp into the cooker and steam, with the rice cooker covered, for about 6 to 8 minutes or until the shrimp turn pink and cook through. Remove and set aside.

4. Clean out the rice cooker and wipe dry. Using the rice cooker pot as the mixing bowl, add the cooked pasta, shrimp, celery, tomatoes, sesame oil, and pepper. Mix well. Garnish with green onions before serving.

Lentil Soup with Pasta

If using dried lentils, separately cook the lentils in stock for about 1 hour or more until they become tender. Canned lentils are more convenient when you want to whip up this dish in less than 30 minutes.

INGREDIENTS | SERVES 3 OR 4

8 cups water, for cooking pasta
1 to 2 teaspoons salt, to taste
½ pound pasta, preferably shell or bowtie pasta
1 tablespoon extra-virgin olive oil
1 tablespoon finely chopped bacon
½ cup finely chopped onions
2 cloves garlic, finely minced
1 stalk celery, finely chopped
1 cup canned lentils, drained
6 cups water or stock
1 stalk celery, finely chopped
Salt and ground black pepper, to taste

Cooking Tip

When is pasta al dente? The only way to tell if the pasta is correctly cooked to the texture you prefer is to sample it while cooking. Al dente means the pasta is firm, yet tender. For strand-shaped pasta, for example, al dente means a tiny uncooked core in the middle of the strand.

1. Add the water to the rice cooker pot, cover, and set to Cook. When the water comes to a boil, lift up the rice cooker lid and add the salt and pasta. Stir the pasta gently to prevent it from sticking to the base of the pot. Cover the rice cooker and allow pasta to cook for about 5 to 6 minutes. The pasta should be slightly undercooked. Dish out, drain, and set aside.

2. Clean out the rice cooker and wipe dry. Add the oil to the rice cooker pot, cover, and set to Cook. When the base of the cooker pot gets warm, add the bacon, onions, garlic, and celery and fry for about 5 minutes until onions turn soft and bacon begins to brown, covering the rice cooker occasionally in the process of cooking.

3. Add the partially cooked pasta and stir to coat it with the bacon mixture.

4. Add the lentils and stock and cover the rice cooker. Bring the mixture to a boil.

5. Once boiling, switch the rice cooker to Warm and continue to simmer for about 8 minutes until the pasta is fully cooked. Add salt and pepper to taste. Ladle pasta with soup into serving bowls.

Spicy Italian Sausage Pasta

*Spicy chorizo sausage also has a lot of flavor.
Use that as a variation in this dish.*

INGREDIENTS | SERVES 2 OR 3

1 tablespoon extra-virgin olive oil
½ cup finely chopped onions
1 clove garlic, finely minced
3 spicy Italian sausages, cut into bite-sized pieces
½ (14½-ounce) can of diced tomatoes, with juice
½ pound fusilli, cooked (see Pasta, page 15)
3 cups fresh baby spinach

1. Add the oil to the rice cooker pot, cover, and set to Cook. When the base of the cooker pot gets warm, add the onions and garlic and fry for about 3 minutes or more, until onions turn slightly soft, covering the rice cooker occasionally in the process of frying.

2. Add sausage and fry for about 3 minutes. Stir and cover the rice cooker occasionally in the process of frying.

3. Stir in the tomatoes and continue to cook for about 2 minutes, covering rice cooker occasionally in the process of cooking.

4. Add the cooked pasta and mix well.

5. Switch rice cooker to Warm and add the spinach. Mix well with pasta and sauce. Serve warm.

Lemon Pasta

This dish can be served warm or cold. It is light and refreshing and makes a wonderful summer dish.

INGREDIENTS | SERVES 2

- 2 tablespoons extra-virgin olive oil
- 2 cloves garlic, finely minced
- 1 teaspoon grated ginger
- ½ teaspoon red chili pepper flakes
- 3 tablespoons lemon juice
- 2 tablespoons water
- Salt and freshly ground black pepper, to taste
- ½ pound thin-strand pasta, cooked (see Pasta, page 15)
- Zest of half a lemon, for garnish
- ¼ cup finely chopped cilantro leaves, for garnish

1. Add the oil to the rice cooker pot, cover, and set to Cook. When the base of the cooker pot gets warm, add the garlic, ginger, and crushed red pepper flakes and fry about 5 minutes until fragrant, covering rice cooker occasionally in the process of frying. Dish out and set aside in deep mixing bowl.

2. Add the lemon juice and water to the garlic and oil mixture as dressing. Season with salt and pepper to taste.

3. Add the pasta and toss well with the dressing. Garnish with lemon zest and cilantro.

Mushroom Pasta

This dish is full of earthy flavors due to the variety of mushrooms. Choose a Chinese vegetable such as bok choy or choy sum, blanch it, and toss it into the final pasta dish.

INGREDIENTS | SERVES 2

- 2 tablespoons extra-virgin olive oil
- 3 shallots, thinly sliced
- 4 fresh shiitake mushroom caps, thinly sliced
- 1 cup white mushrooms, thinly sliced
- 1 cup brown mushrooms, thinly sliced
- 1 (14½-ounce) can diced tomatoes, with juice
- 1 cup water
- Salt and ground black pepper, to taste
- ½ pound fusilli, cooked (see Pasta, page 15)
- ¼ teaspoon dried oregano, for garnish

1. Add the oil to the rice cooker pot, cover, and set to Cook. When the base of the cooker pot gets warm, add the shallots and fry until shallots turn slightly soft.

2. Add the mushrooms, followed by the tomatoes and water. Mix well. Cover the rice cooker and set to Cook. When the sauce mixture starts to simmer, switch the rice cooker to Warm and continue to simmer for 10 to 15 minutes or until the mushrooms become tender.

3. Add salt and black pepper to taste. Add the cooked pasta and mix well. Garnish with oregano before serving.

Macaroni with Chinese Meat Sauce

Due to its shape and size, macaroni can also be a good pasta choice for stir-fries.

INGREDIENTS | SERVES 2

2 tablespoons oil
3 shallots, thinly sliced
1 cup frozen edamame (green soybeans), thawed
½ pound ground beef
½ teaspoon oyster sauce
1 cup hot water
½ pound macaroni, cooked (see Pasta, page 15)
Salt and ground white pepper, to taste
1 green onion, thinly sliced, for garnish

1. Add the oil to the rice cooker, cover, and set to Cook. When the base of the cooker pot gets warm, add the shallots and beans and fry about 5 minutes until shallots are slightly caramelized.

2. Add the ground beef (breaking up into smaller bits) and fry briskly for about 8 minutes, covering the rice cooker occasionally in the process of frying, until beef cooks through.

3. Add the oyster sauce and water to the pot, cover the rice cooker, and cook for about 1 minute; then switch to Warm and simmer for about 8 to 10 minutes until the beef completely cooks through.

4. Add the cooked macaroni and mix well with the beef mixture. Season with salt and white pepper to taste. Garnish with green onions before serving.

Benefits of Edamame

Edamame (green soybeans) are high in proteins and vitamins A, B, and C. They are sometimes known as "Protein of the Mountains," as soybeans offer a complete protein profile containing all essential amino acids.

Spinach and Pine Nut Pasta

As a variation, you can add 1 tablespoon raisins to complement the savory taste of the bacon.

INGREDIENTS | SERVES 2

1 tablespoon extra-virgin olive oil
1 tablespoon finely chopped bacon
3 shallots, finely sliced
6 cups tightly packed fresh baby spinach
½ pound fusilli, cooked (see Pasta, page 15)
1 cup pine nuts

1. Add the oil to the rice cooker pot, cover, and set to Cook. When the base of the cooker pot gets warm, add the bacon and shallots and fry for about 5 minutes until shallots turn soft and bacon begins to brown, covering the rice cooker occasionally in the process of frying.

2. Add the spinach and fry briskly until spinach just cooks, stirring and covering rice cooker occasionally in the process of frying. Dish out in a deep mixing bowl and toss with cooked pasta and pine nuts.

Pasta and Tuna Salad

Bowtie or ribbon pasta work well in this pasta salad recipe.

INGREDIENTS | SERVES 2

1 tablespoon finely chopped bacon
1 cup finely diced green beans
1 cup diced cherry tomatoes
½ pound bowtie pasta, cooked (see Pasta, page 15)
1 tablespoon extra-virgin olive oil
1 tablespoon lemon juice
¼ cup finely chopped cilantro leaves
Salt and freshly ground black pepper, to taste
1 cup canned tuna flakes

1. Turn the rice cooker to Cook. When the base of the cooker pot gets warm, add the bacon, green beans, and tomatoes. Fry for about 5 minutes until green beans turn tender and bacon begins to brown, covering the rice cooker occasionally in the process of frying. Dish out in a deep mixing bowl.

2. Combine cooked pasta with the green bean mixture.

3. In a separate bowl, combine the olive oil, lemon juice, and cilantro leaves and season with salt and black pepper.

4. Pour the dressing over the pasta. Top with tuna flakes and serve.

Cooking Tip

You can cut down on the amount of fat in this recipe by omitting the olive oil in the dressing.

CHAPTER 8

Oodling Noodles

Chilled Soba in
Green Onion Dressing
105

Warm Soba and Japanese
Mushrooms in Ginger Dressing
106

Soba in Tahini Sauce
107

Summer Soba with Spinach
and Mushrooms
108

Kimchi Soba Soup
109

Smoked Salmon with Soba
110

Udon in Mildly
Spiced Cauliflower
111

Stir-Fry Black Pepper
Chicken Udon
112

Ground Beef and
Mushrooms Yakiudon
113

Tom Yum Glass Noodles
114

Stir-Fry Glass Noodles with
Mushrooms and Celery
115

Garlic-Infused Glass Noodles
with Tiger Shrimp
116

Black Vinegar Ground
Meat Noodles
117

Spicy Bean Noodles
118

Noodles in Creamy Egg Gravy
119

Stir-Fry White Pepper Noodles
120

Nyonya-Style Noodles
121

Chicken Mushroom Noodles
122

Rice Noodles with Beef
123

Chilled Soba in Green Onion Dressing

Have this dish warm or cold according to your preference. Chilled soba is definitely recommended during summer.

INGREDIENTS | SERVES 2 OR 3

1 tablespoon water
1 tablespoon shoyu
½ teaspoon mirin
1 teaspoon sesame oil
½ cup finely chopped green onions
6 cups water
½ pound dried soba noodles
8 to 10 cups water with ice, for cold-water bath
2 tablespoons toasted sesame seeds (Cooking Tip, page 29)

1. In a bowl, combine the water, shoyu, mirin, and sesame oil. Ladle the dressing into serving bowls. Then portion the green onions into the serving bowls.

2. Add the 6 cups water to the rice cooker, cover the cooker, and set to Cook. When the water boils, add noodles and stir gently to prevent sticking to the base of the pot. Allow noodles to cook for 5 minutes or more until cooked.

3. Drain the noodles and plunge them into the cold-water bath for 3 to 5 minutes.

4. Place the noodles in the serving bowls containing the dressing, and toss to combine. Garnish with toasted sesame seeds before serving.

Do You Know?
Buckwheat flour is commonly dark, due to the husks left in the flour during milling. Buckwheat, which is often used in Japan to make traditional buckwheat soba noodles, is often considered an excellent health food because it is loaded with B vitamins.

Warm Soba and Japanese Mushrooms in Ginger Dressing

Be sure to use sufficient unsalted boiling water for cooking dried soba noodles. If cooked in too little water, the noodles will become starchy and sticky. Also, take note that overcooking soba noodles will render them mushy.

INGREDIENTS | SERVES 2 AS A MAIN DISH

2 teaspoons grated ginger
1 tablespoon finely chopped green onions
1 teaspoon shoyu
1 teaspoon sesame oil
2 tablespoons water
6 cups water
1 (3½-ounce) pack Japanese beech mushrooms
½ pound dried soba noodles

1. In a bowl, combine grated ginger, green onions, shoyu, sesame oil, and 2 tablespoons water. Ladle half the dressing into serving bowls. Set the remaining half aside to "dress" the mushrooms.

2. Add 6 cups water to the rice cooker, cover, and set to Cook. When the water boils, add the mushrooms and blanch for 15 to 20 seconds until the mushrooms turn tender. Dish out mushrooms and place in the mixing bowl with the remaining dressing. Toss well to coat the mushrooms.

3. Cover the rice cooker again and return the water to a boil. When boiling, lift up the rice cooker lid and add the noodles, stirring gently to prevent sticking to the base of the pot. Allow noodles to cook for 5 minutes or more until al dente or cooked.

4. Drain the noodles and divide among the serving bowls containing the dressing. Toss to combine. Top the noodles with the mushrooms and serve warm.

Soba in Tahini Sauce

Tahini is simply sesame seed butter, stone-ground from sesame seeds.

INGREDIENTS | SERVES 4 AS A SIDE DISH

6 cups water

½ pound dried soba noodles, break dried noodles in half

8 to 10 cups water with ice, for cold-water bath

3 tablespoons tahini

1 teaspoon sesame oil

1 teaspoon grated gingerroot, with juice

1 tablespoon warm water

1 cup finely shredded carrot, drained of excess moisture

1 cup finely shredded cucumber, drained of excess moisture

Cooking Tip

A cold-water bath removes the starch in the noodles, which is especially helpful when the noodles are served chilled.

1. Add the water to rice cooker, cover, and set to Cook. When the water boils, lift up the rice cooker lid, add the noodles, and stir gently to prevent sticking to the base of the pot. Allow noodles to cook for 3 minutes or more until al dente.

2. Drain the noodles and plunge them into the cold-water bath for 3 to 5 minutes. Drain and set aside in serving bowls.

3. In a separate mixing bowl, make tahini sauce by combining tahini, sesame oil, ginger, and warm water.

4. Add the tahini sauce, carrots, and cucumber to the noodles. Toss gently and serve.

Summer Soba with Spinach and Mushrooms

Try this recipe with cha soba, a popular summer soba variety. These are soba noodles with a light-green tinge. Green tea powder is added to the buckwheat flour mix to make these tea-flavored noodles.

INGREDIENTS | SERVES 2

2 cups warm water
3 tablespoons shoyu
1 tablespoon mirin
1 teaspoon grated ginger
1 teaspoon sesame oil
6 cups water
3 cups tightly packed fresh baby spinach
1 cup thinly sliced fresh shiitake mushroom caps
½ pound dried soba noodles
8 to 10 cups water with ice, for cold-water bath

1. In a mixing bowl, combine the warm water, shoyu, mirin, ginger, and sesame oil. Chill the dressing in the refrigerator for 30 minutes to 1 hour.

2. Add 6 cups water to the rice cooker, cover, and set to Cook. When the water boils, add the spinach and blanch for 10 seconds. Dish out and set aside to cool.

3. Place mushrooms in the water and blanch for 15 to 20 seconds until the mushrooms turn tender. Dish out and set aside to cool.

4. Cover the rice cooker again and return the water to a boil. When boiling, lift up the rice cooker lid and add the noodles, stirring gently to prevent sticking to the base of the pot. Allow noodles to cook for 5 minutes or more until al dente.

5. Drain the noodles and plunge them into the cold-water bath for 3 to 5 minutes. Drain and set aside in serving bowls.

6. Top the noodles with the spinach and mushrooms. Serve with the chilled dressing on the side as a dipping sauce.

Kimchi Soba Soup

Add raw shrimp or beef slices to enhance the flavor of this soup. Add either of these ingredients during Step 2 when the water boils.

INGREDIENTS | SERVES 3 OR 4 AS A SIDE DISH

6 cups water
½ pound dried soba noodles
4 to 5 cups water
½ block soft tofu (about 5 ounces), cut into ½-inch cubes
1 cup finely shredded kimchi
1 sheet of nori (Japanese seaweed), shredded

Do You Know?
Similar to kelp, nori is considered a sea vegetable. Sea vegetables contain a wide range of minerals such as iodine, vitamin K, folate, iron, and calcium.

1. Add the water to the rice cooker, cover, and set to Cook. When the water boils, add noodles and stir gently to prevent sticking to the base of the pot. Allow noodles to cook for 5 minutes or more until al dente. Drain the noodles and set aside in serving bowls.

2. Clean out the rice cooker and wipe dry. Add 6 cups water to the rice cooker pot, cover, and set to Cook. When the water boils, add the tofu, switch the rice cooker to Warm, and allow it to simmer for 2 to 3 minutes.

3. Stir in kimchi and simmer for another 3 minutes. Ladle over noodles and serve. Garnish with nori.

Smoked Salmon with Soba

Soba can be made fresh with buckwheat flour, water, and a binder. Specialty Japanese stores may sell soba noodles fresh. However, the dried ones have a longer shelf life and can be easily found in major supermarkets. Buy fresh soba only if using it within two to three days of purchase.

INGREDIENTS | SERVES 2 OR 3

- 6 cups water
- ½ pound dried soba noodles
- 8 to 10 cups water and ice, for cold-water bath
- 2 cups water
- 2 tablespoons shoyu
- 3 tablespoons mirin
- 2 teaspoons brown sugar
- ½ teaspoon salt
- 2 tablespoons bonito flakes
- 1 teaspoon grated ginger
- ¼ pound smoked salmon slices
- 1 sheet nori (Japanese seaweed), shredded as garnish

1. Add 6 cups water to the rice cooker, cover, and set to Cook. When the water boils, add noodles and stir gently to prevent sticking to the base of the pot. Allow noodles to cook for 5 minutes or more until al dente. Drain the noodles and plunge them into the cold-water bath for 3 to 5 minutes. Set aside.

2. Clean out rice cooker and wipe dry. Cover and set to Cook. Add 2 cups water, shoyu, mirin, sugar, and salt. Cover the rice cooker and allow mixture to come to a simmer.

3. Add bonito flakes and ginger and stir well. Switch off rice cooker and let stand for 5 minutes.

4. Strain mixture into serving bowls and portion the noodles into the bowls. Top with smoked salmon slices and garnish with nori before serving.

Udon in Mildly Spiced Cauliflower

Udon is a white, thick noodle made from wheat flour. Packaged fresh udon is usually found in the refrigerated foods section in supermarkets, alongside other fresh noodles.

INGREDIENTS | SERVES 3 OR 4

5 cups water
1 pound cauliflower florets
2 (7-ounce) packs fresh udon
1 tablespoon butter, divided use
2 shallots, thinly sliced
2 cloves garlic, finely minced
1 teaspoon grated ginger
½ teaspoon cumin seeds
¼ teaspoon mustard seeds
½ tablespoon curry powder
½ teaspoon turmeric
1 cup water
Salt and freshly ground black pepper, to taste
¼ teaspoon red chili pepper flakes
1 tablespoon finely chopped cilantro

Cooking Tip

If cooking dried udon, refer to the manufacturer's package for instructions. Typically, dried udon is boiled for 10 to 12 minutes. The Japanese refer to the al dente quality of noodles as *koshi*, meaning "substance." Noodles with "substance" should be tender with no hard core, and the noodle surface should be slippery yet not overly soft.

1. Add the water to the rice cooker, cover, and set to Cook. When the water boils, add the cauliflower florets and blanch for 30 seconds. Dish out and set aside to cool. Leave the remaining water in the cooker.

2. Cover the rice cooker and return the water to a boil. When boiling, add noodles to blanch. Stir gently to prevent sticking to the base of the pot. Allow noodles to cook for about 2 minutes, until noodles are separated. Drain the noodles and set aside.

3. Clean out the rice cooker and wipe dry. Add ½ tablespoon butter to the rice cooker, cover, and set to Cook. When the base of the rice cooker gets warm, add the shallots and fry until shallots turn fairly soft.

4. Add garlic, ginger, cumin, and mustard seeds and fry for about 5 minutes until fragrant.

5. Stir in cauliflower, curry powder, turmeric, and 1 cup water. Cover rice cooker and cook until the mixture returns to a boil.

6. Lift up the rice cooker lid and add the remaining ½ tablespoon butter, salt, pepper, and chili flakes. Stir well and allow mixture to simmer at Warm, with the rice cooker covered, for about 10 minutes.

7. About 1 minute before serving, add the cilantro and mix well. Combine the noodles and cauliflower mixture in a deep bowl and toss gently before serving.

Stir-Fry Black Pepper Chicken Udon

Udon noodles have a thicker and firmer texture than soba noodles and are better for stir-fries.

INGREDIENTS | SERVES 2 OR 3

- 1 teaspoon oyster sauce
- 1 teaspoon dark soy sauce
- ½ teaspoon brown sugar
- 1 teaspoon freshly ground black pepper
- 2 cups water, divided use
- 5 cups water, to blanch and separate the noodles
- 2 (7-ounce) packs fresh udon
- 3 tablespoons vegetable oil
- 1 medium-sized onion
- 2 cloves garlic, finely minced
- 1 teaspoon grated ginger
- 1 chicken breast or thigh, sliced into thin strips
- 3 cups tightly packed shredded round or napa cabbage
- Salt and freshly ground black pepper, to taste

1. In a bowl, combine oyster sauce, soy sauce, brown sugar, black pepper, and 1 cup water. Stir well and set aside as gravy mixture.

2. Add 4 to 5 cups water to the rice cooker, cover, and set to Cook. When the water boils, add the noodles to blanch. Stir gently to prevent sticking to the base of the pot. Blanch noodles for about 1 minute until noodles are separated. Drain the noodles and set aside.

3. Clean out the rice cooker and wipe dry. Add the oil to the rice cooker, cover, and set to Cook. When the base of the rice cooker gets warm, add the onions and fry about 5 minutes until slightly soft.

4. Add garlic and ginger and fry about 5 minutes until fragrant, covering the rice cooker occasionally in the process of frying. Add chicken and cabbage and fry for 3 to 5 minutes until chicken partially cooks through (turns brown at the surface), covering rice cooker occasionally in the process of frying. Dish out and set aside, leaving the remaining oil in the rice cooker.

5. Add the prepared gravy mixture to the pot, cover rice cooker, and cook for 1 to 2 minutes until mixture bubbles.

6. Return the cabbage and chicken mixture to the gravy, stir in remaining 1 cup water, and cook for 2 to 3 minutes until chicken cooks through, switching to Warm if gravy mixture bubbles too vigorously.

7. When sauce reduces and thickens, add the udon noodles and toss well with the gravy. Add salt and pepper to taste. If you haven't already, switch the rice cooker to Warm and allow noodles to simmer until they absorb most of the gravy. Serve warm.

Ground Beef and Mushrooms Yakiudon

Yakiudon is stir-fried udon in soy-based sauce. This recipe uses ground beef and mushrooms as the main ingredients, inspired by Japanese teppanyaki. Substitute ground turkey or other ground meat for the ground beef as preferred, and try a variety of mushrooms to add depth to the stir-fry.

INGREDIENTS | SERVES 2 OR 3

5 cups water
2 (7-ounce) packs fresh udon
2 tablespoons vegetable oil
½-inch piece fresh ginger, thinly shredded
½ pound ground beef
1 (3½-ounce) pack Japanese beech mushrooms
1 teaspoon dark soy sauce
½ cup water
2 green onions, sliced into finger-length pieces
Salt and freshly ground black pepper, to taste

Do You Know?

While yakiudon is stir-fry made with udon, yakisoba is not stir-fry made with soba. Yakisoba actually uses ramen noodles in the stir-fry.

1. Add the water to the rice cooker, cover, and set to Cook. When the water boils, add the noodles to blanch. Stir gently to prevent sticking to the base of the pot. Blanch for about 1 minute until noodles are separated. Drain the noodles and set aside.

2. Clean out the rice cooker and wipe dry. Add oil to the rice cooker, cover, and set to Cook. When the base of the rice cooker gets warm, add the ginger, beef, mushrooms, and soy sauce and stir-fry for 3 to 5 minutes till beef partially cooks through (turns from red to brownish), covering rice cooker occasionally in the process of frying.

3. Add ½ cup water, cover the rice cooker, and continue to cook for about 8 minutes. When the mixture starts to simmer and beef cooks through, add the green onions and udon noodles and toss well. Add salt and pepper to taste. Switch the rice cooker to Warm and allow noodles to simmer until they absorb the sauce mixture. Serve warm.

Tom Yum Glass Noodles

Glass noodles are also known by many other names such as cellophane noodles, bean thread noodles, and mung bean vermicelli. Glass noodles are so-called because of their translucent appearance when cooked.

INGREDIENTS | SERVES 2

4 cups water
2 small bunches bok choy
2 tablespoons vegetable oil
2 shallots, thinly sliced
2 tablespoons vegetable oil
2 shallots, thinly sliced
1 lemongrass, bruised bottom half
¼ pound ground pork
1 teaspoon Tom Yum paste
3 cups water
4 medium-sized shrimp, peeled and deveined
½ of a 7-ounce block firm tofu, cut into ½-inch cubes
¼ pound glass noodles, soaked in warm water for 10 minutes or until softened

Cooking Tip

Glass noodles absorb moisture like a sponge. Do not simmer them for too long in a soup base or they will absorb too much liquid and turn soft and mushy. If cooking a dish with gravy, simmering glass noodles for too long will make you lose all the gravy!

1. Add the water to the rice cooker, cover, and set to Cook. When the water boils, add the bok choy to blanch for 15 to 20 seconds until the bok choy becomes tender. Dish out and set aside.

2. Clean out the rice cooker and wipe dry. Add the oil to the rice cooker, cover, and set to Cook. When the base of the rice cooker gets warm, add the shallots and lemongrass and fry for about 5 minutes until fragrant, covering rice cooker occasionally in the process of frying.

3. Add the ground pork (break into smaller bits) and Tom Yum paste and fry for 5 to 8 minutes, covering rice cooker occasionally in the process of frying.

4. Add 2 to 3 cups water, cover rice cooker, and allow mixture to come to a boil. When boiling, add the shrimp and tofu, cover the rice cooker, and simmer for 5 minutes until shrimp turn pink. Remove the shrimp (with help of kitchen tongs) and set aside.

5. Add glass noodles into the Tom Yum mixture, cover rice cooker, and allow to come to a simmer.

6. Once simmering, immediately dish out glass noodles into serving bowls, top noodles with shrimp and bok choy, and ladle remaining soup over noodles. Serve immediately.

Stir-Fry Glass Noodles with Mushrooms and Celery

Do not confuse glass noodles (typically made from mung beans) with rice vermicelli.

INGREDIENTS | SERVES 2

1 teaspoon oyster sauce
1 teaspoon dark soy sauce
½ teaspoon sugar
2 cups water or stock, divided use
2 tablespoons vegetable oil
2 cloves garlic, finely minced
2 cups brown cremini mushrooms, diced
1 stalk celery, diced
Salt, ground black pepper, and white pepper, to taste
¼ pound glass noodles, soaked in warm water for 10 minutes or until softened
1 teaspoon finely chopped cilantro leaves, for garnish

1. Mix oyster sauce, soy sauce, sugar, and 1 cup water in a bowl. Set aside as sauce.

2. Add the oil to the rice cooker, cover, and set to Cook. When the base of the rice cooker gets warm, add the garlic, followed by mushrooms and celery. Fry about 5 minutes until fragrant, covering rice cooker occasionally in the process of frying.

3. Add the sauce mixture, cover the rice cooker, and cook until slightly bubbling. Add remaining 1 cup water, cover the rice cooker, and simmer the mixture for about 5 minutes, switching to Warm if mixture bubbles too vigorously.

4. Add salt and pepper to taste. Lift up rice cooker lid, add the glass noodles, mix well, and allow noodles to absorb the sauce mixture.

5. Ladle into serving bowls and garnish with cilantro before serving.

Garlic-Infused Glass Noodles with Tiger Shrimp

Tiger shrimp, also known as black tiger shrimp, have firm-textured meat and work well in different methods of cooking, including steaming. Most Asian consumers prefer to purchase these shrimp whole, with the heads still on.

INGREDIENTS | SERVES 2 AS A SIDE DISH

¼ pound glass noodles, soaked in warm water for 10 minutes or until softened

8 shells-on, deveined tiger shrimp, or other large-sized shrimp

1 tablespoon Fried Garlic Slices (page 284)

1 tablespoon finely chopped green onions, divided use

1 teaspoon garlic oil

1 tablespoon Chinese cooking wine

Ground white pepper, to taste

Cooking Tip

Save time during a work week by frying the garlic over the weekend. Store fried garlic and garlic oil in an airtight container in the fridge. On a normal work day, thaw the shrimp from freezer to fridge in the morning; and in the evening, set the properly sliced shrimp to steam with make-ahead fried garlic and garlic oil.

1. Place softened warm glass noodles onto individual serving plates.

2. Fill the rice cooker pot with water to about the 4-cup mark. Cover the rice cooker and set to Cook.

3. Make a tiny slit on each of the shrimp, front and back. This allows you to "straighten" the shrimp. Arrange the straightened shrimp side by side, front-side up, on a plate that will fit into the steamer insert or basket. Sprinkle the fried garlic and half the green onions on the shrimp, and then drizzle the shrimp evenly with the garlic oil and Chinese cooking wine. When the water in the rice cooker boils, place the steamer insert or basket that holds the plate of shrimp into the rice cooker and steam, with the rice cooker covered, for 10 to 12 minutes or more, until the shrimp turn pink and cook through.

4. Divide the shrimp among the serving plates with glass noodles and ladle the garlic-infused shrimp gravy over the noodles. Garnish with remaining green onions and ground white pepper and serve.

Black Vinegar Ground Meat Noodles

Chinese Zhajiang and Korean Jajangmyeon are different types of meat sauces. The Chinese Zhajiang is a meat sauce made with spicy beans, while the Korean Jajangmyeon is a sweeter version. Here is a version with black vinegar added, similar to a popular minced meat noodle dish sold by Singapore's street vendors.

INGREDIENTS | SERVES 2

- 1 tablespoon dark soy sauce
- 1 teaspoon oyster sauce
- 1 teaspoon brown sugar
- 4 to 5 cups water, divided use
- ½ pound dried Chinese noodles (flat noodles preferred); refer to package for cooking instructions
- 2 tablespoons vegetable oil
- 1 clove garlic, finely minced
- ½ pound ground pork
- 2 shallots, thinly sliced
- 6 fresh shiitake mushroom caps, thinly sliced
- Salt and ground white pepper, to taste
- 1 tablespoon black vinegar (balsamic), or more as preferred

Sauce or Topping?
Zhajiang noodles are usually served with meat sauce topping over the noodles, and patrons toss the topping with the noodles before eating. There are also other kinds of meat sauces that are mixed and/or stir-fried with the noodles before serving.

1. Mix soy sauce, oyster sauce, sugar, and 1-cup water in a bowl. Set aside as sauce mixture.

2. Add 3 cups water to the rice cooker, cover, and set to Cook. When the water boils, add the noodles and stir gently to prevent sticking to the base of the pot. Allow noodles to cook for 8 minutes or more until al dente. Drain the noodles and set aside.

3. Clean out the rice cooker and wipe dry. Add the oil to the rice cooker, cover, and set to Cook. When the base of the rice cooker gets warm, add the garlic and fry about 5 minutes until fragrant.

4. Add the pork and lightly fry about 8 minutes until the pork surface turns brown, covering the rice cooker occasionally in the process of frying. Dish out the pork and set aside.

5. Add the shallots and mushrooms and fry 2 to 3 minutes, until shallots turn soft, covering the rice cooker occasionally in the process of frying.

6. Add the sauce mixture, cover the rice cooker, and allow to come to a slight simmer. When simmering, switch to Warm and continue to simmer for 10 to 15 minutes until mushrooms become soft. Return the pork to the rice cooker and continue to simmer at Warm for 15 to 20 minutes until pork cooks through. Add salt and pepper to taste and drizzle 1 tablespoon black vinegar into the mixture during the last 2 minutes.

7. Add the noodles to the rice cooker and mix well with the ground meat mixture. Add more black vinegar if desired and mix well with the noodles.

Spicy Bean Noodles

If you can't find dried Chinese noodles in supermarkets near you, substitute instant Chinese noodles. Cook the instant noodles according to package instructions and set aside in serving bowls.

INGREDIENTS | SERVES 2 OR 3

5 cups water

½ pound dried Chinese noodles, or 3 (3-ounce) packs dried instant noodles

2 tablespoons vegetable oil

¼ pound ground pork

1 clove garlic, finely minced

1 green onion, finely chopped

1 tablespoon hot chili bean paste

2 cups water

1 cup finely shredded cucumber, drained of excess moisture, for garnish

1. Add the water to the rice cooker, cover, and set to Cook. When the water boils, add the noodles and stir gently to prevent sticking to the base of the pot. Cover rice cooker and allow noodles to cook for about 3 minutes, referring to packet instructions as a guide. Drain the noodles and set aside in serving bowls.

2. Clean out the rice cooker and wipe dry. Add oil to the rice cooker, cover, and set to Cook. When the base of the rice cooker gets warm, add the ground pork and fry for 4 to 5 minutes until pork surface turns brown, covering rice cooker occasionally in the process of frying. Dish out the pork and set aside. Leave the remaining oil in the pot.

3. Add garlic, green onions, and bean paste to the pot and continue frying for 2 minutes. Add 2 cups water, cover rice cooker, and allow the sauce mixture to come to a simmer.

4. Once simmering, return the pork to the rice cooker and continue to simmer at Warm for 15 to 20 minutes until pork cooks through.

5. Ladle the sauce over the noodles and garnish with cucumber before serving.

Noodles in Creamy Egg Gravy

In Hong Kong, this dish is popularly known by the Cantonese name Wat Dan Hor. Wat Dan *means "smooth silky eggs," and* Hor *refers to the kind of noodle used, typically flat rice noodles.*

INGREDIENTS | SERVES 2

6 cups water
½ pound dried Chinese noodles
2 tablespoons vegetable oil
6 shrimp, peeled, deveined, and diced into bite-sized pieces
2 cloves garlic, finely minced
1 teaspoon grated ginger
¼ pound chicken thigh, cut to thin strips about ¼-inch thick
4 fresh shiitake mushroom caps, diced
1 cup broccoli florets, blanched
½ tablespoon oyster sauce
2 cups hot water
Salt and ground white pepper, to taste
1 egg, lightly whisked

Cooking Tip

For creamy and smooth egg gravy over savory dishes, do not allow the eggs to cook on high heat, either in the rice cooker or in a pan on the stovetop. Turn down the heat and stir in the whisked egg slowly, using chopsticks to stir the eggs in one direction. This technique is often used when making Chinese egg-drop soup, in which the egg is added during the last few seconds of cooking.

1. Add the water to the rice cooker, cover, and set to Cook. When the water boils, add the noodles and stir gently to prevent sticking to the base of the pot. Cover rice cooker and allow noodles to cook for about 5 minutes. Drain the noodles and set aside in serving bowls.

2. Clean out the rice cooker and wipe dry. Add the oil to the rice cooker, cover, and set to Cook. When the base of the cooker pot gets warm, add the shrimp and fry about 8 minutes until almost cooked (when shrimp turn pink). Dish out shrimp and set aside. Leave the remaining oil in the pot.

3. Add the garlic, ginger, and chicken to the pot. Fry for about 8 minutes until the chicken pieces turn brown on the surface, covering rice cooker occasionally in the process of frying.

4. Add the mushrooms, broccoli, oyster sauce, and 2 cups water; stir well. Cover the rice cooker and allow mixture to come to a simmer. Once simmering, switch to Warm and continue to simmer for 8 to 10 minutes until chicken cooks through.

5. Stir the shrimp into the pot. Season with salt and white pepper to taste.

6. With the rice cooker still at Warm, slowly add the whisked egg, swirling the egg gently in one direction using a chopstick. The heat remaining in the cooked mixture will cook the egg to a runny, smooth consistency. Ladle the mixture on top of the noodles and serve.

Stir-Fry White Pepper Noodles

You can substitute rice vermicelli for the noodles in this dish. Before using the vermicelli, soak in warm water to soften it. No cooking is required for the softened rice vermicelli prior to stir-frying it.

INGREDIENTS | SERVES 2 OR 3

- 1 teaspoon oyster sauce
- 1 teaspoon dark soy sauce
- 2 tablespoons warm water
- ¼ pound thin pork slices, about ¼-inch thick slices
- 1 teaspoon dark soy sauce, for seasoning pork
- ¼ teaspoon white pepper
- 1 teaspoon Chinese cooking wine
- 6 cups water
- ½ pound dried Chinese noodles (thicker strands preferred)
- 2 tablespoons vegetable oil
- 3 shallots, thinly sliced
- 2 cloves garlic finely minced
- 1 pound round or napa cabbage, thinly shredded
- 1 carrot, thinly shredded
- 1 cup water or stock, or more (adjust during cooking)
- Salt, to taste
- ½ teaspoon white pepper
- 1 tablespoon finely chopped cilantro, for garnish

1. Mix oyster sauce, soy sauce, and water in a bowl. Set aside as sauce.

2. Season the pork with dark soy sauce, pepper, and Chinese cooking wine and set aside to marinate in the fridge while preparing noodles and the rice cooker.

3. Add 5 to 6 cups water to the rice cooker, cover, and set to Cook. When the water boils, add noodles and stir gently to prevent sticking to the base of the pot. Allow noodles to cook until al dente. Drain the noodles and set aside.

4. Clean out the rice cooker and wipe dry. Add oil to the rice cooker, cover, and set to Cook. When the base of the rice cooker gets warm, add the pork and fry for about 8 to 10 minutes until pork surface turns brown, covering rice cooker occasionally in the process of frying. Dish out and set aside. Leave the remaining oil in the pot.

5. Add the shallots and garlic to the pot and fry about 5 minutes until shallots turn slightly soft.

6. Add the cabbage and carrots and mix well. Cover the rice cooker and cook for 5 minutes or more until the vegetables become slightly soft and tender.

7. Add the sauce mixture, 1 cup of water or stock, and the pork. Mix well, cover the rice cooker, and allow it to come to simmer. Once simmering, add salt to taste, switch rice cooker to Warm, and continue simmer for 8 to 10 minutes.

8. Add the cooked noodles and white pepper. Mix well and allow to simmer, covered for about 5 to 8 minutes until gravy reduces. Garnish with cilantro and serve.

Nyonya-Style Noodles

This noodle dish is a Peranakan or Straits Chinese favorite. In Peranakan culture, nyonya refers to the female descendants of early Chinese immigrants. There is no special reason why this dish is named Nyonya-Style Noodles. Perhaps it's just that the females are known to be good cooks.

INGREDIENTS | SERVES 2 OR 3

6 cups water

¼ pound fresh yellow noodles (round and fat noodles preferred)

2 tablespoons vegetable oil

2 cloves garlic, finely minced

½ tablespoon mashed fermented salted soybeans

½ pound shredded napa cabbage

6 to 8 shrimp, peeled and deveined

3 cups Shrimp Stock (page 17)

¼ pound rice vermicelli, soaked in warm water for 10 minutes, or until softened

¼ pound fresh mung bean sprouts

Salt and ground white pepper, to taste

1 tablespoon finely chopped green onions, for garnish

Cooking Tip

The best noodles for this dish are the fresh yellow noodles usually found in the refrigerator section in Asian supermarkets, alongside the wonton wrappers and tofu. However, fresh yellow noodles may be hard to find. If unavailable, use spaghetti noodles. Cook spaghetti noodles as you normally would and use them as required in the recipe.

1. Add the water to the rice cooker, cover, and set to Cook. When the water boils, add the noodles to blanch. Stir gently to prevent sticking to the base of the pot. Blanch for about 1 minute until noodles are separated. Drain the noodles and set aside.

2. Clean out the rice cooker and wipe dry. Add oil to the rice cooker, cover, and set to Cook. When the base of the rice cooker gets warm, add the garlic and mashed salted soybeans and fry for about 5 minutes until fragrant.

3. Add the cabbage and shrimp and fry for 5 to 8 minutes until vegetables become slightly soft and shrimp cook through (turn pink), covering the rice cooker occasionally in the process of frying.

4. Add the yellow noodles, rice vermicelli, bean sprouts, and shrimp stock. Mix well, cover rice cooker, and let it simmer about 3 to 5 minutes. Switch to Warm and allow simmer for 5 to 8 more minutes. Season with salt and white pepper. Garnish with green onions and serve.

Chicken Mushroom Noodles

Substitute bok choy or choy sum for the Kai Lan. Broccoli or broccolini make good substitutions as well.

INGREDIENTS | SERVES 2

½ pound chicken thigh, sliced into thin strips
½ teaspoon dark soy sauce
1 teaspoon Chinese cooking wine
½ teaspoon sesame oil
5 cups water
1 small bundle Kai Lan
2 to 3 packs instant noodle bundles
2 tablespoons vegetable oil
2 shallots, thinly sliced
1 clove garlic, finely minced
4 to 6 fresh shiitake mushroom caps, thinly sliced
2 cups water or Chicken Stock (page 16)
Ground white pepper, to taste

1. Season the chicken with soy sauce, Chinese cooking wine, and sesame oil and set aside to marinate in the fridge while preparing the vegetables and noodles.

2. Add the water to the rice cooker, cover, and set to Cook. When the water boils, add the Kai Lan and blanch for 30 seconds. Dish out and set aside.

3. Cover the rice cooker and return to a boil. When boiling, add the noodles to cook, stirring gently to prevent sticking to the base of the pot. Allow noodles to cook for 5 minutes or till they are firm yet not overcooked. Drain the noodles and divide them among the serving plates. Top the noodles with the Kai Lan.

4. Clean out the rice cooker and wipe dry. Add the oil to the rice cooker, cover, and set to Cook. When the base of the rice cooker gets warm, add the shallots and fry for about 3 minutes until slightly soft. Add the garlic and fry for about 3 minutes until fragrant.

5. Add the marinated chicken and the mushrooms. Mix well and fry for 2 minutes until chicken surface turns brown, covering the rice cooker occasionally in the process of cooking.

6. Add the water or stock, cover the rice cooker, and allow the mixture to come to a simmer. When simmering, add the pepper, switch to Warm, and continue simmer for 5 minutes or more until chicken cooks through and the sauce slightly reduces (thickens).

7. Ladle the chicken mushroom sauce over the noodles and serve immediately.

Rice Noodles with Beef

Substitute thin strips of chicken for the beef and green beans for the broccoli, if preferred.

INGREDIENTS | SERVES 2

2 tablespoons vegetable oil
½ pound ground beef
1 clove garlic, finely minced
1 tablespoon black bean paste
¼ pound broccoli florets, blanched
2 tablespoons water
½ pound dried rice stick noodles, soaked in warm water for 10 minutes or until softened
1 tablespoon dark soy sauce
2 green onions, thinly sliced, divided use

Cooking Tip

Rice stick noodles are also known as flat (wide) rice noodles, and are available fresh or dried in supermarkets. Rice stick noodles tend to stick together during stir-frying, and it may be hard to separate the strands in the rice cooker. Whether the noodles are fresh or dried, soak them in warm water before stir-frying to soften and loosen up the strands. Substitute cooked instant Chinese noodles if preferred.

1. Add the oil to the rice cooker, cover, and set to Cook. When the base of the rice cooker gets warm, add the ground beef and fry for about 10 to 12 minutes until the beef completely cooks through, covering the rice cooker occasionally in the process of frying. Dish out and set aside, leaving the remaining oil in the pot.

2. Add the garlic, black bean sauce, broccoli, and water to the pot and stir-fry for 2 to 3 minutes until vegetables become tender, covering the rice cooker occasionally in the process of cooking.

3. When vegetables are tender, add the noodles, soy sauce, and half the green onions. Mix well.

4. Return the beef to the pot and mix well with the noodles. Garnish with remaining green onions before serving.

CHAPTER 9

Fish

Steamed Fish in Tangy
Ginger Sauce
125

Steamed Halibut with
Mushrooms and Tofu
126

Steamed Whole Fish with
Ham and Shiitake Mushrooms
127

Lemongrass Steamed Fish
128

Steamed Fish in Spicy Thai-Style
Yogurt Sauce
129

Steamed Fish with Ginger
and Green Onions
130

Pan-Fried Salmon
130

Cod and Shiitake Mushrooms
in Wine Sauce
131

Pan-Fried Fish in Chinese
Black Bean Sauce
132

Salmon Fillet with Oyster Sauce
133

Pan-Fried Fish in Soy and
Ginger Sauce
134

Halibut with Mango Salsa
135

Fish in Creamy Pistachio
Pesto Sauce
136

Stir-Fried Fish Slices with Ginger
and Green Onions
137

Codfish with Ginger and
Coconut Sauce
138

Fish Curry
139

Tandoori Fish
140

Fish Burger
141

Steamed Fish in Tangy Ginger Sauce

If the fish fillet is thick, it may take a longer time to steam and cook. Cut a few slits on a thicker fillet so the time required for steaming is about the same as it would be for a thinner fillet.

INGREDIENTS | SERVES 2

1 teaspoon grated ginger
¼ cup chopped cilantro leaves
1 teaspoon sesame oil
1 tablespoon lime (or lemon) juice
½ teaspoon brown sugar
2 firm white fish fillets (such as cod or sea bass), about ½-inch thick

1. Mix ginger, cilantro, sesame oil, lime juice, and brown sugar in a bowl. Set aside as sauce.

2. Fill the rice cooker pot with water to about the 4-cup mark. Cover the rice cooker and set to Cook.

3. Place the fish on a shallow plate that will fit in the steamer insert or basket and pour the prepared sauce mixture over the fish. Cover the top of the plate with plastic wrap, to prevent excess condensation during steaming. Allow fish to marinate until the water in the rice cooker boils.

4. When the water in the rice cooker boils, place the steamer insert or basket with the plate of fish into the cooker. Steam for 8 to 10 minutes until the fish cooks through, keeping the rice cooker covered during steaming.

Steamed Halibut with Mushrooms and Tofu

If Japanese brown beech (buna shimeji) mushrooms are not available, substitute fresh shiitake mushrooms, thinly sliced.

INGREDIENTS | SERVES 2

1 medium-sized halibut (or cod) fillet, about ¾ pound
¼ teaspoon salt
¼ teaspoon ground white pepper
½ tablespoon Chinese cooking wine
1 teaspoon sesame oil
½ teaspoon grated ginger
1 (10½-ounce) pack soft tofu, cut to 0.6-inch cubes
1 cup Japanese brown beech (buna shimeji) mushrooms
1 green onion, chopped
1 red chili pepper, seeded and julienned, for garnish
½ cup chopped cilantro leaves, for garnish
1 teaspoon Fried Golden Shallots (page 284), for garnish

1. Season the fish with salt, white pepper, Chinese cooking wine, sesame oil, and grated ginger. Set aside to marinate while you go on to the next step.

2. Fill the rice cooker pot with water to about the 4-cup mark. Cover the rice cooker and set to Cook.

3. Place the tofu pieces on a shallow plate that will fit in the steamer insert or basket. Top with the mushrooms and half of the green onions, and place the marinated fish on top. Cover the top of the plate with plastic wrap, to prevent excess condensation when the fish is steamed.

4. When the water in the rice cooker boils, place the steamer insert or basket with the plate of fish into the rice cooker, and steam for 10 to 12 minutes until the fish cooks through, keeping the rice cooker covered during steaming.

5. Garnish with red chili, remaining green onions, cilantro, and fried shallots.

Animal, Vegetable, and Soy Protein Sources

Although vegetable and soy proteins are relatively low in fat, they are considered incomplete proteins because they do not have a balanced combination of all the amino acids. Animal protein such as fish, on the other hand, is considered a complete protein.

Steamed Whole Fish with Ham and Shiitake Mushrooms

Use luncheon ham or honey-baked ham according to your preference. Bacon strips cut into smaller pieces can be used as a substitute as well. However, bacon typically has a higher salt content than ham, and should be used sparingly.

INGREDIENTS | SERVES 2

- 1 medium-sized whole fish (such as sea bass or snapper), about 1 pound
- ¼ teaspoon salt
- ¼ teaspoon ground white pepper
- ½ tablespoon Chinese cooking wine
- 1 teaspoon sesame oil
- ½ teaspoon grated ginger
- 2 slices ham, each cut into 4 to 6 smaller slices
- 4 to 6 fresh shiitake mushroom caps, thinly sliced
- 1 green onion, chopped, for garnish

1. Cut 2 or 3 slanted slits on the fish. Season fish lightly with the salt, white pepper, Chinese cooking wine, sesame oil, and grated ginger. Insert ham slices and mushrooms into each slit. Set aside to marinate while you go on to the next step. Also set aside any remaining ham and mushrooms.

2. Fill the rice cooker pot with water to about the 4-cup mark. Cover and set to Cook.

3. Place the fish on a shallow plate that will fit in the steamer insert or basket and scatter the remaining ham and mushrooms over the plate. Cover the top of the plate with plastic wrap to prevent excess condensation when the fish is steamed.

4. When the water in the rice cooker boils, place the steamer insert or basket with the plate of fish into the rice cooker, and steam for 12 to 15 minutes until the fish cooks through, keeping the rice cooker covered during steaming.

5. Garnish with green onions before serving.

Lemongrass Steamed Fish

In this recipe the lemongrass releases a very light citrus aroma in the process of steaming. Lemongrass combines well with the cilantro, ginger, garlic, and shallots.

INGREDIENTS | SERVES 2

2 firm white fish fillets (such as cod or sea bass), about ½-inch thick
¼ teaspoon salt
¼ teaspoon ground white pepper
½ tablespoon Chinese cooking wine
2 teaspoons grated ginger
2 stalks lemongrass, each cut into half, and the bottom white part bruised
1 green onion, chopped, for garnish
½ cup chopped cilantro leaves, for garnish
1 fresh red chili pepper, seeded and julienned, for garnish

Sustainable Fish Sources

Visit *www.seafoodwatch.org* and download a pocket guide of sustainable seafood sources. Take the pocket guide along when you go shopping for groceries. Your next fish selection and purchase will be a smart one.

1. Season the fish with the salt, white pepper, Chinese cooking wine, and grated ginger. Set aside to marinate while you go on to the next step.

2. Fill the rice cooker pot with water to about the 4-cup mark. Cover and set to Cook.

3. Place the fish and lemongrass on a plate that will fit in the steamer insert or basket. Cover the top of the plate with plastic wrap to prevent excess condensation when the fish is steamed.

4. When the water in the rice cooker boils, place the steamer insert or basket with the plate of fish into the rice cooker, and steam for 8 to 10 minutes until the fish cooks through, keeping the rice cooker covered during steaming.

5. Garnish with green onions, cilantro, and red chili before serving.

Steamed Fish in Spicy Thai-Style Yogurt Sauce

Bird's eye chili pepper, just about one inch long, is fiery hot. Bird's eye chili adds significant "heat" to many Southeast Asian food recipes. You can substitute red chili pepper, depending on availability and personal preference.

INGREDIENTS | SERVES 2

¼ cup Thai chili sauce

½ cup plain yogurt

1 stalk lemongrass, bottom white half bruised, thinly sliced

1 bird's eye chili pepper (or 1 red chili), seeded and thinly sliced

1 clove garlic, grated

½ cup chopped cilantro leaves

1 tablespoon lime (or lemon) juice

1 teaspoon brown sugar

2 firm white fish fillets (such as sea bass, sole, snapper), about ½-inch thick

¼ teaspoon salt

¼ teaspoon ground white pepper

1. Mix the Thai chili sauce, yogurt, lemongrass, chili, garlic, cilantro, lime juice, and brown sugar in a bowl. Set aside as sauce.

2. Season the fish with the salt and white pepper. Set aside.

3. Fill the rice cooker pot with water to about the 4-cup mark. Cover and set to Cook.

4. Place the fish on a shallow plate that will fit in the steamer insert or basket. Cover the top of the plate with plastic wrap to prevent excess condensation when the fish is steamed.

5. When the water in the rice cooker boils, place the steamer insert or basket with the plate of fish into the rice cooker, and steam for 8 to 10 minutes until the fish cooks through, keeping the rice cooker covered during steaming.

6. Drizzle prepared sauce over cooked fish before serving.

Steamed Fish with Ginger and Green Onions

Ginger eliminates the "fishy" smell that comes from steaming fish. It also adds a special flavor, zest, and aroma to this simple dish.

INGREDIENTS | SERVES 2

2 firm white fish fillets (such cod or sea bass), about ½-inch thick
¼ teaspoon salt
¼ teaspoon ground white pepper
½ tablespoon Chinese cooking wine
1 teaspoon sesame oil
1-inch piece ginger, thinly sliced
1 green onion, cut into 2-inch lengths
½ tomato, cut into wedges

1. Season the fish with the salt, white pepper, Chinese cooking wine, and sesame oil. Set aside to marinate while you go on to the next step.

2. Fill the rice cooker pot with water to about the 4-cup mark. Cover the rice cooker and set to Cook.

3. Place the fish on a shallow plate that will fit in the steamer insert or basket. Top the fish with the ginger and green onions. Surround the fish with the tomatoes. Cover the top of the plate with plastic wrap to prevent excess steam condensation during steaming.

4. When the water in the rice cooker boils, place the steamer insert or basket with the plate of fish into the rice cooker, and steam for 8 to 10 minutes until the fish cooks through, keeping the rice cooker covered during steaming.

Health Benefits of Ginger

Ginger is a good source of vitamin C, magnesium, potassium, copper, and manganese. It is also known to stimulate gastric juices, and provide soothing effects for colds and coughs.

Pan-Fried Salmon

Fish oil is beneficial to overall health as it provides omega-3 fatty acids. Salmon, which is readily available, is an excellent food source of this essential nutrient.

INGREDIENTS | SERVES 2

2 salmon fillets, about ½-inch thick
¼ teaspoon salt
¼ teaspoon freshly ground black pepper
1 teaspoon corn flour
2 tablespoons extra-virgin olive oil

1. Cut 2 or 3 shallow slanted slits on the fish. Season both sides of the fish with salt and black pepper, and then pat both sides with corn flour.

2. Add oil to the rice cooker, cover, and set to Cook. When the base of the cooker pot gets warm, add the salmon and pan-fry on one side, for about 5 to 8 minutes, keeping the rice cooker covered until salmon cooks through (turns pinkish-orange).

Cod and Shiitake Mushrooms in Wine Sauce

Substitute shiitake mushrooms with a medley of white and brown beech Japanese mushrooms. These mushrooms are subtly earthy and go very well with the sauce.

INGREDIENTS | SERVES 2

1 medium-sized cod fillet (or any firm white thick-cut fillet), about ¾ pound
¼ teaspoon salt
¼ teaspoon ground white pepper
1 teaspoon corn flour, divided use
½ cup water, divided use
1 teaspoon grated ginger
1 tablespoon Chinese cooking wine
2 tablespoons vegetable oil
1 green onion, cut into 2-inch lengths
3 to 4 fresh shiitake mushroom caps, thinly sliced
¼ teaspoon sesame oil

1. Season both sides of the fish with salt and white pepper, and then pat both sides with ½ teaspoon of the corn flour.

2. Mix ¼ cup of the water, remaining corn flour, grated ginger, and Chinese cooking wine in a bowl. Set aside as sauce.

3. Add the oil to the rice cooker, cover, and set to Cook. When the base of the cooker pot gets warm, add the fish fillet and pan-fry each side for 3 to 5 minutes, with rice cooker covered when frying each side. When fish is cooked (turns opaque), dish out and set aside. Leave the remaining oil in the pot.

4. Add the green onions and mushroom slices to the pot. Fry about 8 minutes until the mushrooms turn soft, covering rice cooker occasionally in the process of frying.

5. Add the remaining water, cover the rice cooker, and allow to simmer for about 2 minutes.

6. Add the prepared sauce mixture, return the fish to the pot, cover the rice cooker, and simmer for 5 minutes until fish completely cooks through, switching to Warm if mixture bubbles too vigorously. Lift rice cooker lid and continue to simmer until sauce reduces (thickens).

7. Drizzle sesame oil over the fish and serve.

Pan-Fried Fish in Chinese Black Bean Sauce

Chinese black beans are soybeans that have turned black under fermentation in salt. The flavor is intense and may be considered pungent by some. Chinese black beans (in bags) or black bean sauce (in jars) can be found in many Asian markets or in the ethnic and international section of many supermarkets.

INGREDIENTS | SERVES 2

2 firm white fish fillets (such as sea bass, sole, or snapper), about ½-inch thick
¼ teaspoon salt
¼ teaspoon ground white pepper
1 tablespoon corn flour
2 tablespoons vegetable oil
2 cloves garlic, minced
½-inch piece ginger, thinly sliced, then minced (alternatively, 1 teaspoon grated ginger)
1 teaspoon Chinese fermented black beans, slightly mashed
1 green onion, chopped
½ cup water
1 tablespoon Chinese cooking wine
1 teaspoon sesame oil

1. Season both sides of the fish with salt and white pepper, and then pat both sides with corn flour.

2. Add the oil to the rice cooker, cover, and set to Cook. When the base of the cooker pot gets warm, add the fish fillets and pan-fry each side for 2 to 3 minutes, with the rice cooker covered. When fish almost cooks through, dish out and set aside. Leave the remaining oil in the pot.

3. Add the garlic, ginger, and mashed Chinese black beans to the pot and fry for 1 minute. Add the green onions and water and fry for an additional 1 minute, covering the rice cooker occasionally in the process of frying. When the sauce slightly reduces, drizzle half of the cooking wine and sesame oil over the sauce mixture.

4. Return the fish fillets to the rice cooker. Cook for about 5 minutes, lifting the cover occasionally to spoon the Chinese black bean sauce over the fish. Do not turn the fish too frequently in the pot, to keep it from flaking into small pieces.

5. Drizzle remaining cooking wine and sesame oil in the pot to complete cooking. Dish out and serve. Best served with steamed rice.

Semi-Homemade "Ready-to-Go" Chinese Black Bean Sauce

Using the amounts given in this recipe, fry Chinese black beans, minced garlic, ginger, and chopped green onions in vegetable oil for about 2 to 3 minutes. Add water and simmer until sauce reduces slightly. Drizzle in the cooking wine and sesame oil to finish off cooking. For make-ahead sauce, the quantity can be scaled up accordingly, and then stored in the refrigerator for about 2 weeks for future use such as in stir-fries.

Salmon Fillet with Oyster Sauce

When pan-frying salmon fillet with the skin on, always fry skin-side down first.

INGREDIENTS | SERVES 2

1 teaspoon oyster sauce
½ teaspoon brown sugar
1 teaspoon grated ginger
½ teaspoon grated garlic
½ cup water
2 salmon fillets, about ½-inch thick
¼ teaspoon salt
¼ teaspoon ground white pepper
1 teaspoon corn flour
2 tablespoons vegetable oil
1 tablespoon finely chopped green onions
2 fresh shiitake mushroom caps, thinly sliced

1. Mix the oyster sauce, brown sugar, grated ginger, garlic, and water in a bowl. Set aside as sauce.

2. Season both sides of the fish with salt and white pepper, and pat both sides with corn flour.

3. Add the oil to the rice cooker, cover, and set to Cook. When the base of the cooker pot gets warm, add the salmon and pan-fry the fish on one side, for about 3 to 5 minutes, with the rice cooker covered until fish cooks through (turns pinkish-orange). Remove and set aside. Leave the remaining oil in the pot.

4. Add the green onions and mushroom slices. Stir in the prepared sauce, cover the rice cooker, and allow to simmer for 1 minute.

5. Return the fish to the pot, cover the rice cooker, and allow to simmer for another minute or until sauce slightly reduces (thickens) and fish completely cooks through.

Pan-Fried Fish in Soy and Ginger Sauce

There is a popular Chinese dish in which a whole fish is deep-fried in a wok of hot oil. This method of cooking provides more depth of flavor and texture but is not often seen as practical to do at home. This recipe introduces a fuss-free way of enjoying this simple fish dish without a huge splatter of oil.

INGREDIENTS | SERVES 2

- 2 tablespoons dark soy sauce
- 1 teaspoon grated ginger
- 1 tablespoon Chinese cooking wine
- 1 teaspoon sesame oil
- ½ teaspoon brown sugar
- ½ cup water
- 2 firm white fish fillets (such as sea bass, sole, or snapper), about ½-inch thick
- ¼ teaspoon salt
- ¼ teaspoon ground white pepper
- 1 tablespoon corn flour
- 2 tablespoons vegetable oil
- 1 green onion, chopped, for garnish

1. Mix dark soy sauce, ginger, Chinese cooking wine, sesame oil, brown sugar, and water in a bowl. Set aside as sauce.

2. Season both sides of the fish with salt and white pepper, and pat both sides with corn flour.

3. Add the oil to the rice cooker, cover, and set to Cook. When the base of the cooker pot gets warm, add the fish fillets and pan-fry each side for 2 to 3 minutes, with the rice cooker covered. When fish cooks through (turns opaque), dish out and set aside.

4. Add the prepared sauce mixture to the pot, cover the rice cooker, and allow to simmer. When simmering, return the fish to the pot, cover the rice cooker, and simmer for 2 to 3 minutes for sauce to infuse with the fish.

5. Garnish with green onions. Best served with steamed rice.

Chinese Soy Sauces

One of the best-known Asian seasonings, soy sauce is brewed from soybeans, wheat, and salt. The most common types of Chinese soy sauces are light soy sauce and dark soy sauce. Light soy sauce appears thin (less viscous) and lighter in color compared to dark soy sauce. Dark soy sauce is richer in taste; it has more malt in the flavor but is less salty than light soy sauce. It usually is used if both color and flavor need to be added to a dish.

Halibut with Mango Salsa

Halibut tends to have a naturally sweet flavor and no fishy smell. Therefore it should be minimally seasoned and paired with a light and refreshing sauce that does not overpower the fish.

INGREDIENTS | SERVES 2

2 (about ¾-pound each) halibut fillet, cut into ¼-inch-thick slices
½ teaspoon salt
½ teaspoon freshly ground black pepper
1 teaspoon corn flour
1 cup finely cubed ripe mango
½ cup finely cubed kiwi
¼ cup finely chopped cilantro leaves
¼ cup thinly sliced shallots (or small red onion)
1 tablespoon lime juice
3 tablespoons extra-virgin olive oil

1. Season the fish slices with the salt and black pepper and coat lightly with corn flour.

2. Mix mango, kiwi, cilantro, shallots, and lime juice in a bowl. Chill to use as dressing.

3. Add the oil to the rice cooker, cover, and set to Cook. When the base of the cooker pot gets warm, add the fish slices (in batches) in a single layer across the pot. Fry each side for about 2 to 3 minutes, with the rice cooker covered, until fish cooks through (turns opaque). Keep the first batches warm while the rest of the fish is frying.

4. Transfer fish slices to a serving plate, and spoon some mango salsa over the fish as dressing.

Fish in Creamy Pistachio Pesto Sauce

Fish that has a stronger fishy smell, such as tilapia, is usually seasoned with more aromatics and goes well with a "heavy" sauce, like this creamy pesto sauce.

INGREDIENTS | SERVES 2

1 cup fresh basil leaves
½ cup shelled pistachios
2 cloves garlic
½ cup grated Parmesan cheese
3 tablespoons extra-virgin olive oil, divided use
2 firm white fish fillets (such as sole, snapper, or tilapia), about ½-inch thick
¼ teaspoon salt
¼ teaspoon freshly ground black pepper
1 tablespoon butter
½ cup whole milk
1 teaspoon plain flour

Pesto Presto!
Use pine nuts or cashew nuts as alternatives to pistachios. The pesto in this recipe may yield more than what is required for the sauce. Store the remaining pesto in the refrigerator for up to 2 weeks and use it as a pasta dressing or sauce. Pesto freezes nicely as well.

1. Combine basil, pistachios, garlic, and cheese in hand-held electronic chopper/blender and process until uniformly chopped. Gradually add 1 to 2 tablespoons of the olive oil while mixing until desired consistency (grainy texture, not puréed). Set aside.

2. Season both sides of the fish with the salt and black pepper. Set aside.

3. Add the butter and remaining olive oil to the rice cooker, cover, and set to Cook. When the base of the cooker pot gets warm, stir in the milk and flour gradually. Cover the rice cooker and allow to simmer, switching the cooker to Warm if the mixture boils vigorously.

4. Add the fish, switch back to the Cook setting if necessary, cover the pot, and allow the fish to simmer in the sauce for about 5 minutes, until cooked through (turns opaque, white, feels firm). If the sauce bubbles too vigorously, switch to Warm and continue to simmer for the remaining time until the fish cooks through and the sauce thickens.

5. Stir in 1 tablespoon of prepared pesto sauce.

6. Remove the fish to a serving plate and pour the creamy pesto sauce over fish. Serve immediately.

Stir-Fried Fish Slices with Ginger and Green Onions

Adding egg white and corn flour in the seasoning helps to provide a protective coating that gives the cooked fish slices a velvety texture and also prevents them from drying out.

INGREDIENTS | SERVES 2

2 firm white fish fillets (such sea bass or snapper), cut into ¼-inch-thick slices
¼ teaspoon salt
½ teaspoon ground white pepper
1 teaspoon dark soy sauce
1 tablespoon Chinese cooking wine
1 tablespoon corn flour
2 tablespoons vegetable oil
2 shallots, thinly sliced
1-inch piece ginger, thinly sliced, then cut into thin strips
1 tablespoon oyster sauce
½ cup water
1 green onion, cut into 2-inch lengths

1. Season the fish slices with salt, white pepper, soy sauce, Chinese cooking wine, and corn flour.

2. Add the oil to the rice cooker, cover, and set to Cook. When the base of the cooker pot gets warm, add the fish slices (in batches) in single layer across the pot. Fry each side for about 2 to 3 minutes, with the rice cooker covered, until cooked through (turns opaque, white and feels firm). Dish out fish slices and set aside. Leave the remaining oil in the pot.

3. Add shallots to the pot and fry about 3 minutes until slightly soft. Add the ginger and stir-fry about 3 minutes until fragrant.

4. Return the fish slices to the pot and add the oyster sauce and water. Mix well, cover the rice cooker, and allow to cook for about 3 minutes, switching to Warm if mixture bubbles too vigorously.

5. Add the green onions and stir-fry for another minute. Dish out and serve.

Codfish with Ginger and Coconut Sauce

Serving the fish with an assortment of blanched vegetables such as broccoli, carrots, and boiled potatoes will make this a perfectly balanced one-dish meal.

INGREDIENTS | SERVES 2

2 firm white fish fillets (such as cod or sea bass), about ½-inch thick
¼ teaspoon salt
¼ teaspoon freshly ground black pepper
1 tablespoon vegetable oil
1 teaspoon grated ginger
½ teaspoon curry powder
½ cup coconut milk

1. Season both sides of the fish with the salt and black pepper. Set aside.

2. Add the oil to the rice cooker, cover, and set to Cook. When the base of the cooker pot gets warm, add the ginger and curry powder. Stir for 1 minute or until fragrant.

3. Stir in the coconut milk and add the fish fillets. Cover the rice cooker and allow to simmer for 8 to 10 minutes, until fish cooks through, switching rice cooker to Warm if the sauce mixture boils too vigorously. Dish out and serve with blanched vegetables and potatoes.

Coconut Milk

The rich taste of coconut milk can be attributed to the high oil content and sugars. Fresh coconut milk is usually not produced in the United States. You can buy canned coconut milk from Asian groceries and markets or the ethnic and international section of many supermarkets. The canned version, however, typically contains water as filler.

Fish Curry

This easy-to-follow recipe is mildly spiced, yet flavorful.

INGREDIENTS | SERVES 2

2 tablespoons vegetable oil
1 small onion, finely diced
1 clove garlic, finely minced
1 teaspoon curry powder
½ teaspoon turmeric
¼ teaspoon paprika
¼ cup water
2 cups coconut milk
2 firm white fish fillets (such as sole, snapper, or tilapia), about ½-inch thick
6 to 8 cherry tomatoes, cut into halves
Salt and black pepper, to taste

1. Add the oil to the rice cooker, cover, and set to Cook. When the base of the cooker pot gets warm, add the onions and fry for about 5 minutes until onions turn soft and tender.

2. Add the garlic and fry about 3 minutes until fragrant, covering the rice cooker occasionally in the process of frying.

3. Add the curry power, turmeric, and paprika and mix well. Stir in the water, followed by the coconut milk. Cover the rice cooker and allow it to come to a simmer.

4. Once simmering, add the fish fillets, cherry tomatoes, and salt and black pepper to taste. Cover the rice cooker and cook for about 10 to 12 minutes, until fish cooks through (turns opaque), switching the setting to Warm if the sauce mixture boils too vigorously.

Tandoori Fish

A tandoor or tandoori actually is a cylindrical clay oven used in Indian slow-roasting or cooking. Due to the marinating spices used for slow-roasting chicken in the clay oven, tandoori has come to mean a specific flavor rather than a method of cooking.

INGREDIENTS | SERVES 2

½ teaspoon salt
½ teaspoon freshly ground black pepper
2 teaspoons grated garlic
2 teaspoons grated ginger
1 teaspoon turmeric
1 teaspoon ground coriander
1 teaspoon cumin
1 teaspoon paprika (or red chili powder)
½ cup plain yogurt
3 tablespoons extra-virgin olive oil
2 firm white fish fillets (such as sole, snapper, or tilapia), about ½-inch thick

1. Combine the salt, black pepper, garlic, ginger, turmeric, coriander, cumin, paprika, yogurt, and 1 tablespoon of the olive oil in a gallon-sized plastic zip-top bag. Add the fish fillets. Seal the bag and turn it a few times to make sure the fillets are coated with the marinade. Refrigerate and allow to marinate for 30 minutes.

2. When ready to cook, add the remaining olive oil to the rice cooker, cover, and set to Cook. When the base of the pot gets warm, add the fish fillets and fry each side for 5 to 8 minutes until fish completely cooks through, keeping the rice cooker covered while frying.

Serving Suggestion

Serve with Mango Chutney (page 285). The chutney adds a fruity sweetness and complements this savory, mildly spiced fish very well.

Fish Burger

This is a quick and easy meal to prepare, but an even quicker method of cooking is to rub some extra-virgin olive oil on the fish, wrap and seal it tightly in foil, and steam it for about 8 minutes in the rice cooker. Drain excess cooking liquid from the steamed fish before putting it in the bun.

INGREDIENTS | SERVES 2

2 firm white fish fillets (such as sole, snapper, or sea bass), about ½-inch thick
¼ teaspoon salt
½ teaspoon freshly ground black pepper
1 teaspoon turmeric
1 teaspoon corn flour
2 sesame seed buns, split into half
2 teaspoons butter, divided use
1 tablespoon extra-virgin olive oil
2 slices Cheddar or Swiss cheese
1 cup alfalfa sprouts

1. If the fish fillets are too long for the buns, slice each fillet in half. Season both sides of the fish with the salt, black pepper, and turmeric, and pat both sides with corn flour. Set aside.

2. Cover the rice cooker and set to Cook. When the base is warm, place the buns in the cooker, split-side down, and "toast" for about 1 minute. Remove and set aside.

3. Add 1 teaspoon of the butter and the olive oil to the rice cooker, cover, and set to Cook. When the base of the cooker pot gets warm, add the fish fillets and fry each side of fish for 3 to 5 minutes until fish completely cooks through (turns opaque), keeping the rice cooker covered while frying.

4. Meanwhile, use the remaining 1 teaspoon of butter to slightly butter one half of each bun. Place a slice of cheese on the bun; arrange alfafa sprouts on the cheese.

5. Remove pan-fried fish from the rice cooker, place in the prepared bun, and serve.

CHAPTER 10

Shrimp, Scallops, and Clams

Chinese Steamed Shrimp with Ginger
143

Tangy Shrimp Curry with Pineapples
144

Shrimp in Wine Ginger Broth
145

Shrimp with Spicy Tomatoes
145

Spicy Shrimp with Basil
146

Shrimp and Shiitake Curry
147

Indian Shrimp Curry
148

Thai Green Curry with Shrimp
149

Sweet and Sour Shrimp
150

Shrimp in Spicy Milk Sauce
151

Salt and Pepper Shrimp
152

Herb and Garlic Shrimp
152

Black Pepper Shrimp
153

Stir-Fried Shrimp with Asparagus
154

Shrimp and Tomato Fried Eggs
155

Shrimp with Colored Bell Peppers
156

Easy Thai-Style Shrimp Cake
156

Buttered Scallops
157

Clam and Corn in Herby Broth
158

Chinese Steamed Shrimp with Ginger

One of the best ways to cook fresh shrimp is to steam them. Steaming will keep the flavors of fresh shrimp intact, unlike boiling, in which the essence of the shrimp is lost to the cooking liquid.

INGREDIENTS | SERVES 3 OR 4

- 1 pound fresh shrimp, shells on and tails on
- ¼ teaspoon salt
- ¼ teaspoon ground white pepper
- ½ teaspoon grated fresh ginger
- ½-inch piece fresh ginger, sliced into thin shreds
- 1 red chili pepper, seeded and julienned to a tiny shred
- 1 egg white, lightly whisked
- 1 tablespoon Chinese cooking wine

Cooking Tip

Adding egg whites toward the end of cooking is not commonly done by home cooks but is often seen in some Chinese restaurants. Surprise diners with this technique at your table and they'll exclaim, "Wow, how did you do that?" This steamed shrimp dish is very delicious, yet so different.

1. Combine the shrimp, salt, pepper, and grated ginger and allow to marinate for 10 minutes.

2. Place the marinated shrimp on a plate that will fit in the steamer insert or basket. Sprinkle the red chili and sliced ginger over the shrimp.

3. Fill the rice cooker pot with water to about the 4-cup mark. Cover the rice cooker and set to Cook. When the water in the cooker boils, place the steamer insert or basket with the plate of shrimp into the rice cooker, and steam for about 5 minutes, keeping the rice cooker covered.

4. Lift up rice cooker lid, gently pour egg white over the shrimp, drizzle the Chinese cooking wine over the shrimp, cover rice cooker, and steam for additional 2 to 3 minutes until shrimp cook through (turn pink).

Tangy Shrimp Curry with Pineapples

A ripe and sweet pineapple is ideal for this dish. However, if that's not available, use canned pineapple instead, draining off the syrup before use.

INGREDIENTS | SERVES 2 OR 3

1 clove garlic
1 stalk lemongrass (white part only)
4 shallots
5 to 6 dried red chili peppers (to taste)
½ tablespoon belacan (prawn paste)
3 tablespoons vegetable oil
½ cup tamarind juice, extracted from tamarind pulp (size of golf ball)
1 tomato, chopped into bite-sized pieces
2 teaspoons curry powder
2 teaspoons brown sugar
2 cups water
1 pound shrimp
1 cup pineapple cubes

Cooking Tip

In a bowl, soak the tamarind pulp in warm water for 10 minutes, squeezing the pulp gently several times while the pulp is soaking to extract the flavor. Stir to mix, and then strain the tamarind liquid, discarding the pulp and seeds.

1. Combine the garlic, lemongrass, shallots, chilies, and belacan in a food processor and blend into a paste.

2. Add the oil to the rice cooker, cover, and set to Cook. When the base of the cooker pot gets warm, add the paste and fry about 5 to 8 minutes until fragrant, covering the rice cooker occasionally in the process of frying.

3. Stir in the tamarind juice, tomatoes, curry powder, brown sugar, and water. Cover the rice cooker and allow it to come to a simmer.

4. Once simmering and the gravy starts to reduce, lift up the rice cooker lid, add the shrimp and pineapples, and cook for about 10 to 12 minutes until the shrimp cook through (turn pink), covering the cooker occasionally in the process of cooking. Serve with steamed rice.

Shrimp in Wine Ginger Broth

This recipe works best with live shrimp, which you can buy from the fishmonger in Asian supermarkets.

INGREDIENTS | SERVES 3 OR 4

1½ to 2 pounds uncooked shrimp shell-on
½ cup Chinese cooking wine
3 cups water
1-inch piece ginger, thinly sliced
¼ cup gojiberries, soaked in warm water for 5 minutes, then drained

1. In a large bowl, combine the shrimp in the Chinese cooking wine. Set aside for 20 minutes in the fridge to marinate.

2. Add the 3 cups water to the rice cooker pot. Cover the rice cooker and set to Cook. When the water in the cooker boils, add the ginger slices and shrimp. Cover the rice cooker and bring shrimp to a simmer until they cook through (turn pink). Dish out the shrimp and set aside.

3. Add the gojiberries, cover the rice cooker, and bring the broth to a simmer. Once simmering, remove impurities switch off the rice cooker. Ladle the broth and gojiberries over the shrimp and serve.

Shrimp with Spicy Tomatoes

You can substitute fresh cherry or plum tomatoes for the canned tomatoes in this recipe. Sun-dried tomatoes work as well.

INGREDIENTS | SERVES 2 OR 3

2 tablespoons vegetable oil
4 shallots, thinly sliced
½ (8-ounce) can diced tomatoes, with juice
1 teaspoon curry powder
½ teaspoon red chili pepper flakes
½ teaspoon grated ginger
½ teaspoon garam masala
¼ teaspoon salt
1 cup water
1 pound shrimp, peeled and deveined

1. Add the oil to the rice cooker pot, cover, and set to Cook. When the base of the cooker pot gets warm, add the shallots and fry about 5 minutes until shallots turn soft.

2. Add the tomatoes, curry powder, and chili flakes and fry for about 3 minutes, covering the rice cooker occasionally in the process of frying.

3. Add the grated ginger, garam masala, salt, and water. Cover rice cooker and allow to come to a simmer.

4. Once simmering, add the shrimp, mix well, and cook for about 8 to 10 minutes until the shrimp cook through (turn pink) and the gravy slightly reduces. Dish out and serve.

Spicy Shrimp with Basil

Basil has a strong flavor and is perfect for different cuisines. It matches well with Chinese flavorings and some common Indian spices.

INGREDIENTS | SERVES 2 OR 3

1 tablespoon butter, divided use
1 onion, thinly sliced
2 cloves garlic, finely minced
½ teaspoon cumin seeds
½ (8-ounce) can diced tomatoes, with juice
1 teaspoon brown sugar
1 cup water
1 tablespoon finely chopped fresh basil
1 pound shrimp, peeled and deveined

Cumin
Cumin is usually seen in two forms: whole (in the form of small seeds) and ground. Its nutty and peppery flavor plays an important role in Mexican, Indian, and Middle Eastern cuisine.

1. Add ½ tablespoon of the butter to the rice cooker pot, cover, and set to Cook. When the base of the cooker pot gets warm, add the onions and fry for about 5 minutes until onions turn soft.

2. Add the garlic and cumin seeds and stir-fry for 1 to 2 minutes, until fragrant, covering the rice cooker occasionally in the process of frying.

3. Add the tomatoes, brown sugar, and water. Cover the rice cooker and allow to come to a simmer.

4. Once simmering, stir in remaining butter, basil, and shrimp. Mix well, and cook for about 8 to 10 minutes until the shrimp cook through (turn pink) and the gravy slightly reduces. Serve with steamed rice.

Shrimp and Shiitake Curry

This is an easy and healthy curry. Ladle it over noodles or simply serve with steamed rice.

INGREDIENTS | SERVES 2

2 tablespoons vegetable oil
1 medium-sized onion, thinly sliced
1 green or red bell pepper, sliced
6 fresh shiitake mushroom caps, cut into halves
½ pound shrimp, peeled and deveined
1 tablespoon curry powder
1 cup thick coconut milk
½ cup water
¼ teaspoon salt, or to taste

Storage Tips

Once canned coconut milk is opened, it can be kept in an airtight container in the refrigerator up to 1 week. It is recommended that you use up the remaining coconut milk as soon as possible, since the high fat content makes it turn rancid quickly.

1. Add the oil to the rice cooker, cover, and set to Cook. When the base of the cooker pot gets warm, add the onions and fry for about 5 minutes until onions are soft.

2. Add peppers, mushrooms, and shrimp and stir-fry for about 5 to 8 minutes, until the shrimp cook through (turn pink), covering the rice cooker occasionally in the process of cooking. Dish out the vegetable-shrimp mixture to a large bowl and set aside. Leave the remaining oil in the pot.

3. Add the curry powder to the pot and stir-fry for about 1 minute. Stir in the coconut milk and water. Cover rice cooker and bring to a simmer.

4. Once simmering, add salt to taste, switch rice cooker to Warm, lift up rice cooker lid, and return vegetable-shrimp mixture to the pot. Stir gently, cover rice cooker occasionally, and allow coconut milk mixture to simmer for about 5 to 8 minutes until gravy thickens.

Indian Shrimp Curry

Serve this curry with Cucumber Raita
(see Make Your Own Cucumber Raita, page 62) and steamed rice.

INGREDIENTS | SERVES 2 OR 3

2 tablespoons vegetable oil
1 medium-sized onion, finely chopped
2 cloves garlic, finely minced
1 teaspoon grated ginger
1 teaspoon cumin seeds
1 teaspoon turmeric
1 teaspoon paprika
½ teaspoon chili pepper flakes
½ (8-ounce) can diced tomatoes, with juice
1 cup coconut milk
½ teaspoon salt
½ pound shrimp, peeled and deveined
2 tablespoons chopped cilantro
1 tablespoon lemon juice

1. Add the oil to the rice cooker, cover, and set to Cook. When the base of the cooker pot gets warm, add the onions and fry for about 5 minutes until onions are soft.

2. Add the garlic, ginger, cumin, turmeric, paprika, and chili flakes and fry for 3 minutes, covering rice cooker occasionally in the process of cooking.

3. Add the tomatoes, coconut milk, and salt. Cover rice cooker and bring to a simmer.

4. Once simmering, slightly tilt the rice cooker lid and continue to simmer for 6 to 8 minutes. Add the shrimp and cilantro. Stir and simmer for about 5 minutes until shrimp cook through (turn pink), covering rice cooker occasionally in the process of cooking.

5. Stir in lemon juice before serving.

Thai Green Curry with Shrimp

As a variation, try adding other fresh or frozen green vegetables such as zucchini, green peas, and snow peas.

INGREDIENTS | SERVES 2 OR 3

- 2 tablespoons vegetable oil
- 1 medium-sized onion, finely chopped
- 1 kaffir lime leaf, finely chopped (or ½ teaspoon lime zest)
- 2 teaspoons Thai green curry paste
- 2 cloves garlic, finely minced
- 1 cup coconut milk
- 1 tablespoon fish sauce
- 1 cup Shrimp Stock (page 17), Chicken Stock (page 16), or Vegetable Stock (page 18)
- ½ tablespoon brown sugar
- ¼ teaspoon salt
- 1 red bell pepper, diced into bite-sized pieces
- 8 to 10 green beans, ends trimmed and diced into bite-sized pieces
- ½ pack (10½-ounce pack) firm tofu, cubed
- ½ pound shrimp, peeled and deveined
- 1 tablespoon lime juice
- 1 tablespoon finely chopped cilantro leaves

1. Add the oil to the rice cooker, cover, and set to Cook. When the base of the cooker pot gets warm, add the onions and fry for about 5 minutes until onions are soft.

2. Add the kaffir lime leaf, curry paste, and garlic and stir well for about 1 minute. Add coconut milk, fish sauce, stock, brown sugar, and salt. Cover rice cooker and bring to a simmer.

3. Once simmering, add the bell peppers, green beans, and tofu. Cover rice cooker and continue to simmer for 6 to 8 minutes, switching to Warm if mixture bubbles too vigorously.

4. Add the shrimp, cover rice cooker, switch back to Cook if necessary, and bring to simmer again until shrimp cook through (turn pink) in about 8 to 10 minutes. If simmering starts before 8 minutes, stir and switch to Warm and continue cooking the shrimp for the remaining 8 to 10 minutes.

5. Stir in lime juice and cilantro before serving.

Cooking Tip

For a spicier curry, use an additional teaspoon of Thai green curry paste and top with seeded and finely sliced Thai red chili pepper.

Sweet and Sour Shrimp

Add small wedges of seeded red, yellow, and green peppers with the peas and pineapples while cooking this dish to provide color and variety.

INGREDIENTS | SERVES 2 OR 3

1 tablespoon ketchup
1 teaspoon brown sugar
½ cup warm water
2 tablespoons vegetable oil
1 pound shrimp, peeled and deveined
2 shallots, thinly sliced
1 teaspoon grated ginger
½ cup frozen peas, thawed
½ cup pineapple cubes
Salt and ground white pepper, to taste

1. Mix the ketchup, brown sugar, and water in a bowl. Set aside as sauce.

2. Add the oil to the rice cooker, cover, and set to Cook. When the base of the cooker pot gets warm, add the shrimp and fry about 8 to 10 minutes until shrimp cook through (turn pink). Dish out and set aside. Leave the remaining oil in the pot.

3. Add the shallots to the pot and fry about 3 minutes until soft.

4. Add the ginger, peas, and pineapple, and stir-fry for 2 to 3 minutes, covering rice cooker occasionally in the process of cooking.

5. Add prepared sauce mixture; stir well. Add salt and pepper to taste, cover rice cooker, and bring to slight simmer.

6. Once simmering, switch to Warm, return shrimp to the pot, and stir well to coat the shrimp with the sauce.

Shrimp in Spicy Milk Sauce

As a variation and for more aroma, use coconut milk instead of whole milk.

INGREDIENTS | SERVES 2 OR 3

1 tablespoon vegetable oil
1 pound shrimp, peeled and deveined
½ tablespoon butter
4 curry leaves
½ teaspoon red chili pepper flakes
1 teaspoon curry powder
1 teaspoon brown sugar
¼ teaspoon salt
¼ cup whole milk

1. Add the oil to the rice cooker, cover, and set to Cook. When the base of the cooker pot gets warm, add the shrimp and fry for about 8 to 10 minutes until shrimp cook through (turn pink). Dish out and set aside.

2. Add the butter to the pot, then the curry leaves and chili flakes and fry for about 5 minutes until fragrant. Add curry powder, brown sugar, and salt.

3. Slowly stir in the milk to dissolve curry powder and brown sugar. Cover the rice cooker and bring mixture to a slight simmer. When simmering and sauce reduces (thickens) in about 5 to 8 minutes, add the shrimp and mix well with the sauce. Serve with steamed rice.

Curry Leaves

Distinctively aromatic due to the presence of volatile essential oils, curry leaves—both fresh and dried—are usually fried in hot oil to release their scent and enticing flavor. Curry leaves provide a subtle spicy flavor not only in curries but also in many legume dishes. In addition to essential oils, curry leaves contain chlorophyll, beta carotene, folic acid, riboflavin, calcium, and zinc.

Salt and Pepper Shrimp

Vary this recipe by adding some red chili pepper flakes to spice things up. You also can use a ground pepper mix of black, red, and Szechuan peppers for added depth and spice.

INGREDIENTS | SERVES 2 OR 3

1 tablespoon butter
1 green onion, sliced into finger-length pieces
1 clove garlic, finely minced
½-inch piece ginger, sliced into thin finger-length shreds
1 teaspoon kosher salt or sea salt
2 teaspoons freshly ground black pepper
1 pound medium-sized shrimp, deveined, shells on, rinsed, and patted dry with paper towels

1. Add the butter to the rice cooker, cover, and set to Cook. When the base of the cooker pot gets warm, add the green onion, garlic, ginger, salt, and pepper and fry for 2 to 3 minutes until butter mixture is fragrant, covering rice cooker occasionally during frying.

2. In a large bowl, pour the butter mixture over the shrimp and toss to coat.

3. Wipe the rice cooker dry, cover, and set to Cook. When the base of the rice cooker gets warm, add the shrimp and dry-fry the shrimp for about 8 to 10 minutes until they cook through (turn pink), stirring and covering the rice cooker occasionally in the process of cooking. When shrimp are cooked, dish out and serve.

Herb and Garlic Shrimp

For a healthier variation, use extra-virgin olive oil instead of butter. You also can try parsley instead of basil as an herb variation.

INGREDIENTS | SERVES 2 OR 3

1 tablespoon butter
2 cloves garlic, finely minced
¼ teaspoon salt
¼ teaspoon black pepper
1 tablespoon finely chopped fresh basil
1 to 2 tablespoons lemon juice
1 pound shrimp, peeled and deveined

1. Add the butter to the rice cooker, cover, and set to Cook. When butter is melted, switch off the rice cooker.

2. In a separate bowl, combine the melted butter, garlic, salt, pepper, basil, lemon juice, and shrimp. Set aside for 30 minutes to marinate in fridge.

3. Switch rice cooker to Cook. When the base of the cooker pot gets warm, add the butter-garlic-shrimp mixture and fry for 5 to 8 minutes until shrimp cook through (turn pink).

Black Pepper Shrimp

This dish combines butter with a lot of pungent seasonings such as ginger and lots of black pepper to create a delicious delicacy. The recipe is also ideal for crab.

INGREDIENTS | SERVES 2 OR 3

- 1 tablespoon oyster sauce
- 1 teaspoon dark soy sauce
- 1 teaspoon brown sugar
- 1 cup water
- 1 tablespoon vegetable oil
- 1 pound tiger shrimp, shells on, tails on, heads on
- 1 tablespoon butter
- 3 cloves garlic, finely minced
- 1 teaspoon grated ginger
- 1 tablespoon freshly ground black pepper

Cooking Tip

Prior to any cooking, set the rice cooker to Cook and dry-fry the black pepper in the heated rice cooker pot until fragrant for about 5 minutes. Remove and set aside. This is similar to an old-fashioned cooking method in which food is "tempered" until fragrant in a heated wok or pan without oil.

1. Mix the oyster sauce, soy sauce, brown sugar, and water in a bowl. Set aside as sauce.

2. Add the oil to the rice cooker, cover, and set to Cook. When the base of the cooker pot gets warm, add the shrimp and fry for about 8 to 10 minutes until shrimp cook through (turn pink), covering rice cooker occasionally in the processing of cooking. Dish out and set aside.

3. Add the butter to the rice cooker; cover the pot. When butter begins to melt, add the garlic and ginger and fry for 5 minutes until fragrant.

4. Add the prepared sauce mixture, cover rice cooker, and bring to a simmer. Once simmering, lift up rice cooker lid and continue to simmer about 8 to 10 minutes until sauce slightly reduces (thickens).

5. Stir in black pepper. Mix well, cover rice cooker, and continue to simmer for about 1 minute.

6. Return shrimp to the pot, stir, and mix well with sauce. Cover rice cooker and bring to a simmer again. Lift up rice cooker lid and cook until shrimp completely cook through and sauce reduces further (thickens). Serve with steamed rice.

CHAPTER 10 **SHRIMP, SCALLOPS, AND CLAMS**

Stir-Fried Shrimp with Asparagus

For a different flavor, try substituting broccoli or a mix of broccoli and cauliflower for the asparagus.

INGREDIENTS | **SERVES 2**

½ pound shrimp, peeled and deveined
¼ teaspoon salt
¼ teaspoon ground white pepper
1 teaspoon Chinese cooking wine
1 teaspoon oyster sauce
¼ cup Chicken Stock (page 16) or water
½ teaspoon corn flour
2 tablespoons vegetable oil, divided use
4 ounces thin asparagus spears, cut into finger-length pieces
1 teaspoon grated ginger

Cooking Tip

Save preparation time by using thin asparagus spears, as they do not need to be peeled. The asparagus also will be more delicate and crisp in texture. The fatter, thicker spears are just as good in terms of flavor; in fact, they are "meatier" than their thinner counterparts. However, more preparation time is required for peeling off the woody and more fibrous stems of thick asparagus spears.

1. In a medium bowl, season the shrimp with salt and pepper. Set aside.

2. In a separate bowl, combine the Chinese cooking wine, oyster sauce, chicken stock or water, and corn flour. Set aside as a sauce.

3. Add 1 tablespoon of the oil to the rice cooker, cover, and set to Cook. When the base of the cooker pot gets warm, add the asparagus and stir-fry for about 1 minute until asparagus turn tender, covering rice cooker occasionally in the process of frying. Remove asparagus and set aside.

4. Add the remaining oil to the rice cooker, cover, and wait until the oil is hot. When hot, add the ginger and fry for 1 minute until fragrant.

5. Add the shrimp and fry for about 5 to 8 minutes until shrimp just cook (just turn pink). Return the asparagus to the rice cooker and mix well.

6. Slowly stir in the prepared sauce mixture and mix well with shrimp. Cover the rice cooker and allow entire mixture to come to a slight simmer. Once simmering, lift up rice cooker lid. Continue to stir and simmer until sauce thickens and shrimp completely cook through in about 3 to 5 minutes. Serve immediately.

Shrimp and Tomato Fried Eggs

*It is not necessary to wash the rice cooker after frying the eggs.
Just clear out some of the egg remnants with a paper towel and continue with the next step.*

INGREDIENTS | SERVES 3 OR 4

2 to 3 eggs
Salt and ground white pepper, to taste
2 drops sesame oil
Salt and ground white pepper to taste, for the shrimp
1 teaspoon Chinese cooking wine
½ pound shrimp, peeled and deveined
4 tablespoons vegetable oil, divided use
1 tomato, thinly sliced into wedges
2 tablespoons water
2 green onions, finely chopped, for garnish

1. Lightly whisk the eggs in a bowl and combine with salt, pepper, and sesame oil. Set aside.

2. In a separate bowl, combine salt, pepper, Chinese cooking wine, and shrimp. Set aside to marinate.

3. Add 3 tablespoons of the oil to the rice cooker, cover, and set to Cook. When the base of the cooker pot gets warm, add the egg mixture and fry until egg just cooks (do not overcook). Dish out and set aside.

4. Clean out rice cooker. Add the remaining oil to the rice cooker, cover, and set to Cook. When the base of the cooker pot gets warm, add the shrimp and fry for about 8 to 10 minutes until shrimp cook through (turn pink).

5. Add the tomato and fry briskly. Add the water, then cover rice cooker and allow it to come to a simmer.

6. Once simmering, lift up rice cooker lid, switch to Warm, return the eggs to the pot, and mix well by breaking up the eggs into small pieces. Fry eggs with shrimp and tomatoes for about 3 to 5 minutes. Garnish with green onions before serving.

Shrimp with Colored Bell Peppers

The variety of bell peppers used not only adds color but gives the meal balanced nutrition.

INGREDIENTS | SERVES 2

1 clove garlic, finely minced
½ teaspoon salt
1 tablespoon finely chopped cilantro leaves
½ pound shrimp, peeled and deveined
2 tablespoons extra-virgin olive oil
½ green bell pepper, seeded and thinly sliced
½ red bell pepper, seeded and thinly sliced

1. Combine garlic, salt, cilantro leaves, and shrimp in a bowl. Set aside for 5 minutes.
2. Add the oil to the rice cooker, cover, and set to Cook. When the base of the cooker pot gets warm, add the seasoned shrimp and stir-fry for about 5 to 8 minutes until shrimp are just cooked (turn pink).
3. Add the bell peppers and stir-fry for 5 to 8 minutes until peppers become tender and shrimp completely cook through. Dish out and serve.

Easy Thai-Style Shrimp Cake

Fried Thai Fish Cake, also known as Tod Mun Pla, is slightly different from steamed Spicy Fish Custard (page 37). This recipe makes a shrimp version of the popular Thai snack.

INGREDIENTS | SERVES 2 OR 3

½ pound shrimp, peeled and deveined
1 tablespoon curry powder
1 tablespoon finely chopped cilantro leaves
3 kaffir lime leaves, sliced into very fine thin strips
¼ teaspoon salt
¼ teaspoon red chili pepper flakes
1 egg white
4 tablespoons vegetable oil, divided use
½ cup corn flour, for coating

1. Mince the shrimp. Combine minced shrimp with curry powder, cilantro, kaffir lime leaves, salt, chili flakes, and egg white to form a smooth shrimp paste. Shape round, flat cakes from the paste and set aside.
2. Add 2 tablespoons of the oil to the rice cooker, cover, and set to Cook. When the base of the cooker pot gets warm, dip the cakes into corn flour to coat evenly on both sides. Add the shrimp cakes to the rice cooker in batches. Fry each side for 3 to 4 minutes, covering rice cooker during frying. When the cakes turn golden brown and crispy, dish out and set aside. Add more oil as you continue to fry batches. Serve cakes warm.

Buttered Scallops

Make sure to work in one batch when pan-frying the scallops, as they release moisture during cooking. If you can't fit all the scallops into the pan base in one batch and it's necessary to pan-fry a second batch, the rice cooker may need to be cleaned and wiped dry thoroughly between batches.

INGREDIENTS | SERVES 2

2 tablespoons butter

6 to 8 large scallops, patted dry with paper towels

Salt and freshly ground black pepper, to taste

1 tablespoon lemon juice

Cooking Tip

Frozen scallops need to be thawed thoroughly before cooking to make sure there is no excess moisture in them. To be sure, use some paper towels to dry the scallops.

1. Add the butter to the rice cooker, cover, and set to Cook. When the butter melts and the base of the cooker pot gets warm, add the scallops in a single layer, sprinkle with salt and pepper (do not turn the scallops), and fry 2 to 3 minutes.

2. When scallops whiten halfway through, turn to the other side and sprinkle with salt and pepper. Fry 2 to 3 minutes without turning, covering the rice cooker during frying.

3. When scallops cook through (fully whiten), add the lemon juice and simmer for another minute. Serve warm.

Clam and Corn in Herby Broth

To safely store clams before they are cooked, put them in a colander set inside a large bowl. Place some dampened paper towels over the clams and keep them in a cold area of your refrigerator for about half a day.

INGREDIENTS | SERVES 3 OR 4

2 tablespoons olive oil
½ tablespoon butter
3 shallots, thinly sliced
2 cloves garlic, finely minced
1 teaspoon grated ginger
2 pounds clams
1 cup canned corn kernels
¼ cup dry white wine
¼ teaspoon freshly ground black pepper
½ cup water or clam stock
1 tablespoon finely chopped fresh basil

Cooking Tip

When clams are cooked (shells open up), use tongs to remove them and set them aside in a bowl. Overcooked clams are rubbery! If the other ingredients, including the broth, need further cooking, continue to simmer them without the cooked clams. Before serving, ladle the broth over the clams.

1. Add the oil and butter to the rice cooker, cover, and set to Cook. When the base of the cooker pot gets warm, add the shallots and fry for about 3 minutes until shallots turn soft.

2. Add the garlic and ginger and fry for about 3 minutes until fragrant, covering rice cooker occasionally in the process of frying.

3. Add the clams, corn, wine, pepper, and water or stock. Cover rice cooker and allow it to come to a simmer (the steam in the rice cooker will cook the clams) for about 5 minutes, until clams show first signs of opening.

4. Continue simmering, cover rice cooker occasionally in the process and check to see if most of the clams have opened. Discard any that do not open. Remove the clams that have opened and set them aside in serving bowls.

5. Add the basil to the broth, stir well, and ladle broth over the clams in serving bowls. Serve with crusty bread for dipping into the broth.

CHAPTER 11

Chicken

Steamed Chicken with Ginger and Green Onions
160

Steamed Chicken with Carrots and Onions
161

Steamed Dark-Sauce Chicken with Mushrooms
162

Chicken Barley Stew
163

Cider Chicken Stew
164

Tea-Flavored Chicken with Chinese Spices
165

Easy Chicken Curry
165

Chicken with Spicy Tomatoes
166

Chicken Jalfrezi
167

Thai Ginger Chicken
168

Three-Cup Chicken
169

Sesame Oil Chicken
170

Chicken in Wine and Shallot Sauce
171

Orange Chicken
172

Citron Honey Chicken
173

Lychee Chicken
174

Stir-Fried Black Pepper Chicken with Sugar Snap Peas
175

Thai Basil Chicken
176

Steamed Chicken with Ginger and Green Onions

Using the steaming method to cook poultry is healthy, but the meat may taste rather bland. Marinate with Chinese seasonings to flavor up the cooked dish. You will be surprised by the result!

INGREDIENTS | SERVES 2 OR 3

2 pieces boneless chicken thigh, sliced to bite-sized pieces
2 teaspoons oyster sauce
1 teaspoon sesame oil
1 tablespoon Chinese cooking wine
1 teaspoon corn flour
4 fresh shiitake mushroom caps, thinly sliced
1 teaspoon grated ginger
1-inch piece ginger, finely shredded
2 green onions, sliced into finger-length pieces

1. Combine the chicken with oyster sauce, sesame oil, Chinese cooking wine, and corn flour and marinate for 30 minutes in the fridge.

2. Fill the rice cooker pot with water to about the 4-cup mark. Cover and set to Cook.

3. While the water is coming to a boil, place half the mushrooms, half the ginger, and half the green onions on a plate that will fit in the steamer insert or basket. Place the chicken on this layer. Then top the chicken with the remaining mushrooms, ginger, and green onions. Cover the top of the plate with plastic wrap, to prevent excess condensation during steaming.

4. When the water in the rice cooker boils, place the steamer insert or basket with the plate of chicken into the rice cooker and steam for 20 to 25 minutes, until chicken cooks through.

Steamed Chicken with Carrots and Onions

The natural sweetness of the carrots and onions that is released during the steaming process complements the savory Chinese seasonings very well. This is another easy, tasty, and healthy recipe.

INGREDIENTS | SERVES 2 OR 3

6 to 8 mid-joint chicken wings
1 teaspoon oyster sauce
1 tablespoon Chinese cooking wine
1 teaspoon dark soy sauce
1 teaspoon sesame oil
½ teaspoon ground white pepper
½ teaspoon brown sugar
10 to 12 baby carrots
½ medium-sized onion, thinly sliced

Cooking Tip

Steam this dish in tightly wrapped foil, to save time washing dishes after a meal.

1. Combine the chicken with the oyster sauce, Chinese cooking wine, soy sauce, sesame oil, pepper, and brown sugar. Marinate for 30 minutes in the fridge.

2. Fill the rice cooker pot with water to about the 4-cup mark. Cover and set to Cook.

3. While the water is coming to a boil, place the marinated chicken, carrots, and onions evenly on a plate that will fit in the steamer insert or basket. Cover the top of the plate with plastic wrap, to prevent excess condensation during steaming.

4. When the water in the rice cooker boils, place the steamer insert or basket with the plate of chicken into the rice cooker and steam for 20 to 25 minutes, until chicken cooks through.

Steamed Dark-Sauce Chicken with Mushrooms

As a variation, canned button mushrooms also work well in this recipe. Look for canned button mushrooms in Asian supermarkets or the ethnic sections in big supermarkets.

INGREDIENTS | SERVES 3 OR 4

10 to 12 mid-joint chicken wings
2 tablespoons dark soy sauce
1 tablespoon oyster sauce
1 teaspoon sugar
¼ teaspoon white pepper
2 teaspoons Chinese cooking wine
2 tablespoons vegetable oil
2 cloves garlic, crushed whole
2 teaspoons grated ginger
8 fresh shiitake mushroom caps, sliced in halves
1 green onion, finely chopped, for garnish

Cooking Tip

Leftovers of this dish taste as good as the freshly prepared recipe and can be reheated the next day while you cook rice to serve with them. Just make sure you know the time required to cook rice in your rice cooker. About 10 minutes before the end of the cooking time, place the leftovers (on a plate or wrapped in foil) on the steamer insert or basket and place it into the rice cooker to reheat while the rice finishes cooking.

1. Combine the chicken with soy sauce, oyster sauce, sugar, pepper, and Chinese cooking wine. Marinate for 15 minutes in the fridge.

2. Add the oil to the rice cooker, cover, and set to Cook. When the base of the cooker pot gets warm, add the garlic and ginger, and fry for about 3 minutes until fragrant.

3. Add the marinated chicken and the mushrooms and fry for 2 to 3 minutes until chicken turns brown on the surface, covering the rice cooker occasionally in the process of cooking. Switch off rice cooker, dish out chicken, and set aside on a plate that will fit in the steamer insert or basket. Cover the top of plate with plastic wrap to prevent excess condensation during steaming.

4. Clean out the rice cooker and wipe dry. Fill the pot with water to about the 4-cup mark. Cover the rice cooker and set to Cook.

5. When the water in the rice cooker boils, place the steamer insert or basket with the plate of chicken into the rice cooker and steam for 15 to 20 minutes, until chicken cooks through.

6. Garnish with green onions and serve with steamed rice or plain Rice Congee (page 14).

Chicken Barley Stew

The liquid used for boiling the barley can be reserved for cooking and even drinking. Stir some honey and lemon juice into the barley water for a refreshing drink, warm or chilled.

INGREDIENTS | SERVES 2

4 cups water

2 ounces washed and cleaned pearl barley, soaked for 4 hours before using

2 tablespoons vegetable oil

1 shallot, thinly sliced

1 clove garlic, finely minced

½ teaspoon grated ginger

1 boneless chicken thigh, sliced to bite-sized pieces

3 cups barley liquid (adjust as needed during cooking)

6 fresh shiitake mushroom caps, thinly sliced

1 cup canned corn kernels, drained

Salt and ground white pepper, to taste

1 tablespoon finely chopped cilantro leaves, for garnish

Benefits of Barley

Barley is high in dietary fiber—both soluble and insoluble. Both types of fiber help to regulate the bowels and protect the body's intestinal systems.

1. Fill the rice cooker pot with 4 cups water. Cover the rice cooker, set to Cook, and bring the water to a boil. Once boiling, add the presoaked barley, cover, and boil for 15 to 20 minutes until barley softens. Strain barley and place in a bowl. Reserve the barley liquid separately for later use.

2. Clean out the rice cooker and wipe dry. Add the oil to the rice cooker, cover, and set to Cook. When the base of the cooker pot gets warm, add the shallots and fry until soft. Add the garlic and ginger and fry for about 3 minutes until fragrant.

3. Add the chicken and fry for 2 to 3 minutes until chicken turns brown on surface, covering rice cooker occasionally in the process of frying.

4. Add the barley and 2 cups reserved barley liquid. Cover rice cooker and allow to come to a simmer.

5. Add the mushrooms, corn, salt, and pepper. Cover the rice cooker and allow to return to a simmer. When bubbling vigorously, lift rice cooker lid, stir for 1 to 2 minutes, then switch to Warm. Cover rice cooker and continue to cook for 10 to 15 minutes until chicken cooks through. Garnish with cilantro.

Cider Chicken Stew

Medium-starch potatoes work well in most potato dishes, including this recipe. Yukon Gold is a common and readily available all-purpose potato.

INGREDIENTS | SERVES 3 OR 4

2 tablespoons vegetable oil

1 medium-sized onion, sliced into bite-sized wedges

4 chicken drumsticks, or 2 chicken legs (thigh and drumsticks)

2 cups baby carrots

1 large potato, cubed to bite-sized chunks

1 teaspoon corn flour

3 cups spiced cider

1 cup water

½ teaspoon ground white pepper

½ teaspoon ground black pepper

Salt, to taste

1. Add the oil to the rice cooker, cover, and set to Cook. When the base of the cooker pot gets warm, add onions and fry for about 5 minutes until onions become soft.

2. Add chicken, carrots, and potatoes, and fry for 2 to 3 minutes until chicken turns brown on the surface, covering rice cooker occasionally in the process of cooking. Sprinkle the corn flour over this mixture and mix well.

3. Add spiced cider, water, white pepper, and black pepper to the 4-cup mark on the rice cooker or enough to immerse the chicken. Cover rice cooker and allow to come to a boil. Once boiling, switch to Warm, add salt, cover rice cooker, and simmer for 1 to 2 hours until chicken cooks through.

Cooking Tip

It is tricky to figure out how to cut or slice chicken to the desired size. Smaller chicken pieces will cook faster than larger pieces, but tend to dry out faster. Thus, for cooking methods such as stir-frying, chicken is usually sliced into thin strips or bite-sized chunks so that they cook quickly before they can dry out. Larger pieces of chicken work well in cooking methods such as steaming, braising, and stewing, since such methods are able to lock in the moisture in the chicken.

Tea-Flavored Chicken with Chinese Spices

Brewed tea can be used as a braising liquid, as in this recipe, or as a seasoning for marinades. The addition of tea helps this dish gain depth of flavor.

INGREDIENTS | SERVES 3 OR 4

3 to 4 cups water, or enough to immerse the chicken
½ cup dark soy sauce
4 cloves garlic, crushed whole
2-inch piece ginger, slightly bruised
3 pieces star anise
2-inch cinnamon stick
1 tablespoon salt
¼ tablespoon brown sugar
2 tea bags (English Tea)
2 pieces chicken leg (thigh and drumstick), or 4 chicken drumsticks

1. Fill the rice cooker pot with water to about the 4-cup mark. Stir in soy sauce, garlic, ginger, star anise, cinnamon, and salt. Cover and set to Cook.

2. When the mixture starts to boil, add the brown sugar and tea bags, stir well, switch to Warm, and simmer for 10 minutes to brew the tea in the sauce mixture. Remove the tea bags.

3. Immerse the chicken into the mixture, cover the rice cooker, set to Cook, and allow it to come to a simmer. Once simmering, switch to Warm and continue to simmer for 2 hours until chicken cooks through. Chop chicken into smaller pieces before serving.

Easy Chicken Curry

For a healthier version of curry that does not use potatoes (since potato is considered a high-carbohydrate food), substitute carrots or apples or a mixture of these.

INGREDIENTS | SERVES 2 OR 3

2 tablespoons vegetable oil
1 onion, thinly sliced
2 boneless chicken thighs, sliced into bite-sized pieces
1 large potato, peeled and cubed into bite-sized pieces
2 tablespoons curry powder
¼ teaspoon red chili pepper flakes
Salt, to taste
1½ cups water
½ cup coconut milk

1. Add the oil to the rice cooker, cover, and set to Cook. When the base of the cooker pot gets warm, add the onions and fry until onions are slightly soft.

2. Add the chicken, potato, curry powder, red chili flakes, salt, and water; stir well. Cover rice cooker and allow to come to a boil.

3. Once boiling, switch to Warm and continue to simmer for 15 to 20 minutes until chicken cooks through. About 5 minutes before end of cooking, stir in coconut milk and simmer at Warm for the remaining 5 minutes.

Chicken with Spicy Tomatoes

If you prefer not to blend the spice paste, you can thinly slice the shallots, finely mince the garlic, use grated ginger and red chili pepper flakes, and fry them in hot oil until fragrant, before adding the chicken.

INGREDIENTS | SERVES 3 OR 4

4 dried whole red chili peppers
4 shallots
2 cloves garlic
½-inch piece ginger
2 tablespoons vegetable oil
2 chicken thighs, sliced to bite-sized pieces
1 teaspoon ground cumin
½ teaspoon turmeric
1 cinnamon stick
1 whole star anise pod
1 whole clove
½ teaspoon salt
½ teaspoon ground black pepper
½ (8-ounce) can diced tomatoes, with juice
½ cup water, adjust accordingly

1. Combine chilies, shallots, garlic, and ginger in a food processor and blend into a paste. Set aside.

2. Add the oil to the rice cooker, cover, and set to Cook. When the base of the cooker pot gets warm, add the chicken and fry about 8 to 10 minutes until chicken turns brown on the surface. Dish out and set aside. Leave the remaining oil in the rice cooker.

3. Add to the pot the spice paste, cumin, turmeric, cinnamon, star anise, clove, salt, and pepper. Fry for 2 to 3 minutes until fragrant.

4. Return the chicken pieces to the pot, stir to coat the chicken with the spices mixture, and stir-fry for about 5 minutes, covering rice cooker occasionally in the process of cooking.

5. Add the tomatoes and water and stir well. Cover rice cooker and allow it to come to a simmer for 2 to 3 minutes. Then, switch the rice cooker to Warm and continue to simmer for 45 minutes to 1 hour until chicken cooks through.

Mortar and Pestle

Instead of a food processor, use a mortar and pestle to get the best flavors out of the spices. The crushing and pounding actions in a mortar and pestle build flavors and give you more control over the texture of the paste.

Chicken Jalfrezi

This dish was originally created using leftover meat with chili peppers added to mask any unpleasant taste. However, the blend of spices turned out so well that it has become a popular dish.

INGREDIENTS | SERVES 2 OR 3

- ½ pound chicken pieces (thigh and breast meat), sliced to bite-sized pieces
- ½ tablespoon grated ginger
- 2 cloves garlic, grated
- ½ teaspoon ground cumin
- ½ teaspoon ground coriander
- ½ teaspoon turmeric
- ¼ teaspoon salt
- 2 tablespoons vegetable oil
- 1 onion, finely chopped
- 2 fresh serrano green chili peppers, seeded
- 1 green bell pepper, seeded and cubed into bite-sized pieces
- 1 tomato, sliced to thin wedges
- 1 tablespoon butter
- 1 teaspoon red chili powder
- ½ (8-ounce) can diced tomatoes, with juice
- ½ cup water
- 1 tablespoon finely chopped cilantro leaves, for garnish

Do You Know?

The heat in chili is caused by capsaicin concentrated in the membranes surrounding the seeds. Seeding the peppers and removing the membranes helps to reduce the heat. The choice of chili determines the heat level as well. The Scoville scale is a measure of the hotness or piquancy of a chili. If you don't like too much heat, tune down to just one fresh serrano green chili in this recipe.

1. Combine the chicken with ginger, garlic, cumin, coriander, turmeric, and salt and leave to marinate in the fridge for at least 30 minutes.

2. Add the oil to the rice cooker, cover, and set to Cook. When the base of the cooker pot gets warm, add the onion and fry until onions turn soft. Add the green chili and bell peppers and fry for about 5 to 8 minutes until fragrant, covering rice cooker in the process of frying.

3. Add tomato wedges and stir well. Cover rice cooker and allow to simmer for 5 minutes, switching to Warm if mixture bubbles too vigorously. Dish out and set aside.

4. Add the butter to rice cooker, cover, and set to Cook. When the butter has melted, add marinated chicken and stir-fry for about 5 minutes until chicken turns brown on the surface.

5. Add chili powder, canned tomatoes (with juice), and water; stir well. Cover rice cooker and allow to simmer for 10 to 12 minutes, until chicken cooks through, switching to Warm if mixture bubbles too vigorously.

6. Stir in the pepper mixture and mix well with chicken. Cover rice cooker and allow to simmer for 5 to 8 minutes, switching to Warm if mixture bubbles too vigorously. Garnish with cilantro.

Thai Ginger Chicken

This dish is not very common in Thai restaurants, but is popular as a stir-fry made at home. This recipe is adapted from a quick hot-wok stir-fry to the more manageable method of cooking in the rice cooker.

INGREDIENTS | SERVES 2 OR 3

1 bunch of cilantro, leaves only
1 to 2 green chili peppers, seeded and sliced
1-inch piece ginger, peeled and thinly sliced
3 tablespoons vegetable oil
½ medium onion, thinly sliced
1 small eggplant, sliced into bite-sized pieces
½ cup coconut milk
1 tablespoon soy sauce
1½ teaspoons salt
2 chicken thighs, sliced into bite-sized pieces
1 cup water (if needed during cooking)

1. Blend cilantro, chilies, ginger, and half the oil in a food processor. Set aside.

2. Add remaining oil to the rice cooker, cover, and set to Cook. When the base of the cooker pot gets warm, add the onion and fry for about 5 minutes until onions turn soft.

3. Add the eggplant and fry for 2 to 3 minutes, covering rice cooker occasionally in the process of cooking.

4. Add the coconut milk, soy sauce, and salt, cover the rice cooker, and bring to a simmer.

5. Stir in the cilantro-ginger paste. Add the chicken, and water if the mixture appears too dry. Cover the rice cooker and continue to simmer for about 15 minutes until chicken cooks through and sauce reduces (thickens), switching to Warm if mixture bubbles too vigorously.

Three-Cup Chicken

The name "Three-Cup" came about because equal amounts of dark soy sauce, Chinese cooking wine, and sesame oil are used in the recipe. This dish is very popular in Taiwan and is usually served in a clay pot.

INGREDIENTS | SERVES 2 OR 3

- ¼ cup dark soy sauce
- 2 tablespoons water
- ¼ cup Chinese cooking wine, divided use
- 1 tablespoon brown sugar
- ¼ cup sesame oil for cooking, divided use
- ½-inch piece fresh ginger, peeled and sliced
- 2 cloves garlic, finely minced
- 8 to 10 mid-joint chicken wings
- 2 stalks Thai basil, leaves only
- 1 fresh red chili pepper, seeded and julienned

Cooking Tip

Because cooking wine is alcohol-based, it evaporates under heat. If the wine is added all at once during the initial cooking, the dish will not be as aromatic as it would be if the wine were added in stages. In Chinese wok cooking, cooking wine is typically added along the sides of the wok so that the heated metal wall evaporates the alcohol and retains the fragrance of the wine. In clay-pot cooking, cooking wine can be added directly onto a heated, covered clay pot toward the end of cooking. The cooking wine will slowly seep from the clay-pot cover into the dish that is being cooked and will sizzle with fragrance and aroma.

1. Combine soy sauce, water, ¼ cup of Chinese cooking wine, and brown sugar in a bowl. Mix well and set aside as sauce.

2. Add 2 tablespoons sesame oil to the rice cooker, cover, and set to Cook. When the base of the cooker pot gets warm, add the ginger and garlic and fry for 3 minutes until fragrant.

3. Add the chicken and sear for about 5 to 8 minutes until it turns brown on the surface, covering rice cooker occasionally in the process of cooking.

4. Add the sauce mixture and stir well. Cover rice cooker and allow it to cook for about 20 minutes, switching to Warm if mixture bubbles too vigorously, until chicken cooks through and sauce slightly reduces (thickens). Add the remaining sesame oil for final touch of aroma.

5. Before serving, switch rice cooker to Cook. Once simmering, add the remaining ¼ cup Chinese cooking wine, fresh basil, and red chili. Mix well and simmer for about 1 minute. Serve with steamed rice.

Sesame Oil Chicken

This dish is quite common as a confinement food, especially in Chinese families. It is known to be a good dish for postnatal mothers, because traditional Chinese medicine utilizes sesame oil and ginger to heal and expel "excess wind" from the guts.

INGREDIENTS | SERVES 2 OR 3

1 tablespoon dark soy sauce
1 teaspoon brown sugar
½ teaspoon ground white pepper
½ cup water
2 tablespoons sesame oil for cooking
2-inch piece ginger, thinly sliced
2 whole chicken thighs, sliced to bite-sized pieces

1. Mix soy sauce, brown sugar, pepper, and water in a bowl and set aside as sauce.

2. Add the sesame oil to the rice cooker, cover, and set to Cook. When the base of the cooker pot gets warm, add the ginger and fry about 5 minutes until fragrant.

3. Add the chicken and stir-fry for 2 to 3 minutes until chicken turns brown on the surface, covering rice cooker occasionally in the process of cooking.

4. Add the sauce mixture. Mix well, cover rice cooker, and allow to simmer for about 15 minutes, until chicken cooks through and sauce slightly reduces (thickens), stirring occasionally and switching to Warm if the mixture bubbles too vigorously.

5. Serve with steamed rice or plain Rice Congee (page 14).

Chicken in Wine and Shallot Sauce

The use of wine in cooking accentuates the flavors and aroma of food, and should not overpower. Dry white wine is recommended when cooking savory dishes.

INGREDIENTS | SERVES 2 OR 3

3 tablespoons extra-virgin olive oil
4 shallots, thinly sliced
2 chicken breasts
1 teaspoon Worcestershire sauce
½ cup Chicken Stock (page 16)
2 tablespoons dry white wine, divided use
2 tablespoons lemon juice
1 teaspoon freshly chopped parsley

Cooking Tip
Chicken breast is lean and tends to dry out easily during cooking. To reduce cooking time, flatten the chicken breast prior to cooking. Wrap the breast with plastic wrap and lay on a chopping board, then pound the chicken breast flat with the base of a pan or a rolling pin.

1. Add the oil to the rice cooker, cover, and set to Cook. When the base of the cooker pot gets warm, add shallots and fry about 3 minutes until slightly soft.

2. Add the chicken and fry each side about 5 minutes, until brown, covering the rice cooker occasionally in the process of frying.

3. Add Worcestershire sauce, chicken stock, and 1 tablespoon wine. Mix well, cover rice cooker, and allow it to come to a simmer. Once simmering, switch to Warm and continue to simmer for about 10 minutes until chicken cooks through.

4. Lift up rice cooker lid, stir in lemon juice and parsley, and sprinkle in remaining wine along the side of the rice cooker. Serve warm.

Orange Chicken

Do not add the orange segments too early or they will break up and the final dish will look mushy. You can choose not to add the orange segments during cooking and instead use them as a garnish.

INGREDIENTS | SERVES 2 OR 3

3 tablespoons extra-virgin olive oil

2 boneless chicken thighs or 2 pieces breast meat, sliced to thin strips

½ onion, thinly sliced

1 clove garlic, finely minced

½ green bell pepper, thinly sliced, julienned

½ red bell pepper, thinly sliced, julienned

Salt and ground black pepper, to taste

1 orange (juice half of the orange and keep remaining half for orange segments)

1 teaspoon orange rind/zest

1 tablespoon water

1. Add the oil to the rice cooker, cover, and set to Cook. When the base of the cooker pot gets warm, add the chicken and fry until chicken turns brown on all sides. Dish out and set aside. Leave the remaining oil in the rice cooker.

2. Add the onions to the pot and fry until slightly soft. Add the garlic and peppers and stir-fry for about 5 minutes until vegetables become tender, covering rice cooker occasionally in the process of cooking.

3. Return the chicken to the pot and mix well with the vegetables for 2 to 3 minutes.

4. Add salt, pepper, orange juice, orange rind/zest, and water to the chicken mixture. Cover rice cooker and allow to simmer for 5 minutes until chicken cooks through and sauce reduces (thickens).

5. Switch rice cooker to Warm, lift up rice cooker lid, add the orange segments, and mix well for 1 minute. Serve warm.

Citron Honey Chicken

Be creative in choosing fruit preserves to use in this recipe. The sweetness will complement the savory flavors of the dish. Marmalade would work well too, and the finished dish would be similar to Orange Chicken (page 172).

INGREDIENTS | SERVES 2 OR 3

2 pieces chicken thigh (½ pound chicken), sliced to bite-sized pieces
1 tablespoon dark soy sauce
½ teaspoon salt
¼ teaspoon sesame oil
½ teaspoon brown sugar
3 tablespoons vegetable oil
2 shallots, thinly sliced
1 clove garlic, finely minced
1 teaspoon grated ginger
Salt and ground white pepper, to taste
1 to 1½ tablespoons citron or yuzu fruit preserve, to taste
1 cup water (adjust as needed during cooking)

1. Combine chicken with soy sauce, salt, sesame oil, and brown sugar. Marinate for 30 minutes in the fridge.

2. Add the vegetable oil to the rice cooker, cover, and set to Cook. When the base of the cooker pot gets warm, add the shallots and fry about 3 minutes until slightly soft. Add the garlic and ginger and fry about 3 minutes until fragrant.

3. Add the chicken, season with salt and pepper, and fry until chicken turns brown on the surface, covering rice cooker occasionally in the process of cooking.

4. Stir in citron or yuzu preserve to coat the chicken. Add water as needed, if mixture appears too dry. Cover rice cooker and allow mixture to simmer for 10 to 15 minutes until chicken cooks through and sauce reduces (thickens). Stir occasionally, switching to Warm if the mixture bubbles too vigorously.

Citron or Yuzu?

Citron and yuzu have stirred up confusion because both names may be used to refer to the same fruit. This recipe does not restrict you to using either citron or yuzu when creating the final dish. Look for citron or yuzu fruit preserve in the supermarkets. Citron honey, which is available in Korean specialty stores and typically is used to make tea, can be a lovely substitute as well.

Lychee Chicken

Fresh lychee smell fragrant and taste sweet. These tropical fruits can be found in Asian supermarkets. Summer is lychee season, but canned lychee is available all year round in the canned fruit section of most supermarkets.

INGREDIENTS | SERVES 2 OR 3

2 pieces chicken thigh, sliced to bite-sized pieces
1 tablespoon dark soy sauce
½ teaspoon salt
¼ teaspoon sesame oil
¼ teaspoon brown sugar
3 tablespoons vegetable oil
2 shallots, thinly sliced
1 clove garlic, finely minced
1 teaspoon grated ginger
Salt and ground white pepper, to taste
½ (20-ounce) can lychee, drained (reserve syrup)
½ cup reserved lychee syrup
1 fresh red chili pepper, seeded and thinly sliced
1 tablespoon ketchup
2 tablespoons water

1. Combine chicken with soy sauce, salt, sesame oil, and brown sugar. Marinate for 30 minutes in the fridge

2. Add the vegetable oil to the rice cooker, cover, and set to Cook. When the base of the cooker pot gets warm, add the shallots and fry about 3 minutes until slightly soft. Add the garlic and ginger and fry about 3 minutes until fragrant.

3. Add the chicken, season with salt and pepper, and fry about 8 to 10 minutes until chicken turns brown on the surface, covering rice cooker occasionally in the process of cooking.

4. Stir in lychee, lychee syrup, chili pepper, ketchup, and water, coating the chicken with this mixture. Cover rice cooker and allow mixture to simmer for 15 to 20 minutes until chicken cooks through and sauce reduces (thickens). Stir occasionally, switching to Warm if mixture bubbles too vigorously.

Cooking Tip

You can use the remaining canned lychee to prepare cold desserts such as fruit cocktails. You can also freeze lychee with water as ice cubes, and then drop these cubes into chilled water as a summer party drink.

Stir-Fried Black Pepper Chicken with Sugar Snap Peas

As a variation, snow peas work perfectly well in this recipe. Snow peas are flat, while snap peas are plump. Both peas have pods that are edible and good for stir-fries.

INGREDIENTS | SERVES 2 OR 3

1 tablespoon corn flour
2 to 3 tablespoons ground black pepper, to taste
1 tablespoon ketchup
1 tablespoon light soy sauce
2 boneless chicken thighs, sliced into thin strips
3 tablespoons extra-virgin olive oil
½ green bell pepper, thinly sliced and julienned
½ red bell pepper, thinly sliced and julienned
3½ ounces sugar snap peas
2 tablespoons water
Salt and ground black pepper, to taste

1. Combine corn flour and black pepper and spread mixture out on a flat surface.

2. Combine ketchup and soy sauce in a bowl; add chicken and stir to coat. Then roll the chicken strips in the black pepper and corn flour mixture to coat evenly. Set aside.

3. Add the oil to the rice cooker, cover, and set to Cook. When the base of the cooker pot gets warm, add the chicken and fry for 8 to 10 minutes until chicken cooks through, covering rice cooker occasionally in the process of cooking.

4. Add the bell peppers and snap peas and fry about 5 to 8 minutes until vegetables become tender.

5. Add the water, mix well, and simmer further for about 5 to 8 minutes. Season with salt and pepper to taste. Serve with steamed rice.

Thai Basil Chicken

This dish is known as Gai (Chicken) Pad (Stir-Fry) Bai Kaprow (Holy Basil). Substitute ground turkey for the chicken if you prefer a leaner meat.

INGREDIENTS | SERVES 2

2 tablespoons vegetable oil
3 shallots, thinly sliced
2 cloves garlic, finely minced
½ pound ground chicken
1 teaspoon fish sauce
1 Thai chili pepper, seeded and thinly sliced
Salt, to taste
½ cup water or Chicken Stock (page 16)
¼ cup chopped fresh basil

1. Add the oil to the rice cooker, cover, and set to Cook. When the base of the cooker pot gets warm, add the shallots and fry about 3 minutes until soft. Add the garlic and fry about 3 minutes until fragrant.

2. Add the ground chicken (break up into smaller bits of meat), fish sauce, chili pepper, and salt. Fry for about 5 minutes until chicken cooks through, stirring and covering the rice cooker occasionally in the process of cooking.

3. Add water or chicken stock, cover the rice cooker, and allow to simmer for 2 to 3 minutes.

4. Switch to Warm, and continue to simmer for about 5 minutes until chicken cooks through. Lift up rice cooker lid and stir in basil before serving.

Types of Basil

The basil commonly seen and used in Asia is the Thai or holy basil. This leaf has jagged edges and a delicate flavor. The sweet basil usually used in Italian and Mediterranean cooking has leaves with round edges and a more pronounced flavor. These two kinds of basil may or may not be a good substitute for each other, depending on the flavors you intend to create for the dish. There is nothing wrong in experimenting with both types in your daily home cooking.

CHAPTER 12

Pork

Steamed Ribs with Garlic in Chinese Black Bean Sauce
178

Steamed Savory Pork with Sweet Pumpkin
179

Steamed Pork Patty
180

Kimchi Pork
180

Chinese Stewed Meatballs
181

Pork Rib Curry
182

Chinese Pork Dumpling (Wonton) Soup
183

Thai Meat Patties
184

Ground Pork with Mushrooms
185

Pork with Potatoes, Peas, and Corn
186

Stir-Fried Pork with Ginger
187

Braised Fragrant Pork
188

Tamarind Pork Slices
189

Pork in Tomato Sauce
190

Steamed Ribs with Garlic in Chinese Black Bean Sauce

Pre-frying the garlic, ginger, and mashed Chinese black beans in hot oil releases their aromas and enhances the flavoring of the ribs.

INGREDIENTS | SERVES 2

1 tablespoon Chinese cooking wine
1 teaspoon brown sugar
1 teaspoon corn flour
1 teaspoon dark soy sauce
¼ teaspoon white pepper
½ pound bone-in pork ribs
1 tablespoon canola oil
2 cloves garlic, minced
½ teaspoon grated ginger
1 teaspoon Chinese black beans, slightly mashed
1 to 2 fresh red chili peppers, seeded and thinly sliced
1 green onion, finely chopped, for garnish

Cooking Tip

This recipe takes about 35 minutes from start to finish, but you can save time and effort by opting for Semi-Homemade "Ready-to-Go" Chinese Black Bean Sauce (page 132). If you have that sauce made in advance, all you will have to do for this dish is marinate the ribs, mix them thoroughly with 1–2 teaspoons of "ready-to-go" sauce, and follow the steaming instructions in Steps 3 and 4 of this recipe.

1. Mix the Chinese cooking wine, brown sugar, corn flour, dark soy sauce, and white pepper in a plastic zip-top bag. Add the ribs to the bag, mix well, and place bag in fridge for about 1 hour.

2. Add the oil to the rice cooker, cover, and set to Cook. When the base of the cooker pot gets warm, add the garlic, ginger, and mashed Chinese black beans, and lightly fry for 2 minutes.

3. Add the marinated ribs and fry with garlic mixture for about 2 minutes, covering rice cooker occasionally in the process of cooking. When the ribs have turned slightly brown on the outside, switch off the rice cooker.

4. Transfer the ribs to a plate that will fit in the steamer insert or basket and top the ribs with the sliced red chilies. Cover the top of the plate with plastic wrap, to prevent excess condensation when the ribs are steamed. Place the plate of ribs into steamer insert or basket.

5. Clean out the rice cooker and wipe dry. Place the pot back into the rice cooker, add water to fill up half the pot, cover rice cooker, and set to Cook. When the water in the pot boils, place the steamer insert that holds plate of ribs into the rice cooker, cover, and cook. Steam the ribs for about 25 minutes.

6. Garnish with green onions before serving. Best served with steamed rice or plain Rice Congee (page 14).

Steamed Savory Pork with Sweet Pumpkin

This is a healthy and fuss-free steamed dish that uses readily available ingredients and seasonings.

INGREDIENTS | SERVES 2 OR 3

½ pound ground pork
2 green onions, finely chopped
2 teaspoons Chinese cooking wine
1 teaspoon dark soy sauce
¼ teaspoon salt
¼ teaspoon ground white pepper
½ teaspoon brown sugar
1 egg
½ teaspoon sesame oil
½ pound pumpkin, peeled and seeded, cut into thin slices

1. Combine all ingredients except pumpkin in a bowl. Set aside to marinate while preparing next step.

2. Add water to the rice cooker to about the 4-cup mark, cover, and set to Cook.

3. Lay pumpkin uniformly on a plate that will fit in the steamer insert or basket. Top pumpkin with pork mixture (use fingers to break into smaller bits). Cover the top of the plate with plastic wrap, to prevent excess condensation when the pork is steamed.

4. When the water in the pot starts to boil, place the steamer insert or basket that holds the plate of pork into the rice cooker, cover, and cook. Steam about 10 to 12 minutes until pork cooks through.

Steamed Pork Patty

As a variation, use dried shiitake mushrooms instead of fresh ones. Before using dried shiitake mushrooms, rehydrate them by soaking in warm water for 15 to 20 minutes.

INGREDIENTS | SERVES 2 OR 3

1 teaspoon dark soy sauce
¼ teaspoon salt
¼ teaspoon white pepper
2 teaspoons Chinese cooking wine
½ teaspoon sesame oil
½ pound ground pork
5 fresh shiitake mushroom caps, finely diced
6 medium-sized shrimp, peeled, deveined, and diced
½ pack (about 5 ounces of a 10½-ounce pack) soft tofu, slightly mashed, drained of excess moisture
1 green onion, finely chopped

1. Combine the soy sauce, salt, pepper, Chinese cooking wine, and sesame oil with ground pork. Then combine mushrooms, shrimp, tofu, and green onions into the ground pork mixture. Combine thoroughly.

2. Shape mixture into a round ball, flatten it slightly into a "block," and place on a plate that fits in the steamer insert or basket.

3. Add water to the rice cooker to fill up half the pot. Cover the pot and set to Cook. When the water boils, place the steamer insert that holds the plate of meat into the rice cooker, cover, and cook. Steam for 20 to 25 minutes until meat cooks through.

Kimchi Pork

As a variation, use thin slices of pork instead of strips.

INGREDIENTS | SERVES 2 OR 3

½ pound pork tenderloin, sliced into thin strips
¼ teaspoon ground white pepper
1 teaspoon Chinese cooking wine
1 tablespoon vegetable oil
1 cup thinly sliced kimchi
3 tablespoons water

1. Marinate pork with pepper and Chinese cooking wine. Set aside.

2. Add the oil to the rice cooker, cover, and set to Cook. When the base of the cooker pot gets warm, add the pork and fry about 8 to 10 minutes until pork turns brown on the surface and is partially cooked, covering the rice cooker occasionally in the process of frying.

3. Add the kimchi, mix well with the pork, and fry briskly, covering rice cooker occasionally in the process of frying. Add water, cover the rice cooker, and allow the pork to cook in the simmering mixture for 8 to 10 minutes until the meat cooks through, switching to Warm if the mixture bubbles too vigorously.

Chinese Stewed Meatballs

The origin of this recipe traces back to a Chinese dish consisting of huge meatballs stewed with vegetables. For easy cooking, the meatballs in this recipe are mini meatballs.

INGREDIENTS | SERVES 3 OR 4

- 1 pound ground pork
- 2 tablespoons dark soy sauce
- 1 teaspoon grated ginger
- ¼ teaspoon salt
- ½ teaspoon ground white pepper
- 2 teaspoons Chinese cooking wine
- ½ teaspoon sesame oil
- 2 green onions, finely chopped, for meatballs
- 1 egg
- ½ cup corn flour
- ½ cup vegetable oil, for frying
- 1-inch piece ginger, thinly sliced
- 1 pound napa cabbage, cut into 2-inch lengths
- 8 fresh shiitake mushroom caps, sliced
- 1 tablespoon dark soy sauce
- ¼ teaspoon ground white pepper
- 2 to 3 cups Chicken Stock (page 16) or water, to immerse and simmer the meatballs
- 1 green onion, finely chopped

Cooking Tip

Shape the meat into small, flat patties instead of making round meatballs. Flat patties are easier to cook through and at the initial stage of browning, the amount of vegetable oil used in frying the meat can be significantly reduced. There is less wastage of vegetable oil, and the final dish is definitely less greasy.

1. Combine ground pork with soy sauce, ginger, salt, white pepper, Chinese cooking wine, sesame oil, green onions, and egg.

2. Form mixture into small round balls (1-inch diameter). Roll the meatballs on a bed of ½ cup corn flour to coat the meat for frying. Set aside.

3. Add the oil to the rice cooker, cover, and set to Cook. When the base of the cooker pot gets warm, add the meatballs and fry about 8 to 10 minutes until they turn slightly golden brown on the surface. Switch off rice cooker. Dish out the meatballs and place on paper towels.

4. Discard the majority of the frying oil, leaving about 2 tablespoons of oil in the pot. Cover rice cooker and set to Cook. When the base of the cooker pot gets warm, add the ginger, cabbage, mushrooms, soy sauce, and white pepper. Fry for 4 to 5 minutes, covering rice cooker occasionally in the process of frying.

5. Add the stock or water, cover rice cooker, and allow it to reach a simmer. When simmering, lift up rice cooker lid, return the meatballs to the rice cooker, cover, and allow the meatballs to cook in simmering mixture for about 20 minutes until the meatballs cook through. Stir occasionally, switching to Warm if mixture bubbles too vigorously. Garnish with green onions and serve warm.

Pork Rib Curry

Surprise your diners by serving pork rib curry instead of the usual chicken curry. It will taste different but still delicious.

INGREDIENTS | SERVES 2 OR 3

1 pound bone-in pork ribs
2 tablespoons curry powder, divided use
½ teaspoon salt
1 tablespoon vegetable oil
2 cloves garlic, finely minced
1 teaspoon grated ginger
2 cups water or more (enough to immerse the ribs)

1. Combine ribs with 1 tablespoon curry powder and salt in a bowl. Marinate in fridge for 30 minutes.

2. Add oil to the rice cooker, cover, and set to Cook. When the base of the cooker pot gets warm, add the garlic, ginger, and remaining curry powder. Lightly fry for 1 to 2 minutes.

3. Add the marinated ribs and fry with garlic mixture for about 2 minutes until ribs turn brown on the surface.

4. Add the water, stir well, cover rice cooker, and allow to reach a simmer. Allow the pork ribs to cook in simmering mixture for about 15 minutes until pork cooks through, stirring and covering the rice cooker occasionally, and switching to Warm if the mixture bubbles too vigorously.

Chinese Pork Dumpling (Wonton) Soup

Dumpling dishes vary widely, all based on the concept of meat wrapped in dough "skin," but often cooked in different ways (boiled, steamed, pan-fried) or with slightly different fillings.

INGREDIENTS | SERVES 3 OR 4 (ABOUT 30 WONTONS)

½ pound ground pork
2 teaspoons dark soy sauce
½ teaspoon salt
¼ teaspoon ground white pepper
2 teaspoons Chinese cooking wine
1 teaspoon sesame oil
2 bunches bok choy, blanched and squeezed dry (to remove moisture), finely chopped
1 egg
30 wonton wrappers
Water, set aside in a bowl for wonton wrapping

Cooking Tip

Wonton wrappers can be found in many Asian supermarkets. The fresh wrappers are usually found in the chiller section, together with tofu and fresh noodles. If you cannot use all of them in one session of cooking, they can be wrapped with plastic wrap, placed in airtight freezer bags, and stored in the freezer for later use.

1. Mix the ground pork with the soy sauce, salt, pepper, Chinese cooking wine, and sesame oil. Add the bok choy and egg to the pork mixture. Combine thoroughly.

2. Wrap the wontons one at a time. Dip your fingers in some water and use them to moisten the edges of each wrapper. Place 1 teaspoon of filling in the center of the wrapper, fold wrapper in half, and seal the edges by crimping, with filling secured in the center.

3. Add water to fill the rice cooker pot to about the 4-cup mark, cover, and set to Cook. When the water in the pot starts to boil, add 10 to 12 wontons and cover rice cooker until the water boils again. Add 1 cup water, cover rice cooker, and bring the water back to a boil. Dish out the wontons. Repeat for subsequent batches (add more water if water has fallen below 4-cup mark). Serve boiled dumplings in chicken soup.

Thai Meat Patties

Fresh water chestnuts may be hard to find in supermarkets, so substitute with canned water chestnuts. If you have difficulties finding canned water chestnuts, substitute jicama (arrowroot) or potatoes.

INGREDIENTS | SERVES 3 OR 4 (ABOUT 14, 2-INCH DIAMETER PATTIES)

1 cup water chestnuts
½ cup chopped cilantro
1 tablespoon chopped fresh basil
1 fresh red chili pepper, seeded and finely chopped
3 cloves garlic, finely minced
1 tablespoon fish sauce
1 tablespoon oyster sauce
½ teaspoon black pepper
1 teaspoon sesame oil
2 teaspoons brown sugar
1 egg
2 teaspoons flour
1 pound ground pork
1 cup vegetable oil, divided use

1. Combine all ingredients except vegetable oil in a bowl. Mix and combine thoroughly. Form into balls of about 1-inch diameter each, and flatten each into about 2-inches diameter patty. Set aside.

2. Add 2 tablespoons of vegetable oil to the rice cooker, cover, and set to Cook. When the base of the cooker pot gets warm, add patties in batches, frying each side about 3 minutes, until brown and cooked through. Cover the rice cooker while frying each side. Repeat for subsequent batches.

Ground Pork with Mushrooms

The flavors of this dish become more intense when leftovers are reheated the next day. You can therefore cook more to intentionally create leftovers.

INGREDIENTS | SERVES 4 TO 6

2 tablespoons dark soy sauce
1 tablespoon oyster sauce
½ tablespoon brown sugar
3 tablespoons warm water
1 tablespoon vegetable oil
1 pound pork
4 shallots, thinly sliced
2 cloves garlic, finely minced
6 fresh shiitake mushroom caps, finely diced
1 cup water
¼ teaspoon salt
¼ teaspoon ground white pepper
2 cups warm water (adjust as needed during cooking)

Cooking Tip

Do not allow the pork to remain in the pot to be cooked with the other ingredients, as overcooked pork will be rubbery and tough. Dish out the partially cooked ground pork, continue with the other stages of cooking, and then return the pork to a simmering mixture to completely cook through at lower heat.

1. In a small bowl, mix soy sauce, oyster sauce, brown sugar, and water. Set aside as sauce.

2. Add the oil to the rice cooker, cover, and set to Cook. When the base of the cooker pot gets warm, add ground pork (break into small bits) and fry about 8 to 10 minutes until pork turns brown on the surface. Dish out the partially cooked pork and set aside. Leave the remaining oil in the pot.

3. Add the shallots to the pot and fry about 3 minutes until soft. Add the garlic and mushrooms and fry about 3 minutes until aromatic.

4. Add 1 cup water, salt, and pepper. Cover rice cooker and allow the mixture to reach a simmer.

5. Once simmering, return partially cooked pork to the pot. Add the sauce and enough water to partially immerse the entire mixture. Stir well, cover the rice cooker, and allow the pork to cook in the simmering mixture for about 20 minutes, stirring occasionally. Switch to Warm if mixture bubbles too vigorously. Keep at Warm before serving with steamed rice.

Pork with Potatoes, Peas, and Corn

Unlike the Ground Pork with Mushrooms (page 185), in which you could scale up on the quantity and cook more, the vegetables in this dish tend to turn mushy when reheated. Therefore, it is recommended that you cook only enough for just one meal.

INGREDIENTS | SERVES 2 OR 3

- 1 tablespoon dark soy sauce
- 1 teaspoon oyster sauce
- 1 teaspoon brown sugar
- 3 tablespoons warm water
- 3 tablespoons vegetable oil
- ½ pound ground pork
- 2 shallots, thinly sliced
- 1 clove garlic, finely minced
- 1 medium-sized potato, diced to ½-inch cubes
- ½ cup frozen peas (or canned)
- ½ cup frozen corn (or canned)
- 1 cup water
- ¼ teaspoon salt
- ¼ teaspoon ground white pepper
- 2 cups warm water (adjust as needed during cooking)

1. In a small bowl, mix soy sauce, oyster sauce, brown sugar, and water. Set aside as sauce.

2. Add the oil to the rice cooker, cover, and set to Cook. When the base of the cooker pot gets warm, add ground pork (break into small bits) and fry until pork turns brown on the surface. Dish out the partially cooked pork and set aside. Leave the remaining oil in the pot.

3. Add the shallots and fry about 3 minutes until soft. Add the garlic, potatoes, peas, and corn and fry about 5 minutes until aromatic, covering rice cooker occasionally in the process of cooking.

4. Add 1 cup water, salt, and pepper. Cover rice cooker and allow the mixture to reach simmer.

5. Once simmering, return the partially cooked pork to the pot. Add the sauce and enough warm water to partially immerse the entire mixture. Stir well, cover the rice cooker, and allow the pork to cook in the simmering mixture for about 20 minutes, switching to Warm if mixture bubbles too vigorously. Keep at warm before serving with steamed rice.

Stir-Fried Pork with Ginger

Toward the end of cooking, drizzle in drops of sesame oil and Chinese cooking wine to add fresh aroma in this dish.

INGREDIENTS | SERVES 2

½ pound pork tenderloin, thinly sliced
1 teaspoon grated ginger
1 teaspoon Chinese cooking wine
¼ teaspoon salt
¼ teaspoon ground white pepper
1 teaspoon corn flour
2 tablespoons dark soy sauce
1 teaspoon oyster sauce
1 teaspoon brown sugar
2 cups warm water
3 tablespoons vegetable oil
2-inch piece ginger, peeled, thinly shredded
1 teaspoon Fried Ginger Strips (page 284), for garnish

Cooking Tip

There is a tendency for meat slices to stick together during the first few seconds of stir-frying. Some Chinese chefs prefer to stir-fry using chopsticks, as the chopsticks are helpful for separating the meat slices while frying. As a home cook, you can try adding a tablespoon of oil when seasoning the meat slices. This will prevent the slices from sticking together when frying. Remember to reduce the amount of vegetable oil used for frying by the amount added while seasoning the meat.

1. Season pork with ginger, Chinese cooking wine, salt, pepper, and corn flour. Set aside.

2. In another bowl, mix soy sauce, oyster sauce, brown sugar, and warm water. Set aside as sauce.

3. Add the oil to the rice cooker, cover, and set to Cook. When the base of the cooker pot gets warm, add the pork and fry for about 8 to 10 minutes until pork turns brown on the surface and is partially cooked. Dish out and set aside. Leave the remaining oil in the pot.

4. Add the ginger to the pot and fry until fragrant. Then add the sauce, mix well, cover rice cooker, and allow mixture to reach simmer.

5. Once simmering, return the pork to the pot, cover the rice cooker, and allow to cook in the simmering mixture for 8 to 10 minutes until pork cooks through, stirring occasionally. Switch to Warm when the mixture bubbles vigorously and when gravy reduces (thickens). Garnish with fried ginger strips.

Braised Fragrant Pork

This is also known as Babi Chin *in Nyonya cuisine.*
Babi *means "pork" in Malay.*

INGREDIENTS | SERVES 2 OR 3

3 tablespoons vegetable oil
6 shallots, thinly sliced
4 cloves garlic, thinly sliced
1 tablespoon coriander seeds
4 pieces star anise
12 to 16 ounces pork belly, sliced to 1-inch cubes
6 fresh shiitake mushroom caps, cut into halves
2 tablespoons dark soy sauce
¼ teaspoon salt
¼ teaspoon ground white pepper
1 teaspoon sugar
3 cups water, or just enough to immerse the pork

1. Add the oil to the rice cooker, cover, and set to Cook. When the base of the cooker pot gets warm, add the shallots and fry about 3 minutes until soft. Add the garlic and fry about 3 minutes until fragrant. Add coriander seeds and star anise and stir-fry for 1 minute, covering rice cooker occasionally in the process of frying.

2. Add the pork, mushrooms, soy sauce, salt, pepper, sugar, and water to the pot. Stir well. Cover rice cooker and bring to a light simmer. When simmering, switch to Warm and simmer for about 2 hours until meat is tender. Stir occasionally.

Cooking Tip

You may find fresh pork belly too gelatinous to be cut into neat cubes. Slicing pork is easier when the meat is still slightly frozen. Remember, you do not necessarily need to wait for meat to completely thaw prior to slicing.

Tamarind Pork Slices

This recipe requires overnight preparation to bring out the most intense flavors. As an alternative, Steps 1 through 3 can be done in the morning, and the actual cooking in the evening.

INGREDIENTS | SERVES 2 OR 3

Boiling water set aside in a deep bowl, to immerse the pork belly for blanching

12 ounces pork belly

2 tamarind pulp (golf-ball size)

½ teaspoon salt

2 teaspoons brown sugar

½ teaspoon ground white pepper

4 tablespoons vegetable oil, divided use (about 2 tablespoons each batch)

Cooking Tip

Ready-made tamarind paste (or juice) can be found in Asian supermarkets or ethnic stores such as Vietnamese and Thai markets. Using these can be a timesaver, especially when you just need the juice for cooking.

1. Immerse the pork in hot boiling water for 15 minutes. Remove the fat that rises to the top. Dish out the pork and set it on a plate for steaming in Step 2.

2. Add water to the rice cooker pot to fill up half the pot, cover, and set to Cook. When the water boils, add the steamer insert that holds the plate of pork (covered with plastic wrap) and steam for 20 to 25 minutes. Remove plate from steamer and set aside the pork to cool.

3. When cooled, place the pork, tamarind pulp, salt, brown sugar, and pepper into a zip-top freezer bag. Rub the pork with the other ingredients to coat evenly. Set aside to marinate in the fridge overnight or at least 4 hours.

4. Before cooking, drain the marinade from the pork. Slice the pork into thin slices.

5. Add about 2 tablespoons oil to the rice cooker, cover, and set to Cook. When the base of the cooker pot gets warm, add the pork in batches and fry for 1 to 2 minutes on each side, until pork slices turn brown and cook through. Cover rice cooker while frying. Remove and serve.

Pork in Tomato Sauce

*Ketchup gives a sweet and sour aspect to this appetizing pork dish.
It can be served with rice and is perfect as a sandwich filler, too.*

INGREDIENTS | SERVES 2

½ pound pork tenderloin, thinly sliced
1 teaspoon dark soy sauce
¼ teaspoon salt
¼ teaspoon ground white pepper
½ teaspoon honey
1 tablespoon ketchup
½ cup water
1 teaspoon corn flour
3 tablespoons vegetable oil

1. Combine the pork with soy sauce, salt, pepper, and honey. Leave to marinate in fridge for 30 minutes.

2. In a separate bowl, combine ketchup, water, and corn flour. Set aside as sauce.

3. Add the oil to the rice cooker, cover, and set to Cook. When the base of the cooker pot gets warm, add the pork and fry about 8 to 10 minutes until browned and partially cooked through. Dish out and set aside. Leave the remaining oil in the pot.

4. Add the prepared sauce to the pot, stir well, cover rice cooker, and allow to reach a simmer. Once simmering, return the pork to the pot, cover rice cooker, allow to reach a simmer, and let it simmer for about 8 to 10 minutes. If mixture bubbles too vigorously, switch to Warm and continue to simmer for the remaining 8 to 10 minutes until the pork cooks through and sauce reduces (thickens).

CHAPTER 13

Beef

Steamed Beef and Cabbage Rolls
192

Beef Stew
193

Mild Beef Curry with Potato and Peas
194

Pumpkin and Beef Curry
195

Spicy Ground Beef with Tomato and Egg
196

Spicy Ground Beef
197

Ground Beef with Peas
198

Beef with Ginger and Green Onions
199

Black Pepper Basil Beef
200

Beef in Mushroom Sauce
201

Beef in Honey Caramelized Onions
202

Stir-Fried Beef in Garlic Black Bean Sauce
203

Mini Beef Burger
204

Steamed Beef and Cabbage Rolls

Use sukiyaki beef (readily available thinly sliced beef) for this recipe to save time on slicing.

INGREDIENTS | SERVES 2 OR 3

10–16 napa cabbage leaves

½ pound beef tenderloin, sliced paper-thin

1 (3½-ounce) pack enoki mushrooms

1. Add water to the 4-cup mark in the rice cooker, cover, and set to Cook. When the water boils, add the napa cabbage, blanch 15 seconds (just to soften the leaves for easy wrapping), remove the leaves, and set aside to cool. Drain excess moisture from the blanched cabbage. Leave the water in the rice cooker for steaming.

2. Lay the cooled cabbage leaves on a flat surface (use 2 leaves to partially overlay each other and to increase the length of the roll). Place beef slices flat on top of the cabbage, and then place a few enoki mushrooms on the beef (it is okay for the enoki mushrooms to protrude from the end of roll). Roll up the cabbage leaves to enclose the beef (do not fold in the ends), similar to sushi rolling. Set aside on a plate that will fit in the steamer insert or basket.

3. With the water remaining in the rice cooker, cover the rice cooker and set to Cook. When the water boils, place the steamer insert or basket that holds the plate of cabbage rolls over the boiling water. Cover the rice cooker and steam for 10 minutes or more until beef cooks through.

Beef Stew

To add more flavor to the beef stew, about 1 tablespoon of diced bacon can sometimes be added to pre-fry with the onions.

INGREDIENTS | SERVES 2 OR 3

1 pound cubed beef stew meat
1 tablespoon corn flour
½ teaspoon salt
2 tablespoons olive oil
1 medium-sized onion, sliced into bite-sized wedges
1 carrot, sliced to bite-sized chunks
2 stalks celery, sliced to bite-sized chunks
2 cups or more warm water (enough to partially immerse the beef cubes)

Cooking Tip

The flour in this recipe not only "seals" the moisture in the beef, it also helps to thicken the stew. Add about 1 cup peeled and cubed potatoes in Step 4 for further thickening.

1. Combine beef, corn flour, and salt in a large zip-top freezer bag. Shake to coat beef with flour.

2. Add the oil to the rice cooker, cover, and set to Cook. When the base of the cooker pot gets warm, add the beef and fry for about 8 to 10 minutes until evenly browned on the surface. Dish out and set aside. Leave the remaining oil in the pot.

3. Add the onions to the pot and fry about 5 minutes until slightly soft, covering the rice cooker occasionally in the process of frying.

4. Return the beef to the pot. Add the carrots, celery, and warm water (enough to partially immerse the beef). Cover and allow mixture to reach a simmer. Once simmering, switch to Warm and continue to simmer 2 hours.

Mild Beef Curry with Potato and Peas

If you want to avoid the high carbohydrates in this dish, leave out the potatoes, but increase the quantity of peas by another half cup so the dish remains substantial.

INGREDIENTS | SERVES 2 OR 3

3 tablespoons vegetable oil
½ pound ground beef
3 shallots, thinly sliced
1 clove garlic, finely minced
1 medium-sized potato, cubed
½ cup frozen peas (or canned)
1 tablespoon curry powder
2 cups warm water (adjust as needed during cooking)
¼ teaspoon salt
¼ teaspoon ground white pepper

1. Add the oil to the rice cooker, cover, and set to Cook. When the base of the cooker pot gets warm, add ground beef (break into small bits) and fry about 8 to 10 minutes until beef turns brown on the surface. Dish out and set aside. Leave the remaining oil in the pot.

2. Add the shallots to the pot and fry about 3 minutes until soft. Add the garlic, potatoes, peas, and curry powder and fry about 5 minutes until aromatic, covering the rice cooker occasionally in the process of cooking.

3. Add the 2 cups water, salt, and pepper. Cover rice cooker and allow the mixture to reach a simmer.

4. Once simmering, return beef to the pot, cover the rice cooker, and allow the beef to cook for about 10 minutes, switching to Warm if the mixture bubbles too vigorously. Keep at Warm before serving with steamed rice.

Pumpkin and Beef Curry

Some supermarkets pre-pack and sell beef based on cooking methods. For example, you may see packaged beef that is labeled "Stew Beef Cubes," good for stew and slow-cooking; or "Beef Fillets," good for stir-fries. Keep on the lookout for such labels to make grocery shopping easier.

INGREDIENTS | SERVES 2 OR 3

2 tablespoons vegetable oil
½ pound beef tenderloin, sliced into thin strips, against the grain
3 shallots, thinly sliced
1 clove garlic, finely minced
1½ cups peeled and seeded pumpkin, cubed
1 tablespoon curry powder
½ cup coconut milk
1 kaffir lime leaf, whole

Do You Know?
Pumpkin seeds are also known as pepitas. These seeds are high in minerals such as manganese, magnesium, and phosphorus. Pumpkin seeds can be roasted and turned into healthy snacks.

1. Add the oil to the rice cooker, cover, and set to Cook. When the base of the cooker pot gets warm, add beef and fry about 8 to 10 minutes until beef turns brown on the surface. Dish out and set aside. Leave the remaining oil in the pot.

2. Add the shallots to the pot and fry 3 minutes until soft. Add the garlic and fry about 3 minutes until fragrant.

3. Add the pumpkin, curry powder, coconut milk, and lime leaf. Cover rice cooker and allow the mixture to reach a simmer.

4. Once simmering, stir the mixture and then return the beef to the pot. Switch to Warm and allow the beef to simmer 10 to 15 minutes until beef cooks through.

5. Remove lime leaf and serve with steamed rice.

Spicy Ground Beef with Tomato and Egg

This recipe traces back to the similar Malay omelet sandwich called Roti John, which was made by topping a toasted French loaf (Roti) with a fried meat mixture.

INGREDIENTS | SERVES 2 OR 3

2 tablespoons vegetable oil
½ pound ground beef
6 shallots, thinly sliced
1 cup canned diced tomatoes, with juice
½ teaspoon ground cumin
1 teaspoon curry powder
¼ teaspoon red chili powder
¼ teaspoon turmeric
½ teaspoon chili pepper flakes
Salt and freshly ground black pepper, to taste
1 egg, lightly whisked

1. Add oil to the rice cooker, cover, and set to Cook. When the base of the cooker pot gets warm, add beef (break into small bits) and fry about 8 to 10 minutes until beef turns brown on the surface. Dish out and set aside. Leave the remaining oil in the pot.

2. Add the shallots to the pot and fry about 3 minutes until soft and almost caramelized.

3. Add all the remaining ingredients except the egg. Fry for about 2 minutes, covering the rice cooker occasionally in the process of frying.

4. Add the egg and fry briskly, breaking egg into small bits and mixing well with the spices.

5. Return the beef to the rice cooker and continue to fry the mixture for 2 to 3 minutes until beef and egg cook completely. Cover the rice cooker and simmer until mixture is almost dry. Keep at Warm before serving.

Spicy Ground Beef

To ensure good-quality ground beef, buy a chuck steak from the supermarket and grind it at home using a food processor.

INGREDIENTS | SERVES 2 OR 3

1 tablespoon vegetable oil
½ pound ground beef
1 tablespoon butter, divided use
4 shallots, thinly sliced
1 clove garlic, finely minced
2 teaspoons grated ginger
1 fresh green chili pepper, seeded and sliced, divided use
½ teaspoon red chili powder
1 tomato, chopped
1 tablespoon finely chopped cilantro, for garnish

1. Add the oil to the rice cooker, cover, and set to Cook. When the base of the cooker pot gets warm, add beef (break into small bits) and fry about 8 to 10 minutes until beef turns brown on the surface and almost cooks through, covering rice cooker occasionally in the process of cooking. Dish out and set aside. Leave the remaining oil in the pot.

2. Add ½ tablespoon of the butter to the pot, and allow to melt. Add the shallots and fry about 3 minutes until soft. Add the garlic and ginger and fry about 3 minutes until fragrant.

3. Add half of the sliced chili, the chili powder, tomato, and remaining butter. Fry for 1 minute, covering the rice cooker occasionally in the process of cooking.

4. Return beef to the pot and fry briskly, covering the rice cooker until beef cooks through completely in about 8 to 10 minutes. Garnish with cilantro and remaining sliced chili, then mix well.

Cilantro or Coriander?

The leaves of this herb are known as cilantro leaves or coriander leaves or Chinese parsley in different parts of the world. The fruits are called coriander seeds. Both the leaves and the dried seeds are used in a wide range of cuisines.

Ground Beef with Peas

As a variation, substitute broccoli florets for the peas. However, to ensure consistency in texture and proper bite with the ground beef, cut the broccoli florets to smaller florets or pieces.

INGREDIENTS | SERVES 2 OR 3

2 tablespoons vegetable oil
½ pound ground beef
2 cloves garlic, finely minced
½ tablespoon oyster sauce
1 cup water
¼ teaspoon ground black pepper
1 cup frozen peas
Salt and ground white pepper, to taste
1 green onion, finely chopped, for garnish

1. Add the oil to the rice cooker, cover, and set to Cook. When the base of the cooker pot gets warm, add beef and fry about 8 to 10 minutes until beef turns brown. Dish out and set aside. Leave the remaining oil in the pot.

2. Add garlic to the pot and fry about 3 minutes until fragrant. Add oyster sauce, water, and pepper; stir well. Cover rice cooker and allow mixture to come to a simmer.

3. Once simmering, add the peas, return the beef to the pot, and add salt and pepper to taste. Cover the rice cooker and allow mixture to continue cooking, until beef cooks through and peas become tender in about 8 to 10 minutes, switching to Warm if mixture bubbles too vigorously. Keep at Warm before serving. Garnish with green onion.

Beef with Ginger and Green Onions

Similar to soy sauce and sesame oil, oyster sauce is one of the essential Chinese seasonings to stock in the pantry. Oyster sauce is usually sold in bottles, and once opened for use in the kitchen, it is best stored in the refrigerator.

INGREDIENTS | SERVES 2

1 teaspoon oyster sauce
½ cup water
2 tablespoons vegetable oil
½ pound beef fillet, thinly sliced
½ medium-sized onion, thinly sliced
1-inch piece ginger, finely shredded
3 green onions, sliced into finger-length pieces
¼ teaspoon ground black pepper

Do You Know?

Spring onions, green onions, and scallions are not exactly the same, although they come from the same onion family. They are different as they are harvested at different stages of the maturing cycle. Therefore, one might be more pungent than the other (for example, spring onions are more pungent than green onions and green onions are more pungent than scallions).

1. Mix oyster sauce and water in a bowl and set aside as sauce.

2. Add the oil to the rice cooker, cover, and set to Cook. When the base of the cooker pot gets warm, add beef and fry about 8 to 10 minutes until beef turns brown on the surface and almost cooks through. Dish out and set aside. Leave the remaining oil in the pot.

3. Add the onions to the pot and fry about 5 minutes until soft. Add the ginger and green onions and fry about 3 minutes until fragrant, covering rice cooker occasionally in the process of frying.

4. Add the sauce, return the beef to the pot, and add the pepper. Fry for about 3 minutes, cover the rice cooker, and simmer for about 5 minutes until beef cooks through and sauce reduces (thickens), switching to Warm if the mixture bubbles too vigorously.

Black Pepper Basil Beef

A constant reminder for you is "always slice beef against the grain." Doing that puts you one step closer to producing tender beef slices in the finished dish.

INGREDIENTS | SERVES 2

½ pound beef sirloin, thinly sliced against the grain
2 teaspoons oyster sauce
1 teaspoon dark soy sauce
½ teaspoon sugar
½ tablespoon ground black pepper
1 egg
1 teaspoon corn flour
2 tablespoons vegetable oil
2 tablespoons water
1 cup fresh basil leaves

1. Combine beef with oyster sauce, soy sauce, sugar, pepper, egg, and corn flour. Marinate for 1 hour in the fridge. Before cooking, drain and reserve about 2 tablespoons of the marinade mixture.

2. Add the oil to the rice cooker, cover, and set to Cook. When the base of the cooker pot gets warm, add beef and fry about 8 to 10 minutes until beef turns brown on the surface.

3. Add the reserved marinade and the water. Cover the rice cooker and continue cooking for about 5 to 8 minutes or more until beef cooks through and sauce slightly reduces (thickens).

4. Add basil leaves, mix well, and stir until sauce reduces further, about 3 to 5 minutes.

Beef in Mushroom Sauce

If you prefer, substitute onions for the leeks. Onions will reduce preparation time, since they do not require much cleaning. However, the flavors brought up by leeks are more subtle compared to onions, which are more pungent.

INGREDIENTS | SERVES 2 OR 3

2 teaspoons dark soy sauce
2 tablespoons Chinese cooking wine
1 teaspoon corn flour
½ cup water
2 tablespoons vegetable oil
½ pound beef sirloin, thinly sliced against the grain
½ leek, thinly sliced
1 clove garlic, thinly sliced
6 fresh shiitake mushroom caps, thinly sliced

Cooking Tip
Leeks contain a lot of grit and dirt and need to be cleaned thoroughly before use. Visit *http://video.about.com/frenchfood/Cleaning-Fresh-Leeks.htm* to learn how to clean leeks.

1. Combine soy sauce, Chinese cooking wine, corn flour, and water in a bowl. Set aside as sauce.

2. Add the oil to the rice cooker, cover, and set to Cook. When the base of the cooker pot gets warm, add beef and fry about 8 to 10 minutes until beef turns brown on the surface. Dish out and set aside. Leave remaining oil in pot.

3. Add the leek, garlic, and mushrooms to the pot and fry for about 2 minutes.

4. Stir in the sauce, cover rice cooker, and allow to reach simmer. Once simmering, return beef to the pot, mix well, and continue to cook for about 5 minutes until beef cooks through and sauce reduces (thickens), switching to Warm if mixture bubbles too vigorously.

Beef in Honey Caramelized Onions

There is a wide variety of honey available on the market. Be creative and try some of the different kinds, such as single-flower honey, clover honey, and even blended honey.

INGREDIENTS | SERVES 2

1 teaspoon oyster sauce
1 teaspoon dark soy sauce
½ teaspoon ground black pepper
1 teaspoon honey
1 cup warm water
½ pound beef fillet
¼ teaspoon salt
½ teaspoon ground black pepper
½ tablespoon corn flour
1 onion, thinly sliced

1. Mix oyster sauce, soy sauce, pepper, honey, and water in a bowl. Set aside as sauce.

2. Combine beef slices with salt, pepper, and corn flour.

3. Add oil to the rice cooker, cover, and set to Cook. When the base of the cooker pot gets warm, add beef and fry about 8 to 10 minutes until beef turns brown and cooks through, covering rice cooker occasionally in the process of cooking. Dish out and set aside. Leave the remaining oil in the pot.

4. Add the onions to the pot and fry about 5 to 8 minutes until onions are fully caramelized, covering rice cooker occasionally in the process of frying.

5. When onions are caramelized, add the sauce, cover the rice cooker, and allow the mixture to simmer until sauce slightly reduces (thickens) in about 3 to 5 minutes. Return the beef to the sauce and allow it to simmer at Warm, with the rice cooker covered, for 5 minutes or more until beef completely cooks through and sauce further reduces.

Stir-Fried Beef in Garlic Black Bean Sauce

You can substitute chicken in this recipe if you prefer white meat to red meat. The dish goes well with steamed rice or over rice vermicelli.

INGREDIENTS | SERVES 2

2 tablespoons vegetable oil
½ pound beef fillet
1 green bell pepper, seeded and thinly sliced
1 clove garlic, finely minced
1 teaspoon grated ginger
1 fresh red chili pepper, seeded and sliced
½ tablespoon black beans, slightly mashed
½ cup water

Cooking Tip

Use the drier salted whole black beans rather than the ready-paste "wetter" version. (Both are available bottled in Asian supermarkets.) When slightly mashed during preparation, the whole black beans add a chunkier texture and more body to the final dish.

1. Add the oil to the rice cooker, cover, and set to Cook. When the base of the cooker pot gets warm, add beef and peppers and fry about 8 to 10 minutes until beef turns brown. Dish out and set aside. Leave the remaining oil in the pot.

2. Add the garlic, ginger, chili pepper, and black beans, and fry about 5 minutes until fragrant.

3. Add the water, cover the rice cooker, and allow to reach a simmer. Return beef and peppers to the pot; mix well. Cook for 5 minutes until beef completely cooks through and sauce reduces (thickens), switching to Warm if the mixture bubbles too vigorously. Serve with steamed rice or over noodles.

Mini Beef Burger

For a healthier version, use leaner meat. However, remember that lean meat will have less flavor and tends to dry out (because it has less fat). The resulting patty will be less tender, less moist, and less juicy when cooked.

INGREDIENTS | SERVES 4

1 pound ground beef
½ onion, grated
1 teaspoon minced garlic
½ teaspoon grated ginger
1 teaspoon Worcestershire sauce
1 teaspoon dried basil
½ teaspoon salt
½ teaspoon ground black pepper
1 egg
4 tablespoons extra-virgin olive oil, divided use (about 2 tablespoons per batch)
4 burger buns, halved
4 slices mozzarella cheese
2 tomatoes, sliced and divided use
8 to 10 lettuce leaves
½ onion, thinly sliced

1. Place the beef, grated onion, garlic, ginger, Worcestershire sauce, basil, salt, pepper, and egg in a large bowl. Mix with your hands until evenly combined. Divide meat mixture into 4 burger patties, each about 3 inches in diameter and ½-inch thick.

2. Add oil to the rice cooker, cover, and set to Cook. When the base of the cooker pot gets warm, add patties (in batches) and fry about 5 minutes on each side or until browned and cooked through. Cover rice cooker while frying (using partial steam to cook the beef). Transfer the cooked patties to a plate, set aside, and cover with foil to keep warm. Repeat with the remaining oil and patties.

3. Place a patty on each burger bun and add cheese, tomatoes, lettuce, and sliced onions, as desired.

CHAPTER 14

Legumes and Beans

Garlic Bean Soup
206

Potato and Pea Soup
207

Vegetable Soup with Pinto Beans
208

Lentil Soup
208

Quick Pea Curry
209

Black Bean Casserole in Tomato Gravy
210

Spicy Green Beans
211

Spicy Pinto Beans with Onions
212

Curried Chickpeas
213

Stir-Fried Mixed Beans
214

Quick Chick-A-Pea
215

Chickpeas with Peppers
215

Thai-Style Lentils
216

Black Bean Patties
217

Garlic Bean Soup

The flavor of garlic can be changed according to how it is prepared. If you add a whole garlic clove without crushing, mincing, or slicing it, it will give flavor without the "bite" (pungency and sharpness) of garlic.

INGREDIENTS | SERVES 3 OR 4

1 cup dry white beans, soaked overnight
1 tablespoon vegetable oil
1 medium-sized onion, thinly sliced
1 teaspoon grated ginger
8 cloves garlic, crushed into a paste
½ teaspoon ground black pepper
Salt, to taste
1 cup warm water
1 cup cooking liquid from boiled beans
½ cup thick coconut milk
2 tablespoons chopped parsley, for garnish

Cooking Tip

Do not mash all the beans unless you favor a completely smooth and creamy soup. When you mash some of the beans, and leave some whole, the soup will turn out chunkier in texture. Create the texture you enjoy.

1. Add soaked beans to the rice cooker pot, and fill with fresh water until totally immersed. Cover rice cooker, set to Cook, and boil about 30 to 45 minutes until beans turn tender (check for tenderness during boiling). Drain. Set aside beans and 1 cup of the cooking liquid.

2. Clean out rice cooker and wipe dry. Add the oil to the rice cooker, cover, and set to Cook. When the base of the cooker pot gets warm, add the onions and fry about 5 minutes until soft. Add the ginger and garlic and fry about 3 minutes until garlic disintegrates further, covering rice cooker occasionally in the process of frying.

3. Add the pepper, salt, water, cooking liquid from boiled beans, and the cooked beans. Partially mash the beans gently with the back of a ladle. Cover the rice cooker and allow to reach a simmer.

4. Once simmering, switch to Warm and continue simmer for about 15 minutes. Before end of cooking, with about 5 minutes to go, stir in coconut milk. Garnish with parsley.

Potato and Pea Soup

Remember to wash your hands, including your fingertips, after seeding and removing the membranes from the chili pepper. The volatile oils from the peppers can irritate your skin and eyes if you unwittingly touch your face with your "spicy" fingers.

INGREDIENTS | SERVES 3 OR 4

2 tablespoons extra-virgin olive oil
1 onion, diced
1 large potato, peeled and diced into ½-inch cubes
2 cloves garlic, crushed
1 teaspoon grated ginger
½ teaspoon ground cumin
½ teaspoon garam masala
½ teaspoon turmeric
4 cups Vegetable Stock (page 18)
1 fresh red chili pepper, finely chopped
1 cup frozen peas
Salt and ground black pepper, to taste
1 tablespoon finely chopped cilantro, for garnish

1. Add the oil to the rice cooker, cover, and set to Cook. When the base of the cooker pot gets warm, add the onions and fry about 5 minutes until soft. Add the potato, garlic, and ginger and fry for about 5 minutes, covering rice cooker occasionally in the process of frying.

2. Add cumin, garam masala, and turmeric and fry for about 1 minute.

3. Stir in vegetable stock and chili pepper. Cover rice cooker and bring to a simmer.

4. Once simmering, switch rice cooker to Warm and continue to simmer for 20 minutes until potatoes start to disintegrate.

5. Add the peas and cook for 5 to 8 minutes until tender. Season with salt and pepper to taste. Garnish with cilantro.

Vegetable Soup with Pinto Beans

As a variation, substitute cannellini beans for the pinto beans.

INGREDIENTS | SERVES 3 OR 4

- 2 tomatoes, diced
- 1 small eggplant, diced
- 1 carrot, peeled and diced
- 1 leek, cleaned thoroughly and sliced into rings
- 1 (15-ounce) can pinto beans, drained, gently rinsed with water, then drained again
- 3 cups Chicken Stock (page 16) or Vegetable Stock (page 18)
- 1 teaspoon dried basil

1. Add all ingredients except the basil to the pot. Cover rice cooker, set to Cook, and bring to boil.
2. Once boiling, switch to Warm and continue to simmer for 20 minutes or until vegetables become tender.
3. Add basil and stir well. Serve warm.

Cooking Tip

Ingredients should be cut and sliced into uniform sizes to ensure uniform cooking time.

Lentil Soup

They are many types of lentils, with brown and red being the most common. Dried lentils need to be soaked overnight before boiling in a fresh batch of water.

INGREDIENTS | SERVES 3 OR 4

- 1 tablespoon butter
- 1 onion, finely chopped
- 2 cloves garlic, crushed
- ½ teaspoon garam masala
- ½ teaspoon turmeric
- ¼ teaspoon red chili powder
- 1 teaspoon ground cumin
- ½ (14½-ounce) can diced tomatoes, drained
- 1 (14½-ounce) can canned lentils, drained, gently rinsed with water, then drained again
- 2 to 3 cups water or stock
- Salt and ground black pepper, to taste
- 1 tablespoon finely chopped cilantro, for garnish

1. Add the butter to the rice cooker, cover, and set to Cook. When the base of the cooker pot gets warm and butter melts, add the onions and fry about 5 minutes until soft. Add the garlic and fry about 3 minutes until fragrant, covering rice cooker occasionally in the process of frying.
2. Add garam masala, turmeric, chili powder, and cumin and fry briskly for 1 minute.
3. Stir in tomatoes, lentils, and water or stock. Cover rice cooker and bring to a simmer.
4. Once simmering, switch to Warm and continue to simmer for about 20 minutes. Season with salt and pepper to taste. Garnish with cilantro and serve with Indian *roti* (bread).

Quick Pea Curry

Garbanzo beans are also called chickpeas. They have a nutty taste and buttery texture. This legume is used in many Middle Eastern and Indian dishes such as hummus and curries.

INGREDIENTS | SERVES 3 OR 4

2 tablespoons vegetable oil
1 onion, finely chopped
1 teaspoon grated ginger
2 cloves garlic, peeled and crushed
2 teaspoons curry powder
½ teaspoon turmeric
½ teaspoon red chili powder
½ pound round cabbage, thinly shredded
1 cup frozen peas
1 (15-ounce) can garbanzo beans, drained, gently rinsed with water, then drained again
2 cups water or Vegetable Stock (page 18)
Salt and ground black pepper, to taste

1. Add the oil to the rice cooker, cover, and set to Cook. When the base of the cooker pot gets warm, add the onions and fry about 5 minutes until slightly soft.

2. Add the ginger, garlic, curry powder, turmeric, and chili powder and fry about 5 minutes until onions become completely soft and the mixture is fragrant, covering the rice cooker occasionally in the process of frying.

3. Add cabbage, peas, and beans and mix well with spices.

4. Add vegetable stock or water, cover rice cooker, and allow to simmer.

5. Once simmering, switch to Warm and simmer for about 30 minutes until cabbage becomes soft. Season with salt and pepper to taste.

Black Bean Casserole in Tomato Gravy

If using canned beans, try buying low-sodium or no-salt versions.

INGREDIENTS | SERVES 4

1 tablespoon vegetable oil
1 onion, finely chopped
1 clove garlic, finely minced
1 teaspoon grated ginger
½ teaspoon turmeric
½ teaspoon ground cumin
1 teaspoon garam masala
½ teaspoon red chili powder
½ (14½-ounce) can diced tomatoes, with juice
1 fresh green chili pepper, seeded and thinly sliced
1 cup water
1 (15-ounce) can black beans, drained, gently rinsed with water, then drained again
Salt and ground black pepper, to taste

1. Add the oil to the rice cooker, cover, and set to Cook. When the base of the cooker pot gets warm, add the onions and fry about 5 minutes until soft, covering the rice cooker occasionally in the process of frying.

2. Add the garlic, ginger, turmeric, cumin, garam masala, and red chili powder and fry about 3 minutes until fragrant.

3. Add tomatoes and green chili. Mix well. Add the water and beans, cover rice cooker, and allow to simmer for about 5 to 10 minutes until gravy slightly reduces (thickens).

4. Once simmering, switch to Warm and continue cooking the black beans for about 5 minutes until they reach a gravy-like consistency. Season with salt and pepper to taste.

Cooking Tip

Canned beans may need to be drained and rinsed thoroughly to reduce their gas-causing properties. Beans cause gas because they contain a sugar, oligosaccharide, that the human body cannot break down. By rinsing the beans, you are trying to remove as much of the gas-causing sugar as possible.

Spicy Green Beans

Turmeric can stain the fingers yellow and subsequently stain your clothes. Be careful when using.

INGREDIENTS | SERVES 2 OR 3

½ tablespoon butter
5 shallots, thinly sliced
2 cloves garlic, finely minced
½ pound green beans, cut into ¼-inch pieces
½ teaspoon cumin seeds
1 teaspoon turmeric
½ teaspoon red chili pepper flakes
Salt and freshly ground black pepper, to taste
3 tablespoons water

1. Add the butter to the rice cooker, cover, and set to Cook. When the base of the cooker pot gets warm and butter melts, add the shallots and fry about 3 minutes until soft. Add the garlic and fry about 3 minutes until fragrant.

2. Add the green beans, mix well, and fry 8 to 10 minutes until green beans turn slightly tender, covering the rice cooker occasionally in the process of cooking.

3. Add cumin, turmeric, and chili pepper flakes; mix well. Add salt and pepper to taste.

4. Add the water, mix well with green beans, cover rice cooker, and cook for about 2 to 3 minutes until water almost evaporates, then switch to Warm for about 15 minutes or more, simmering the green beans until completely soft.

Spicy Pinto Beans with Onions

"Pinto" means "painted" in Spanish, and it perfectly describes the colorful nature of this bean, which when dried is light beige with a reddish brown splash. When cooked, the colored variation disappears, and the beans exhibit a shade of creamy pink.

INGREDIENTS | SERVES 2 OR 3

½ tablespoon butter
3 shallots, thinly sliced
1 clove garlic, finely minced
1 teaspoon ground cumin
½ teaspoon turmeric
½ carrot, diced into ¼-inch cubes
3 tablespoons water
1 (14½-ounce) can pinto beans, drained, gently rinsed with water, then drained again
Salt and ground black pepper, to taste

1. Add the butter to the rice cooker, cover, and set to Cook. When the base of the cooker pot gets warm and the butter melts, add the shallots and fry about 3 minutes until soft. Add the garlic and fry about 3 minutes until fragrant, covering rice cooker occasionally in the process of frying.

2. Add the cumin, turmeric, and carrots. Fry briskly about 3 minutes and mix well.

3. Add the water, cover rice cooker for about 5 minutes, and allow carrots to cook and become softer.

4. Add the pinto beans, cover rice cooker, and allow mixture to cook slightly for about 5 minutes. Switch to Warm for about 10 minutes until carrots turn completely soft. Season with salt and pepper to taste.

Benefits of Turmeric

Part of the ginger family, turmeric is used extensively in Southeast Asian cooking, especially in Indian cuisine. Turmeric is also believed to act as an anti-inflammatory agent. The yellow-orange pigment in turmeric, called curcumin, is known to be the primary pharmacological agent in this spice, which is often used in traditional Chinese and Indian medicine.

Curried Chickpeas

Fresh curry leaves are the best in terms of flavor and aroma. Curry leaves have a short storage life. Store them in an airtight plastic bag in the refrigerator for up to two weeks.

INGREDIENTS | SERVES 2 OR 3

½ tablespoon butter
3 shallots, thinly sliced
1 clove garlic, finely minced
3 curry leaves
½ tablespoon curry powder
½ teaspoon cumin seeds
½ teaspoon turmeric
½ teaspoon red chili powder
1 (14½-ounce) can garbanzo beans, drained, gently rinsed with water, then drained again
Salt and ground black pepper, to taste

1. Add the butter to the rice cooker, cover, and set to Cook. When the base of the cooker pot gets warm and the butter melts, add the shallots and fry about 3 minutes until soft.

2. Add the garlic and curry leaves and fry about 3 minutes until fragrant, covering rice cooker occasionally in the process of frying.

3. Add the curry powder, cumin seeds, turmeric, and chili powder, and fry briskly for about 3 minutes.

4. Add the beans, mix well, and fry for about 2 minutes. Season with salt and pepper to taste. Cover rice cooker for about 2 minutes, then switch to Warm and simmer for 10 to 12 minutes. Stir occasionally.

Stir-Fried Mixed Beans

A can of mixed beans provides variety, color, and a balanced profile of minerals and fiber from the bean family.

INGREDIENTS | SERVES 3 OR 4

2 tablespoons extra-virgin olive oil
1 medium onion, finely chopped
1 clove garlic, finely minced
2 stalks celery, diced
1 carrot, diced
1 (14½-ounce) can mixed beans, drained, gently rinsed with water, then drained again
2 medium zucchini, diced
1 tomato, diced
3 tablespoons water
½ teaspoon dried basil
Salt and ground black pepper, to taste

Cooking Tip
When slicing or dicing vegetables such as carrots, celery, and zucchini, it is best to slice or dice at a bias to expose a larger surface area during cooking, resulting in shorter cooking time.

1. Add the oil to the rice cooker, cover, and set to Cook. When the base of the cooker pot gets warm, add the onions and fry about 5 minutes until onions are slightly soft. Add the garlic and fry about 3 minutes until fragrant.

2. Add the celery and carrots and fry for 2 to 3 minutes, covering the rice cooker occasionally in the process of cooking.

3. Add the beans, zucchini, tomatoes, and water; mix well. Cover rice cooker and allow to reach a slight simmer. Stir occasionally.

4. Switch to cooker to Warm and simmer about 10 to 12 minutes until vegetables turn tender. Add the basil, mix well, and then season with salt and pepper to taste.

Quick Chick-A-Pea

This is an extremely simple and tasty recipe that can be made in less than 10 minutes.

INGREDIENTS | **SERVES 2 OR 3**

2 tablespoons extra-virgin olive oil
3 shallots, thinly sliced
1 clove garlic, finely minced
1 teaspoon grated ginger
1 (14½-ounce) can chickpeas, drained, gently rinsed with water, then drained again
1 cup frozen peas, thawed
1 green onion, finely chopped
1 fresh red chili pepper, seeded and thinly sliced
Salt and ground black pepper, to taste

1. Add the oil to the rice cooker, cover, and set to Cook. When the base of the cooker pot gets warm, add the shallots and fry about 3 minutes until slightly soft. Add the garlic and ginger and fry about 3 minutes until fragrant.
2. Add the chickpeas and frozen peas and mix well. Cover rice cooker and cook for 1 to 2 minutes. Stir occasionally.
3. Add the green onions and chili; mix well. Season with salt and pepper to taste.

Chickpeas with Peppers

For best results, dice the bell pepper instead of slicing, so that the consistency of the final dish, especially in the shape of the beans and peppers, remains.

INGREDIENTS | **SERVES 2 OR 3**

2 tablespoons extra-virgin olive oil
3 shallots, thinly sliced
1 clove garlic, finely minced
1 teaspoon grated ginger
1 red bell pepper, seeded and diced
1 (14½-ounce) can garbanzo beans, drained, gently rinsed with water, then drained again
Salt and ground black pepper, to taste
1 teaspoon finely chopped cilantro, for garnish

1. Add the oil to the rice cooker, cover, and set to Cook. When the base of the cooker pot gets warm, add the shallots and fry about 3 minutes until soft. Add the garlic and ginger and fry about 3 minutes until fragrant.
2. Add the bell peppers and beans and fry about 5 to 8 minutes until peppers turn tender, covering rice cooker in the process of cooking. Season with salt and pepper to taste. Garnish with cilantro.

Thai-Style Lentils

The corn kernels add a hint of sweetness and color contrast to this dish. Omitting this ingredient will not affect the "Thai factor."

INGREDIENTS | SERVES 3 OR 4

2 tablespoons extra-virgin olive oil
3 shallots, thinly sliced
1 clove garlic, finely minced
1 teaspoon grated ginger
2 kaffir lime leaves, whole
1 Thai chili pepper, seeded and finely chopped
1 (14½-ounce) can lentils, drained, gently rinsed with water, then drained again
1 cup corn kernels, drained
1 tablespoon finely chopped cilantro, divided use
Salt and freshly ground black pepper, to taste
1 teaspoon lime juice

Cooking Tip
The kaffir lime leaves may be quite difficult to chew. Add them whole to give aroma and flavor to the dish, and then remove the leaves before serving.

1. Add the oil to the rice cooker, cover, and set to Cook. When the base of the cooker pot gets warm, add the shallots and fry about 3 minutes until slightly soft.

2. Add the garlic, ginger, lime leaves, and chili and fry about 3 minutes until fragrant, covering rice cooker occasionally in the process of frying.

3. Add the lentils, corn, and ½ tablespoon cilantro. Mix well and fry for about 3 minutes, covering rice cooker occasionally in the process of cooking.

4. Season with salt and pepper to taste. Remove the lime leaves, drizzle in the lime juice, and garnish with remaining cilantro before serving.

Black Bean Patties

In addition to being perfect finger-friendly vegetarian snacks, these patties make healthy vegetarian burgers as well.

INGREDIENTS | SERVES 2 OR 3

1 (15-ounce) can black beans, drained, gently rinsed with water, then drained again

½ green bell pepper, seeded and chopped

½ medium-sized onion, cut into wedges

3 cloves garlic

1 teaspoon cumin

1 teaspoon red chili powder

1 egg

4 tablespoons vegetable oil, divided use (about 2 tablespoons per batch)

1. Mash the beans in a large bowl with a fork until thick and pasty.

2. Blend the bell peppers, onion, and garlic in a food processor to produce a finely grated mixture.

3. Combine the bell pepper mixture with the mashed beans, followed by cumin, chili powder, and egg. Use your fingers to evenly combine the mixture until it is sticky and holds together. Form into patties and set aside.

4. Add oil to the rice cooker, cover, and set to Cook. When the base of the cooker pot gets warm, add patties (in batches), and fry each side for about 3 minutes or until browned. Cover rice cooker while frying. Repeat with the remaining oil and patties.

CHAPTER 15

Eggs

Easy Chinese Savory
Egg Custard
219

Japanese Tea-Bowl Egg
(*Chawanmushi*)
220

Tea-Flavored Eggs
221

Eggs with Caramelized Onions
222

Egg Curry
223

Egg with French Beans
224

Shrimp Foo Yong
225

Egg with Pork and Cilantro
226

Onion and Green Chili Omelet
227

Scrambled Eggs with Spices
228

Indian Cheese Omelet
229

Green Onion and Potato Frittata
230

Summer Frittata
231

Easy Chinese Savory Egg Custard

The chicken stock used in this recipe produces a smooth-textured, flavorful egg custard.

INGREDIENTS | SERVES 2

2 eggs, whisked
Salt and ground white pepper, to taste
¼ cup Chicken Stock (page 16)
2 drops sesame oil
1 teaspoon finely chopped green onions, for garnish

Cooking Tip
Use a sieve to strain the whisked egg to remove egg-white strands and foam. It will improve the quality and texture of the egg custard.

1. Fill the rice cooker pot with water to about the 3-cup mark. Cover the rice cooker and set to Cook.

2. In a bowl suitable for placing into the steamer insert or basket of the rice cooker, whisk the eggs with salt and pepper. Add chicken stock to the whisked egg mixture. Stir to combine and DO NOT whisk again. Cover or seal the bowl containing the egg mixture with foil. Place the bowl in the steamer insert or basket.

3. When the water in the rice cooker boils, place the steamer insert or basket with the bowl of eggs into the rice cooker. Steam, with the rice cooker covered, for 10 minutes until the egg custard sets.

4. When ready to serve, drizzle sesame oil on top of the egg custard and garnish with green onions.

Japanese Tea-Bowl Egg (*Chawanmushi*)

This is a popular appetizer in Japanese cuisine. Chawan means "tea-bowl," and mushi means "steaming." Thus Chawanmushi means "Steamed in a Tea-Bowl."

INGREDIENTS | SERVES 2

½ cup dashi stock
½ teaspoon Japanese soy sauce (shoyu)
½ teaspoon mirin
¼ teaspoon salt
2 eggs
2 small fresh shiitake mushroom caps, thinly sliced, divided use
2 shrimp, peeled, deveined, and diced, divided use
2 teaspoons finely chopped green onions, divided use

1. Set the rice cooker to Cook. Add the dashi stock, Japanese soy sauce, mirin, and salt to the pot. Cover the pot and bring to a simmer for about 5 minutes.

2. Switch off rice cooker, pour out dashi mixture, and allow it to cool to room temperature.

3. Clean out the rice cooker. Fill the pot with water to about the 3-cup mark. Cover the rice cooker and set to Cook.

4. In a separate bowl, whisk the eggs and add the cooled dashi mixture to the eggs. Sieve the whisked egg mixture to remove remnants of egg-white strands. Set aside.

5. Divide shiitake, shrimp, and green onions into two *chawanmushi* cups, or teacups. Fill each cup ¾ full with the egg mixture. Cover and seal the cups with foil. Place the cups in the steamer insert or basket.

6. When the water in the rice cooker boils, place the steamer insert or basket with the cups into the rice cooker. Steam, with the rice cooker covered, for about 10 minutes until the egg custard sets.

Tea-Flavored Eggs

Also known as tea leaf eggs, these are commonly sold as savory snacks by street vendors or in night markets in China, Hong Kong, Taiwan, and other Chinese communities.

INGREDIENTS | SERVES 4 TO 6

4 cups water
6 eggs, at room temperature
1 tablespoon light soy sauce
4 tablespoons dark soy sauce
2 tablespoons black tea leaves
1 cinnamon stick
2 pieces star anise
1 teaspoon brown sugar

Cooking Tip

If not consumed immediately, remove the eggs from heat after simmering for two hours, and allow them to sit for two more hours in the braising liquid. The longer they are allowed to sit, the more flavorful they are.

1. Fill the rice cooker pot with 4 cups water, or enough water to cover the eggs. Cover the rice cooker and set to Cook. Bring the water to a boil.

2. Once boiling, gently add the eggs to boil for about 10 minutes. When eggs are hard-boiled and cooked, remove them from the hot water and rinse them in a separate cold-water bath.

3. When eggs are cooled, gently crack the shells using the back of a teaspoon, to introduce "crack lines" throughout the egg. Do not peel off the eggshell. The "cracked" eggshell should be intact with the egg.

4. Return the "cracked" eggs to the water in the pot, and add the soy sauce, black tea, cinnamon stick, star anise, and brown sugar. Cover rice cooker and allow the tea mixture to simmer.

5. Once simmering, switch rice cooker to Warm and simmer eggs in tea mixture for about 2 hours.

Eggs with Caramelized Onions

Always check for the expiration date on the egg carton. If you're not a frequent user of eggs, buy them in smaller cartons so they will not go bad before you can consume them. Store eggs in the refrigerator until ready to use.

INGREDIENTS | SERVES 2

4 cups water
2 eggs, at room temperature
1 tablespoon vegetable oil
3 shallots, thinly sliced
½ teaspoon grated ginger
¼ teaspoon curry powder
¼ teaspoon ground cumin
1 tablespoon water
Salt and ground black pepper, to taste

1. Fill the rice cooker pot with 4 cups water or enough water to cover the eggs. Cover the rice cooker, set to Cook, and allow to come to a boil.

2. Once boiling, gently add the eggs to boil for about 10 minutes. When eggs are cooked, remove them from the hot water and rinse them in a separate cold-water bath. Once cooled, peel the hard-boiled eggs and slice each egg in half. Set the eggs aside on a serving plate, cut-side up.

3. Clean out the rice cooker and wipe dry. Add the oil to the rice cooker, cover, and set to Cook. When the base of the cooker pot gets warm, add the shallots and fry about 3 minutes until slightly soft.

4. Add the ginger, curry powder, cumin, water, salt, and pepper. Fry for about 3 minutes until the shallots are completely caramelized, covering the rice cooker occasionally in the process of frying.

5. Ladle the caramelized shallot mixture over the eggs and serve with steamed rice.

Egg Curry

When intending to boil eggs, always take them out of the refrigerator ahead of time and allow them to come to room temperature. Cold eggs will crack when dropped in boiling water.

INGREDIENTS | SERVES 2

4 cups water
3 eggs, at room temperature
1 tablespoon vegetable oil
1 medium-sized onion, thinly sliced
1 clove garlic, finely minced
½ teaspoon grated ginger
1 teaspoon red chili powder
¼ teaspoon turmeric
¼ teaspoon ground coriander
½ (14½-ounce) can diced tomatoes, with juice
1 fresh green chili pepper, seeded and chopped
1 cup water

Cooking Tip

Instead of adding whole boiled eggs to the spicy gravy, you can slice the eggs into halves or quarters. Part of the egg yolk will disintegrate in the gravy and thicken the curry. However, if adding sliced eggs, do not stir excessively or the entire curry will become too mushy and will not look presentable.

1. Fill the rice cooker pot with 4 cups water or enough water to cover the eggs. Cover the rice cooker, set to Cook, and bring the water to boil. Once boiling, gently add the eggs for about 10 minutes. When eggs are cooked, remove them and set aside to cool. When cooled, peel the hard-boiled eggs and slice each egg in half. Set aside.

2. Clean out the rice cooker and wipe dry. Add the oil to the rice cooker, cover, and set to Cook. When the base of the cooker pot gets warm, add the onions and fry about 5 minutes until slightly soft.

3. Add the garlic, ginger, chili powder, turmeric, and coriander and fry about 3 minutes until fragrant, covering rice cooker occasionally in the process of frying.

4. Add the tomatoes, chili, and water. Cover rice cooker and allow mixture to simmer.

5. Once simmering, add the boiled eggs, cover rice cooker, and cook for 1 minute, then switch to Warm and cook for another 2 to 3 minutes. Serve with steamed rice.

Egg with French Beans

Substitute long beans for the French beans if you prefer.

INGREDIENTS | SERVES 2

3 eggs
¼ teaspoon dark soy sauce
¼ teaspoon ground white pepper
2 tablespoons vegetable oil
½ pound French green beans, diced to small pieces
Salt and ground white pepper, to taste

1. In a small bowl, whisk the eggs with soy sauce and pepper. Set aside.

2. Add oil to the rice cooker, cover, and set to Cook. When the base of the cooker pot gets warm, add the green beans, sprinkle in salt and pepper to taste, and fry for about 5 minutes, covering rice cooker occasionally in the process of frying, until green beans have turned slightly tender.

3. Gently pour in the whisked eggs so that they spread evenly across the surface of the pot and cover the green beans. Allow the eggs to cook on one side for 3 to 5 minutes until slightly browned, then flip to the other side to complete cooking in about 3 minutes, covering the rice cooker in the process of cooking the eggs.

4. When eggs have cooked and set, switch off rice cooker, dish out, and serve.

Shrimp Foo Yong

Traditionally, this dish is a deep-fried pancake filled with eggs, vegetables, and leftover meat or seafood. Today, the cooking method has changed to pan-frying, especially when this dish is homemade.

INGREDIENTS | SERVES 2

2 tablespoons vegetable oil

12 to 16 shrimp, peeled, deveined, and diced (into about ½-inch pieces)

3 eggs

¼ teaspoon dark soy sauce

¼ teaspoon ground white pepper

2 green onions, sliced into finger-length pieces

Cooking Tip

You do not need to restrict yourself to leftover ingredients when making this dish. Use fresh ingredients to match up with the fresh eggs!

1. Add the oil to the rice cooker, cover, and set to Cook. When the base of the cooker pot gets warm, add the shrimp and fry about 8 to 10 minutes until shrimp turn pink and almost cooked. Dish out and set aside to cool. Leave the remaining oil in the pot.

2. In a bowl, whisk the eggs with soy sauce and pepper. Add the green onions and cooled shrimp and whisk gently to combine.

3. Cover the rice cooker, set to Cook, and heat the oil that remains in the pot. When base of pot is warm, gently pour in the egg mixture and fry, breaking up the eggs while cooking, covering the rice cooker in the process of frying the eggs. Once the eggs are cooked through, dish out and serve.

Egg with Pork and Cilantro

As an alternative, use ground beef or chicken.

INGREDIENTS | SERVES 2

3 eggs
¼ teaspoon dark soy sauce
¼ teaspoon ground white pepper
2 tablespoons vegetable oil
¼ pound ground pork
Salt and ground white pepper, to taste
1 tablespoon finely chopped cilantro leaves

Cooking Tip

As an alternative cooking step, you can dish out the cooked pork to cool. Then add the pork, seasoning, and cilantro leaves into the whisked egg mixture and whisk to combine all the ingredients. This will take more time since you need to wait for the pork to cool. However, it might be easier to control the cooking process as the entire egg mixture is added all at the same time and fried at the same temperature.

1. In a small bowl, whisk the eggs with soy sauce and pepper. Set aside.

2. Add oil to the rice cooker, cover, and set to Cook. When the base of the cooker pot gets warm, add the pork (break into small bits and spread evenly across the pot) and fry about 10 to 12 minutes until pork is cooked, covering rice cooker occasionally in the process of frying. Season with salt and pepper to taste.

3. Gently pour in the eggs so that the eggs spread evenly across the pot surface and cover the pork bits. Sprinkle in cilantro and allow the eggs to cook on one side for 3 to 5 minutes until slightly browned, covering the rice cooker in the process of cooking the eggs. When egg has cooked and set, switch off the rice cooker, dish out, and serve.

Onion and Green Chili Omelet

If you want your eggs fluffier, add 1 to 2 tablespoons more milk when you whisk the eggs.

INGREDIENTS | SERVES 2 OR 3

4 eggs
2 tablespoons whole milk
1 fresh green chili pepper, seeded and finely chopped
Salt, to taste
¼ teaspoon freshly ground black pepper
2 tablespoons vegetable oil
½ onion, finely chopped

Cooking Tip

To make sure the omelet is presented nicely (and not broken to pieces), try not to move the eggs too much when frying. As the eggs begin to set on the base of the pot, try lifting the eggs slightly at the edge to allow uncooked portions of the egg to flow underneath to be cooked.

1. In a bowl, lightly whisk the eggs, milk, chili, salt, and pepper to combine. Set aside.

2. Add the oil to the rice cooker, cover, and set to Cook. When the base of the cooker pot gets warm, add the onions and fry about 5 minutes until slightly soft, covering rice cooker occasionally in the process of frying.

3. Gently pour in the whisked eggs so that they spread evenly across the pot surface. Cover rice cooker, lifting the lid occasionally to monitor. When the omelet is almost cooked in 5 to 8 minutes, fold it in half in the rice cooker, cover rice cooker, switch the cooker to Warm, and allow to cook for 30 seconds longer.

4. Transfer omelet onto a plate and serve immediately.

Scrambled Eggs with Spices

In Parsi cuisine this is also known as akoori. Another variant is pora, which refers to "Parsi omelet."

INGREDIENTS | SERVES 3 OR 4

5 eggs
2 tablespoons whole milk
Salt and ground black pepper, to taste
1 tablespoon butter, divided use
2 shallots, thinly sliced
1 clove garlic, finely minced
1 fresh green chili pepper, seeded and chopped
1 tomato, peeled and diced
Pinch (less than ¼ teaspoon) of ground turmeric
¼ teaspoon ground cumin
1 tablespoon finely chopped cilantro leaves, divided use

1. In a bowl, lightly whisk the eggs, then stir in milk, salt, and pepper to combine. Set aside.

2. Add ½ tablespoon of the butter to the rice cooker, cover, and set to Cook. When the base of the cooker pot gets warm and butter melts, add the shallots and fry about 3 minutes until slightly soft.

3. Add the garlic and chili and fry for about 3 minutes, covering rice cooker occasionally in the process of frying.

4. Add remaining butter, tomatoes, turmeric, and cumin. Stir well for about 5 to 8 minutes until tomatoes release their juices, covering rice cooker in the process of frying the tomatoes and spices.

5. Add the whisked eggs and ½ tablespoon cilantro, stirring occasionally to fluff up. Cook the eggs evenly for about 3 to 5 minutes until a creamy, moist consistency, switching rice cooker to Warm if the heat is too high and seems to be drying out the eggs.

6. Transfer eggs to serving plate and garnish with remaining cilantro. Serve with toasted bread or Indian *roti* (bread).

Indian Cheese Omelet

As a variation, use heavy cream instead of whole milk to produce a fluffy omelet with a richer taste.

INGREDIENTS | SERVES 2

2 eggs
3 tablespoons whole milk
¼ teaspoon garam masala
1 fresh green chili pepper, seeded and chopped
Salt, to taste
¼ teaspoon freshly ground black pepper
1 tablespoon butter
1 tablespoon grated Parmesan cheese
2 slices Cheddar cheese

Garam Masala

Garam masala is a blend of fragrant and aromatic Indian spices including cumin seeds, fennel seeds, coriander seeds, cardamom seeds, black peppercorns, and turmeric. You should buy garam masala and other spice blends in small amounts because they do not keep long and gradually lose their aroma.

1. In a small bowl, lightly whisk the eggs, milk, garam masala, chili, salt, and pepper. Set aside.

2. Add the butter to the rice cooker, cover, and set to Cook. When the base of the cooker pot gets warm and butter melts, gently pour in the egg mixture so that the eggs spread evenly across the pot surface. Cook the egg about 5 to 8 minutes on one side, covering rice cooker in the process.

3. Sprinkle the Parmesan cheese on the eggs and lay the Cheddar slices on top of the eggs. Fold the omelet in half and cover the rice cooker for about 30 seconds to melt the cheese. When the cheese melts, switch off rice cooker and transfer the omelet onto a serving plate.

Green Onion and Potato Frittata

For a higher nutritional value (or if you dislike the pungency of green onions), substitute fresh baby spinach.

INGREDIENTS | SERVES 2

4 cups water
1 medium-sized potato
2 eggs
3 tablespoons whole milk
1 tablespoon finely chopped green onions
Salt and freshly ground black pepper, to taste
1 tablespoon butter, divided use
2 slices Cheddar cheese

1. Fill the rice cooker pot with 4 cups water. Cover the rice cooker and set to Cook. When water boils, add the potato and boil for 15 minutes.

2. Lightly whisk the eggs, milk, green onions, salt, and pepper in a bowl. Set aside.

3. Once the potatoes are cooked in the rice cooker, remove the potato and set aside to cool. When cooled, peel and cut the potato into ½-inch cubes. Set aside.

4. Clean out the rice cooker and wipe dry. Add ½ tablespoon of the butter to the rice cooker, cover, and set to Cook. When the base of the cooker pot gets warm and the butter melts, add the potato cubes and fry for 2 to 3 minutes, spreading the potatoes evenly across the pot.

5. Add the remaining butter. When it melts, gently pour in the egg mixture so that the egg spreads evenly across the pot surface. Cook the egg on one side for about 5 to 8 minutes, covering the rice cooker during this process. When egg is almost cooked (cooked on one side but still runny on top), add the Cheddar cheese, cover rice cooker, and allow cheese to melt.

6. After the cheese melts and the runny portions of the egg are cooked, transfer egg onto serving plate and serve immediately.

Summer Frittata

Traditionally, a frittata is partially cooked on the stovetop, broiled to finish, and served open-faced. Today, however, the term "frittata" is often used to describe a thick omelet.

INGREDIENTS | SERVES 2

2 eggs

2 tablespoons whole milk

Salt and freshly ground black pepper, to taste

3 tablespoons extra-virgin olive oil

1 cup fresh corn kernels

½ green bell pepper, seeded and finely diced

½ red bell pepper, seeded and finely diced

1 teaspoon butter

Cooking Tip

Make use of seasonal ingredients to create your own repertoire of seasonal frittatas. How about an asparagus frittata in spring, cabbage and onion frittata in fall, and cauliflower and butternut squash frittata in winter?

1. In a small bowl, lightly whisk the eggs, milk, salt, and pepper. Set aside.

2. Add the oil to the rice cooker, cover, and set to Cook. When the base of the cooker pot gets warm, add the corn and peppers and fry for 2 to 3 minutes, spreading the vegetable mixture evenly across the pot.

3. Add the butter. When it melts, gently pour in the egg mixture so that the egg spreads evenly across the pot. Cook the egg, covering the rice cooker during this process. When the egg is fully cooked in about 8 to 10 minutes, transfer the frittata to a plate and serve immediately.

CHAPTER 16

Tofu

Steamed Tofu Balls
233

Steamed Tofu with Ground Pork
234

Spinach Tofu in Mushroom Sauce
235

Tofu Casserole
236

Tofu with Hot Shallot Oil
236

Tofu Curry
237

Mapo Tofu
238

Tofu with Shrimp, Meat, and Mushrooms
239

Marinated Scrambled Tofu with Peppers and Onions
240

Tofu with Butternut Squash
241

Tofu with Bean Sprouts and Spices
241

Tofu Patties
242

Steamed Tofu Balls

A healthy and protein-packed dish you can even enjoy on its own.

INGREDIENTS | SERVES 2

Ingredients

½ (10½-ounce) block firm tofu, drained of excess moisture
¼ pound ground chicken
1 egg white
Pinch (less than ¼ teaspoon) of salt
¼ teaspoon ground white pepper
½ teaspoon corn flour
3 fresh shiitake mushroom caps, sliced thinly
Ground white pepper, to taste

Cooking Tip

Use a denser tofu such as firm tofu in this recipe, since soft tofu has a higher moisture content. The high moisture content in soft tofu will make tofu balls lose their firm structure and they will not look presentable.

1. Fill the rice cooker pot with water to about the 3-cup mark. Cover the rice cooker and set to Cook.

2. Mash tofu in a bowl, then combine with ground chicken, egg white, salt, pepper, and corn flour. Mix well. Shape tofu mixture into round balls, and place evenly across a plate that will fit in the steamer insert or basket. Sprinkle mushrooms over the tofu balls. Cover the plate with plastic wrap and set aside.

3. When the water in the rice cooker boils, place the steamer insert or basket with the plate of tofu balls into the rice cooker. Cover rice cooker for about 10 minutes until the chicken is cooked.

4. Add a dash of white pepper to the steamed dish before serving.

Steamed Tofu with Ground Pork

As a variation, cut the tofu into small cubes and steam with the fried pork mixture as directed. The flavors will penetrate deeper within the tofu.

INGREDIENTS | SERVES 2

1 (10-ounce) block soft tofu, drained of excess moisture
1 teaspoon Chinese cooking wine
2 teaspoons dark soy sauce
½ teaspoon brown sugar
¼ teaspoon sesame oil
¼ teaspoon ground white pepper
2 tablespoons water
1 tablespoon vegetable oil
½ pound ground pork
1 tablespoon finely chopped green onions, divided use
1 fresh red chili pepper, seeded and thinly sliced, for garnish

1. Place the tofu on a plate that will fit in the steamer insert or basket. Set aside.

2. Mix Chinese cooking wine, soy sauce, brown sugar, sesame oil, pepper, and water in a bowl. Set aside as sauce.

3. Add the oil to the rice cooker, cover, and set to Cook. When the base of the cooker gets warm, add the shallots and fry about 3 minutes until fragrant.

4. Add the ground pork (break up into even, small bits), ½ tablespoon of the green onions, and prepared sauce mixture. Mix well, cover the rice cooker, and allow to simmer for 30 seconds. Switch off rice cooker. Ladle the pork mixture over the tofu.

5. Clean the rice cooker and wipe dry. Add water to the rice cooker to fill up half the pot, cover, and set to Cook. When the water boils, place the steamer insert or basket holding the tofu and pork into the rice cooker, cover, and steam for about 10 minutes until pork cooks through. Garnish with remaining green onions and red chili.

Spinach Tofu in Mushroom Sauce

You can also use frozen spinach for this dish. Thaw the frozen spinach according to package instructions and then continue with this recipe.

INGREDIENTS | SERVES 2 OR 3

1 (10-ounce) block soft tofu, drained of excess moisture

2 cups tightly packed, coarsely chopped baby spinach

2 teaspoons oyster sauce

½ teaspoon dark soy sauce

1 teaspoon brown sugar

1 cup water

1 tablespoon vegetable oil

1 (1½-ounce) pack Japanese beech mushrooms

Cooking Tip

Soft tofu has a high moisture content (almost 90 percent). To drain effectively, place paper towels over the tofu to absorb the moisture.

1. Fill the rice cooker pot with water to about the 3-cup mark. Cover the rice cooker and set to Cook.

2. Place tofu on a plate that will fit in the steamer insert or basket. Arrange chopped spinach on top of the tofu and cover the plate with plastic wrap.

3. In a small bowl, mix oyster sauce, soy sauce, brown sugar, and water. Set aside as sauce.

4. When the water in the rice cooker boils, place the steamer insert or basket with the plate of tofu in the rice cooker, and steam for about 3 minutes until the spinach is soft and cooked. Remove steamer insert and set spinach tofu aside.

5. Clean the rice cooker and wipe dry. Add the oil to rice cooker, cover, and set to Cook. When base of rice cooker gets warm, add the mushrooms, followed by sauce mixture. Cover rice cooker and allow to reach a simmer. Once simmering, switch to Warm and simmer for 5 minutes until mushrooms are cooked.

6. Ladle the mushroom sauce over the steamed spinach tofu and serve immediately.

Tofu Casserole

Add about ½ cup of diced zucchini for a wider variety of vegetables in this casserole. Then cut down broccoli florets to ½ cup.

INGREDIENTS | SERVES 4

½ tablespoon oyster sauce
½ teaspoon dark soy sauce
1 teaspoon brown sugar
¼ teaspoon ground white pepper
½ cup water
1 tablespoon vegetable oil
2 cloves garlic, thinly sliced
1 cup diced celery
1 cup broccoli florets
1 cup cauliflower florets
1 (10-ounce) block firm tofu, cubed into bite-sized pieces

1. In a small bowl, mix oyster sauce, soy sauce, brown sugar, pepper, and water. Set aside as sauce.

2. Add oil to the rice cooker, cover, and set to Cook. When the base of the pot gets warm, add the garlic and fry about 3 minutes until fragrant.

3. Add the celery, broccoli, cauliflower, and tofu and fry for 3 minutes until vegetables are slightly tender, covering rice cooker occasionally in the process of frying.

4. Stir in sauce mixture, mix well with vegetables and tofu, cover rice cooker at Cook, and allow to reach a simmer.

5. Once simmering, switch to Warm and continue simmer for 5 to 10 minutes until all the vegetables are tender. Serve with steamed rice.

Tofu with Hot Shallot Oil

To save time you can use ready-made fried shallots, found in some Asian supermarkets.

INGREDIENTS | SERVES 2 OR 3

1 (10-ounce) pack soft tofu, drained, and sliced to about 1-inch cubes
1 teaspoon dark soy sauce
½ teaspoon Worcestershire sauce
1 red chili pepper, seeded and thinly sliced
2 tablespoons finely chopped green onions
1 tablespoon Fried Golden Shallots (page 284)
1 teaspoon sesame oil
1 tablespoon vegetable oil

1. Place tofu on a plate. Drizzle soy sauce and Worcestershire sauce over the tofu. Top with chili, green onions, and fried shallots.

2. Add the sesame oil and vegetable oil to the rice cooker, cover, and set to Cook. Heat the oil about 3 to 5 minutes until almost smoking (covering rice cooker will induce smoking). Pour the hot oil over the tofu. Serve immediately with steamed rice.

Tofu Curry

This tofu vegetable curry is a milder and sweeter curry and uses ready available peanut butter instead of making peanut paste from scratch.

INGREDIENTS | SERVES 2 OR 3

1 tablespoon vegetable oil
3 shallots, chopped
2 cloves garlic, finely minced
1 teaspoon grated ginger
1 teaspoon curry powder
½ teaspoon turmeric
½ teaspoon ground cumin
1 fresh red chili pepper, seeded
1 cup water
2 tablespoons chunky peanut butter
1 cup coconut milk
2 kaffir lime leaves
1 teaspoon brown sugar
1 (10-ounce) block firm tofu, drained and cut into 1-inch cubes
1 green bell pepper, cut to bite-sized wedges
1 red bell pepper, cut to bite-sized wedges
Salt, to taste

1. Add the oil to the rice cooker, cover, and set to Cook. When the base of the cooker pot gets warm, add the shallots and fry about 3 minutes until slightly soft.

2. Add the garlic, ginger, curry powder, turmeric, cumin, and chili and fry about 3 minutes until fragrant, covering rice cooker occasionally in the process of frying.

3. Stir in the water, peanut butter, coconut milk, lime leaves, and brown sugar. Stir well to mix. Cover the rice cooker at Cook and bring to a simmer.

4. Once simmering, add the tofu, bell peppers, and salt. Continue to simmer on Warm with the rice cooker covered, stirring occasionally, for about 10 minutes until bell peppers are tender. Served with steamed rice.

Cooking Tip
Use fresh kaffir leaves if possible for best results. Frozen leaves work second best. If you do not have kaffir leaves, substitute about 2 to 3 tablespoons fresh lime juice and 1 to 1½ teaspoons finely grated lime peel.

Mapo Tofu

Typically, in Chinese restaurants you will see a thin, oily, shocking-red film in this dish due to the addition of red chili oil.

INGREDIENTS | SERVES 2 OR 3

1 tablespoon vegetable oil
½ pound ground pork
2 shallots, thinly sliced
½ teaspoon grated ginger
1 clove garlic, finely minced
1 tablespoon hot bean chili paste
1 teaspoon Chinese cooking wine
1 cup water
1 (10-ounce) pack soft tofu, drained, and cubed (about 1-inch cubes)
Ground white pepper, to taste
1 tablespoon finely chopped green onions, for garnish

Cooking Tip

Do not stir too frequently after adding the tofu, or you may end up with an overly mushy tofu dish.

1. Add the oil to the rice cooker, cover, and set to Cook. When the base of the cooker pot gets warm, add the ground pork (break into small even bits) and fry about 8 to 10 minutes until pork turns pink on the surface. Dish out and set side. Leave the remaining oil in the pot.

2. Add the shallots to the pot and fry about 3 minutes until slightly soft.

3. Add the ginger, garlic, chili paste, and Chinese cooking wine and fry for 2 minutes until fragrant. Stir in water, cover rice cooker, and bring to a simmer.

4. Once simmering, return the pork to the rice cooker, add the tofu, cover rice cooker, and allow mixture to come to a simmer again. If the mixture boils too vigorously, switch to Warm and continue simmering for 5 minutes.

5. Sprinkle with pepper and stir well. Garnish with green onions before serving.

Tofu with Shrimp, Meat, and Mushrooms

Depending on personal preferences, you can also use soft or firm tofu to replace medium-firm tofu in this recipe.

INGREDIENTS | SERVES 3 OR 4

1 tablespoon vegetable oil
¼ pound ground pork
1 clove garlic, finely minced
½ teaspoon grated ginger
4–6 medium-sized shrimp, peeled, deveined, and diced
4 fresh shiitake mushroom caps, diced to cubes
1 teaspoon oyster sauce
½ cup water
1 (10-ounce) pack medium-firm tofu, sliced to ½-inch cubes
Salt and ground white pepper, to taste
1 teaspoon finely chopped green onions, for garnish

1. Add the oil to the rice cooker, cover, and set to Cook. When the base of the cooker pot gets warm, add the ground pork (break into small even bits) and fry about 8 to 10 minutes until pork turns pink on the surface. Dish out and set side. Leave the remaining oil in the pot.

2. Add the garlic and ginger to the pot and fry about 3 minutes until fragrant.

3. Add the shrimp and mushrooms and fry for 2 to 3 minutes until shrimp turn pink, covering rice cooker in the process of cooking.

4. Add the oyster sauce and water. Stir well, cover rice cooker, and allow to reach a simmer.

5. Once simmering, return pork to the pot and add the tofu, salt, and pepper. Cover rice cooker and allow to reach a simmer again in about 8 to 10 minutes. If the mixture boils too vigorously, switch to Warm and continue to simmer for the remaining 10 minutes.

6. Garnish with green onions before serving.

Marinated Scrambled Tofu with Peppers and Onions

You can buy ready-marinated tofu from Asian supermarkets. The tofu usually is pre-marinated in five-spice powder.

INGREDIENTS | SERVES 2 OR 3

1 (10-ounce) block firm tofu, sliced to 1-inch cubes
3 cloves garlic, finely minced
1 tablespoon dark soy sauce
¼ teaspoon ground white pepper
¼ teaspoon ground black pepper
2 tablespoons vegetable oil
½ onion, thinly sliced
½ green bell pepper, diced

Cooking Tip
Finely minced garlic, compared to thinly sliced garlic or whole cloves, releases a lot more flavor for marinating purposes. In order to release full flavor for marinating, try crushing the garlic, then mincing it.

1. Place tofu cubes and garlic in a bowl and combine with soy sauce, white pepper, and black pepper. Set aside to marinate for 15 minutes.

2. Add the oil to the rice cooker, cover, and set to Cook. When the base of the cooker pot gets warm, add the onions and fry about 5 minutes until soft. Dish out and set side. Leave the remaining oil in the pot.

3. Drain the tofu (discard marinade). Add tofu to the pot and fry for 2 to 3 minutes. Add the bell peppers and fry for 2 to 3 minutes until bell peppers are slightly tender, covering rice cooker in the process of cooking.

4. Toward end of cooking, return the onions to the pot, mix well and cook for another 3 minutes, covering rice cooker in the process of cooking. Dish out and serve.

Tofu with Butternut Squash

Slice the butternut squash into smaller cubes to reduce cooking time.

INGREDIENTS | SERVES 2 OR 3

2 tablespoons vegetable oil
3 shallots, thinly sliced
1 clove garlic, finely minced
½ teaspoon grated ginger
1½ cups peeled and diced butternut squash (diced into ½-inch cubes)
½ teaspoon cumin seeds
2 tablespoons water
¼ teaspoon ground black pepper
1 (10-ounce) block firm tofu, sliced into ½-inch cubes, drained
1 tablespoon finely chopped cilantro, divided use

1. Add the oil to the rice cooker, cover, and set to Cook. When the base of the cooker pot gets warm, add the shallots, garlic, ginger, butternut squash, and cumin seeds. Fry for 3 to 5 minutes, until shallots and butternut squash turn slightly soft, covering rice cooker occasionally in the process of cooking.

2. Add the water and pepper. Mix well, cover rice cooker, and allow butternut squash to cook for about 8 to 10 minutes until tender, switching to Warm if the moisture begins to dry off.

3. Once the butternut squash becomes tender, add the tofu and ½ tablespoon cilantro. Gently mix well and cover rice cooker for about 1 minute. Garnish with remaining cilantro before serving.

Tofu with Bean Sprouts and Spices

As a variation, you can use soybean sprouts instead of mung bean sprouts in this recipe.

INGREDIENTS | SERVES 2 OR 3

1 tablespoon vegetable oil
2 shallots, thinly sliced
½ teaspoon grated ginger
½ teaspoon turmeric
½ teaspoon ground cumin
¼ teaspoon red chili pepper flakes
½ tablespoon butter
Salt and ground black pepper, to taste
1 (10-ounce) block firm tofu, sliced into bite-sized cubes (about 1 inch), drained
3 tablespoons water
3 cups mung bean sprouts

1. Add the oil to the rice cooker, cover, and set to Cook. When the base of the cooker pot gets warm, add the shallots and fry about 3 minutes until slightly soft.

2. Add the ginger, turmeric, cumin, chili flakes, butter, salt, and pepper. Fry about 5 minutes until fragrant, covering rice cooker occasionally in the process of frying.

3. Add the tofu, water, and bean sprouts. Mix well, cover rice cooker, and allow to reach a simmer.

4. Once simmering, switch to Warm and cook about 5 to 8 minutes until mixture is almost dry.

Tofu Patties

You can add ½ cup mashed white beans (canned) while mashing the tofu to make the patties more substantial.

INGREDIENTS | SERVES 2 TO 3

1 (10-ounce) block firm tofu, drained
2 shallots, chopped
½-inch piece ginger, sliced
½ teaspoon turmeric
½ teaspoon cumin seeds
1 teaspoon Worcestershire sauce
Salt and ground black pepper, to taste
1 egg
1 teaspoon corn flour
4 tablespoons vegetable oil, divided use (about 2 tablespoons each batch)

1. In a large bowl, mash the tofu with a fork until thick and pasty.

2. Combine shallots, ginger, turmeric, cumin seeds, Worcestershire sauce, salt, and pepper in a food processor and blend to a smooth texture.

3. Mix blended mixture into mashed tofu. Add egg and corn flour into the mixture. Mix with your fingers until evenly combined and mixture is sticky and holds together. Drain excess liquid. Form into patties and set aside.

4. Add oil to the rice cooker, cover, and set to Cook. When the base of the cooker pot gets warm, add the patties (in batches), and fry each side for about 3 minutes or until browned. Cover rice cooker while frying. Repeat with the remaining oil and patties.

CHAPTER 17

Vegetables

Steamed Napa Cabbage
with Ham
244

Snow Peas with Bell Peppers
244

Steamed Eggplant
245

Easy Chinese Vegetable Stew
246

Stir-Fried Long Beans
247

Stir-Fried Chinese Cabbage
248

Stir-Fried Asparagus
with Scallops
248

Curry Vegetables
249

Indian Potato and Cauliflower
(*Aloo Gobi*)
250

Cabbage and Cauliflower Curry
with Peas
251

Indian Braised Okra
251

Indian Eggplant Stew
252

Brussels Sprouts in Oyster Sauce
253

Buttered Brussels Sprouts
254

Kale with Mushrooms
254

French Green Beans and
Carrots with Herbs
255

Creamed Spinach
255

Buttered Kai Lan with Shallots
256

Swiss Chard with Raisins
257

Okra Stew
258

Steamed Napa Cabbage with Ham

Steamed napa cabbage can never be tasteless and bland when savory ham combines with the sweetness of the cabbage. Substitute deli ham for the Canadian bacon if preferred.

INGREDIENTS | SERVES 4

1 teaspoon oyster sauce

½ cup warm water

1 medium-sized (12 to 16 ounces) napa cabbage, separated into whole leaves and blanched

2 slices Canadian bacon, cut into thin strips

1. Fill the rice cooker pot with water to about the 4-cup mark. Cover and set to Cook.
2. Stir the oyster sauce and warm water in a bowl. Set aside as sauce.
3. Assemble the cabbage leaves on a plate that fits into the steamer insert or basket, layering Canadian bacon strips among and in between the blanched cabbage leaves. Pour the sauce over the cabbage.
4. When the water in the rice cooker boils, place the steamer insert or basket that holds the plate of cabbage into the rice cooker. Steam, with the rice cooker covered, for 10 to 12 minutes or more, until the leaves soften.

Snow Peas with Bell Peppers

The ends of the pea pods may be fibrous. Prior to using, trim off the tips at both ends of the pod.

INGREDIENTS | SERVES 2

1 tablespoon vegetable oil

1 clove garlic, finely minced

4 fresh shiitake mushroom caps, cut into halves

8 ounces snow peas

3 tablespoons water

½ green bell pepper, seeded and sliced (about ½-inch thick)

½ red bell pepper, seeded and sliced (about ½-inch thick)

Salt and ground white pepper, to taste

1. Add oil to the rice cooker, cover, and set to Cook. When the base of the cooker pot gets warm, fry the minced garlic about 3 minutes until fragrant.
2. Add the mushrooms and fry about 2 to 3 minutes, stirring and covering the rice cooker occasionally in the process of frying.
3. Add snow peas and continue frying for 2 to 3 minutes, adding the water gradually. Cover rice cooker occasionally in the process of frying.
4. Add the green and red bell peppers, mix well, and fry for 3 to 5 minutes, covering rice cooker occasionally in the process. Add salt and white pepper to taste and serve.

Steamed Eggplant

Eggplant is known as aubergine or brinjal in different parts of the world.

INGREDIENTS | SERVES 4

½ teaspoon light soy sauce
1 teaspoon sesame oil
2 tablespoons warm water
3 tablespoons hot water
2 small eggplants, ends trimmed, cut lengthwise into 4 slices each
2 teaspoons grated ginger

Cooking Tip
Eggplant is known for its ability to absorb oil during cooking and may turn out greasy if cooked the wrong way. Steaming is definitely a healthy method of cooking eggplant.

1. Fill the rice cooker pot with water to about the 4-cup mark. Cover the rice cooker and set to Cook.

2. Meanwhile, stir the soy sauce, sesame oil, and hot water in a bowl. Set aside as sauce.

3. Arrange the eggplant slices, cut-side up, evenly across a plate that fits in the steamer insert or basket. Top with the grated ginger.

4. When the water in the rice cooker boils, place the steamer insert or basket that holds the plate of eggplant into the rice cooker. Steam, with the rice cooker covered, for 10 to 15 minutes or more, until the eggplant softens and cooks through.

5. Drizzle the sauce over the steamed eggplant before serving.

Easy Chinese Vegetable Stew

This dish is often referred to as Lo Han Chai, and is also known as Buddha's Delight. If you are strictly vegetarian, replace the oyster sauce with a vegetarian version, or simply omit it.

INGREDIENTS | SERVES 3 OR 4

1 teaspoon oyster sauce

2 teaspoons brown sugar

½ cup warm water

2 tablespoons vegetable oil

1 tablespoon salted soybeans, mashed with back of spoon

1 head round or napa cabbage, leaves separated, rinsed, and cut into about 2-inch long slices

8 fresh shiitake mushroom caps, cut into halves

½ (10-ounce) pack of firm tofu, sliced to the length of cabbage slices

1 cup warm water (adjust as needed during cooking)

3 ounces mung bean vermicelli, soaked in warm water for 5 minutes to soften

Salt and ground white pepper, to taste

1. Mix oyster sauce, brown sugar, and ½ cup warm water in a bowl. Set aside as sauce.

2. Add the oil to the rice cooker, cover, and set to Cook. When the base of the cooker pot gets warm, add the salted soybeans and fry about 3 minutes until fragrant.

3. Add the cabbage, followed by mushrooms and tofu, and mix well. When cabbage softens, stir in the sauce mixture, mix well, cover rice cooker, and allow to reach a simmer.

4. Once the mixture is simmering, switch to Warm and simmer, covered, for about 15 or more minutes until vegetables and mushrooms soften, adding water (adjust accordingly from 1 cup) if mixture is too dry. Stir occasionally.

5. Stir in vermicelli and simmer for another 2 to 3 minutes. Add salt and pepper to taste before serving.

Stir-Fried Long Beans

This recipe is adapted from the classic Szechuan dish Four-Season Long Beans, or Szechuan Sautéed Long Beans. In the original recipe the long beans are deep-fried. This version eliminates the deep-frying, making it easier to prepare at home.

INGREDIENTS | SERVES 2

1 tablespoon vegetable oil
2 cloves garlic, finely minced
1 teaspoon grated ginger
½ pound ground pork
8 ounces long beans, blanched, then cut into finger-length pieces
1 green onion, finely chopped

1. Add oil to the rice cooker, cover, and set to Cook. When the base of the cooker pot gets warm, add the garlic and ginger and fry about 3 minutes until fragrant.

2. Add the ground pork (break up into smaller bits) and fry for 8 to 10 minutes until browned and cooked through. Dish out and set aside. Leave the remaining oil in the pot.

3. Add the long beans to the pot and fry for 5 to 8 minutes until soft and tender, covering rice cooker occasionally in the process of frying.

4. Return the pork to the pot and fry with the long beans for additional 2 to 3 minutes. Add the green onions and mix well before serving.

Stir-Fried Chinese Cabbage

This dish is typically made by stir-frying cabbage and Chinese dried shrimp. Because the dried shrimp may not be readily available, this recipe substitutes shallots and slightly caramelizes them for extra flavor.

INGREDIENTS | SERVES 2 OR 3

1 tablespoon vegetable oil
5 shallots, thinly sliced
2 cloves garlic, finely minced
1 head (12 to 16 ounces) Chinese cabbage, thinly sliced
Salt and ground white pepper, to taste
3 tablespoons water

1. Add oil to the rice cooker, cover, and set to Cook. When the base of the cooker pot gets warm, fry shallots about 3 minutes until slightly caramelized.

2. Add the garlic and cabbage and fry for 3 to 4 minutes until cabbage slightly softens, covering rice cooker occasionally in the process of frying. Add salt and white pepper and mix well.

3. Add the water, cover rice cooker, and allow to simmer for 10 to 15 minutes, until cabbage softens further and is cooked through. Switch to Warm if mixture starts to dry out too quickly.

Stir-Fried Asparagus with Scallops

If you do not want to bite on thin slices of ginger while enjoying this dish, substitute grated ginger.

INGREDIENTS | SERVES 2

1 tablespoon vegetable oil
4 jumbo scallops, sliced into quarters
6 ounces thin asparagus, cut into finger-length pieces
½-inch piece ginger, thinly sliced
2 tablespoons water
Salt and ground white pepper, to taste

1. Add oil to the rice cooker, cover, and set to Cook. When the base of the cooker pot gets warm, add the scallops and fry each side, with rice cooker covered, for 1 to 2 minutes until scallops are cooked through (fully whitened). Dish out and set aside. Leave the remaining oil in the pot.

2. Add the asparagus and sliced ginger to the pot and fry for about 2 to 3 minutes.

3. Add the water and allow asparagus to simmer until tender, stirring and covering rice cooker occasionally. Add salt and white pepper to taste.

4. Return the scallops to the pot and mix well with the asparagus before serving.

Curry Vegetables

This dish can be made into another popular dish known as Lontong, *which is essentially the curry vegetables with* ketupat *(rice cakes) added.*

INGREDIENTS | SERVES 3 OR 4

8 dried red chili peppers, soaked in warm water for 10 minutes
5 shallots, chopped
4 cloves garlic, peeled
1-inch piece ginger, peeled
2 tablespoons curry powder
1 cup coconut milk, divided use
3 cups Vegetable Stock (page 18)
3 to 4 tablespoons vegetable oil
½ (10-ounce) pack firm tofu, cut to 2-inch squares, ½-inch thick
1 pound long beans, cut into finger-length pieces
1 carrot, sliced into bite-sized chunks
½ pound round cabbage, coarsely chopped
3 cups water (adjust as needed during cooking)
2 hard-boiled eggs, sliced into quarters, for garnish

Cooking Tip

For a more authentic version of this dish, *galangal* (Thai ginger) should be used. Galangal is aromatic and more pungent than ginger. This recipe has been adapted to the ingredients that are readily available in most supermarkets.

1. Drain the chilies and combine them with the shallots, garlic, ginger, and curry powder in a food processor. Grind to create a smooth curry paste and set aside.

2. In a small bowl, mix ½ cup coconut milk with the vegetable stock and set aside.

3. Add the oil to the rice cooker, cover, and set to Cook. When the base of the cooker pot gets warm, add the tofu and slightly fry about 5 to 8 minutes until brown on both sides. Remove and cut into smaller bite-sized pieces. Leave the remaining oil in the pot.

4. Add the curry paste to the pot and fry about 3 minutes until fragrant. Add the mixture of coconut milk and stock, cover rice cooker, and bring to a slight simmer.

5. Once simmering, add the long beans, carrots, cabbage, browned tofu, and 2 cups water and bring to a boil.

6. Once boiling, add remaining 1 cup water, switch to Warm, and simmer for about 12 to 15 minutes until vegetables are just tender but still firm.

7. Add remaining coconut milk and continue to simmer for about 5 minutes.

8. Remove from heat and garnish with hard-boiled eggs.

Indian Potato and Cauliflower (*Aloo Gobi*)

Quite simply, Aloo means potatoes, and Gobi means cauliflower. This is a popular dish in Indian cuisine. It is best served with basmati rice or Indian roti (bread).

INGREDIENTS | **SERVES 3 OR 4**

3 tablespoons vegetable oil
3 shallots, thinly sliced
½-inch piece ginger, finely minced
2 cloves garlic, finely minced
1 large potato, boiled, peeled, and cubed (about 1-inch cubes)
3 cups cauliflower florets, blanched
½ cup diced tomatoes, with juice
½ teaspoon cumin seeds
½ teaspoon garam masala
¼ teaspoon red chili powder
½ teaspoon turmeric
½ cup water
Salt and freshly ground black pepper, to taste
1 tablespoon coarsely chopped cilantro leaves and stems

1. Add the oil to the rice cooker, cover, and set to Cook. When the base of the cooker pot gets warm, add the shallots and fry about 3 minutes until soft.

2. Add the ginger and garlic and continue frying about 3 minutes.

3. Add the cubed potatoes and blanched cauliflower florets, followed by tomatoes, cumin seeds, garam masala, chili powder, and turmeric. Mix to ensure that the potatoes and cauliflower are well coated with the spices and fry about 5 to 8 minutes. Cover rice cooker occasionally in the process of frying.

4. Stir in the water, cover rice cooker, and bring to a simmer. Add salt and pepper to taste.

5. Once simmering, switch to Warm and continue to cook for about 10 to 12 minutes until cauliflower becomes tender and potatoes start to turn soft and able to break up easily. Add cilantro and mix well before serving.

Cabbage and Cauliflower Curry with Peas

To keep this recipe as simple as possible, you could use only one kind of vegetable, either the cabbage or the cauliflower, and just use more of it.

INGREDIENTS | SERVES 3 OR 4

- 3 tablespoons vegetable oil
- 1 onion, finely chopped
- 3 cloves garlic, finely minced
- 1 tablespoon curry powder
- 1 teaspoon ground turmeric
- ½ teaspoon red chili flakes
- 3 cups cauliflower florets
- 8 ounces round cabbage, thinly sliced (about ½-inch thick)
- 1 cup frozen peas, thawed
- 1 cup water
- Salt and freshly ground black pepper, to taste
- ½ cup coconut milk

1. Add the oil to the rice cooker, cover, and set to Cook. When the base of the cooker pot gets warm, add the onion, garlic, curry powder, turmeric, and chili flakes and fry for about 3 to 4 minutes until onion turns slightly soft and the mixture is fragrant, covering rice cooker occasionally in the process of cooking.

2. Add the cauliflower, cabbage, peas, water, salt, and pepper. Mix well. Cover the rice cooker and allow it to come to a slight simmer. Cook for about 15 minutes, switching to Warm if the mixture bubbles too quickly or starts to dry out.

3. Toward end of cooking, slowly stir in coconut milk. Mix well and simmer for 2 minutes before serving.

Indian Braised Okra

Use grated garlic and ginger instead of minced to reduce preparation time.

INGREDIENTS | SERVES 2 OR 3

- ½ tablespoon butter
- 3 shallots, thinly sliced
- ½ pound fresh okra, cubed (about ½-inch cubes)
- ½-inch piece ginger, finely minced
- 2 cloves garlic, finely minced
- ½ cup diced tomatoes, with juice
- ½ teaspoon cumin
- ½ teaspoon turmeric
- ½ cup water
- Salt and black pepper, to taste

1. Add the butter to the rice cooker, cover, and set to Cook. When the base of the cooker pot gets warm, add the shallots and fry about 3 minutes until soft.

2. Add the okra, followed by all the remaining ingredients. Cover and cook for about 5 minutes, stirring occasionally.

3. Switch the rice cooker to Warm. With the rice cooker covered, simmer for 12 to 15 minutes, stirring occasionally until okra is tender. Serve with either rice or Indian *roti* (bread).

Indian Eggplant Stew

Stewing is a good method to cook eggplants since you can control the amount of fat. Use 2 to 3 tablespoons extra-virgin olive oil instead of butter for a healthier recipe.

INGREDIENTS | SERVES 2 OR 3

½ tablespoon butter
3 shallots, thinly sliced
2 cloves garlic, finely minced
½-inch piece ginger, finely minced
½ teaspoon ground cumin
½ teaspoon turmeric
½ teaspoon red chili pepper flakes
1 medium-sized eggplant, cubed (about 1-inch cubes)
½ (14½-ounce) can diced tomatoes, with juice
3 tablespoons water or Vegetable Stock (page 18)
Salt and ground black pepper, to taste

1. Add the butter to the rice cooker, cover, and set to Cook. When the base of the cooker pot gets warm, add the shallots, garlic, ginger, cumin, turmeric, and red chili flakes and fry for about 5 minutes until shallots are soft, covering rice cooker occasionally in the process of frying.

2. Add the eggplant and mix well with the spices. Cook for about 5 minutes, stirring and covering rice cooker occasionally in the process of cooking.

3. Add the tomatoes, water or stock, salt, and pepper. Mix well, switch to Warm, cover the rice cooker, and simmer for about 15 minutes or more, stirring occasionally until eggplant is tender. Serve with either rice or Indian *roti* (bread).

Brussels Sprouts in Oyster Sauce

Undercooked Brussels sprouts usually taste slightly bitter and may turn off many people.

INGREDIENTS | SERVES 2 OR 3

8 Brussels sprouts, cut into halves
1 teaspoon oyster sauce
½ cup warm water
1 tablespoon vegetable oil
1 clove garlic, finely minced
½ teaspoon grated ginger
Salt and ground white pepper, to taste

Cooking Tip

Brussels sprouts seldom come in uniform sizes. To prepare the bigger sprouts for cooking, use a paring knife to cut a small cross at the bottom, about ½-inch deep into the sprouts. This will ensure that the bigger sprouts cook faster than they otherwise would and all the sprouts will be cooked evenly in the same amount of time.

1. Place Brussels sprouts on a plate that will fit into the steamer insert or basket. Set aside.

2. Fill the rice cooker pot with water to about the 4-cup mark, cover, and set to Cook.

3. In a small bowl, mix the oyster sauce with warm water. Set aside as sauce.

4. When the water in the rice cooker boils, place the steamer insert or basket that holds the plate of Brussels sprouts into the rice cooker and steam, with the rice cooker covered, for 3 to 4 minutes until sprouts slightly soften. Drain excess water from the Brussels sprouts and set aside.

5. Clean out rice cooker and wipe dry. Add the oil to the rice cooker, cover, and set to Cook. When the base of the cooker pot gets warm, add garlic and ginger, followed by Brussels sprouts, placed cut-side down. Fry for 2 to 3 minutes, covering the rice cooker occasionally in the process of cooking.

6. Add the sauce mixture, salt, and pepper, and mix well. Allow to simmer for 1 to 2 minutes, switching to Warm if mixture bubbles too vigorously.

Buttered Brussels Sprouts

As this recipe uses only a few basic ingredients, try to play on the spice factor by mixing white and black pepper to give more depth, flavor, and aroma to the dish.

INGREDIENTS | **SERVES 2 OR 3**

8 Brussels sprouts, cut into halves
½ tablespoon butter
Salt and freshly ground black pepper, to taste

1. Place Brussels sprouts on a plate that fits into the steamer insert or basket. Set aside.

2. Fill the rice cooker pot with water to about the 4-cup mark. Cover the rice cooker and set to Cook. When the water in the rice cooker boils, place the steamer insert or basket that holds the plate of Brussels sprouts into the rice cooker and steam, covered, for 3 to 4 minutes until sprouts slightly soften. Drain excess water from the Brussels sprouts and set aside.

3. Clean out the rice cooker and wipe dry. Add the butter to the rice cooker, cover, and set to Cook. When the base of the cooker pot gets warm, add Brussels sprouts, cut-side down, and fry for about 2 to 3 minutes until tender. Before serving, add salt and freshly ground black pepper. Toss well.

Kale with Mushrooms

Add pine nuts to give an added crunch and texture to this otherwise soft-textured dish.

INGREDIENTS | **SERVES 2**

2 tablespoons extra-virgin olive oil
4 cups tightly packed, finely chopped kale
4 ounces cremini mushroom caps, thinly sliced
½ cup water (adjust as needed during cooking)
Salt and freshly ground black pepper, to taste

1. Add the oil to the rice cooker, cover, and set to Cook. When the base of the cooker pot gets warm, add the kale and mushrooms, and pan-fry for about 2 to 3 minutes, until the vegetables become tender. Add water if mixture is too dry.

2. Add salt and pepper and toss well for another 1 to 2 minutes before serving.

French Green Beans and Carrots with Herbs

When Asians refer to long beans, they usually mean Chinese long beans or yard-long beans. These are different from the shorter-length green beans or French green beans. The taste is different as well, so it may be tricky if you choose to substitute.

INGREDIENTS | SERVES 2

1 tablespoon olive oil
1 clove garlic, grated
1 teaspoon grated ginger
8 ounces French green beans, cut into finger-length pieces
1 cup shredded carrots
2 tablespoons water
½ teaspoon dried oregano

1. Add the oil to the rice cooker, cover, and set to Cook. When the base of the cooker pot gets warm, add garlic and ginger, followed by beans and carrots. Pan-fry for about 2 to 3 minutes, covering rice cooker occasionally in the process of frying.

2. Gradually stir in the water, cover rice cooker, and allow to simmer for 2 to 3 minutes until beans and carrots become tender and cook through, switching to Warm if the mixture bubbles too vigorously or dries out too quickly.

3. Before serving, sprinkle dried oregano over the vegetables. Best served as a side dish with a main course of grilled fish.

Creamed Spinach

If using fresh baby spinach, make sure the moisture from blanching the spinach is fully drained. You must try to remove as much moisture as possible so that it will not affect the creamy consistency of the final dish.

INGREDIENTS | SERVES 2

1 tablespoon butter
¼ cup finely chopped shallots
½ pound frozen spinach, thawed
¼ cup heavy cream
Salt and freshly ground black pepper, to taste

1. Add the butter to the rice cooker, cover, and set to Cook. When the base of the cooker pot gets warm, add the shallots and pan-fry for about 2 to 3 minutes, until shallots turn soft and slightly caramelize.

2. Add the spinach and cook, stirring about 5 minutes, just until the liquid is released.

3. Slowly add the cream and cook about 8 to 10 minutes until cream reduces by almost half, covering rice cooker in the process of cooking. Switch to Warm and simmer for about 2 to 3 minutes, stirring occasionally until the mixture is thick and creamy.

4. Add salt and pepper and stir well into the creamed mixture. Remove from the heat and serve immediately.

Buttered Kai Lan with Shallots

Also known as Chinese broccoli or Chinese kale, Kai Lan has slightly bitter leaves and thick stems. It is a popular vegetable, especially in Cantonese cuisines. This recipe uses some butter to bring a richer taste and aroma to the dish.

INGREDIENTS | SERVES 2

1 tablespoon extra-virgin olive oil
½ tablespoon butter
4 shallots, thinly sliced
3 small bundles Kai Lan, stalks and leaves separated
½ cup water (adjust as needed during cooking)
Salt, to taste

Cooking Tip

The thick stems of Kai Lan take a long time to cook compared to the leaves. It is important to cook the stems first, then add the leaves toward the end of cooking. This will ensure that the vegetable is uniformly cooked.

1. Add the oil to the rice cooker, cover, and set to Cook. When the base of the cooker pot gets warm, add the butter and shallots and pan-fry for about 3 to 4 minutes, until shallots turn soft and slightly caramelized, covering rice cooker occasionally in the process of frying. Remove and set aside. Leave the remaining oil in the pot.

2. Add the Kai Lan stalks to the pot and pan-fry for about 2 minutes, covering the rice cooker occasionally in the process of cooking.

3. Add the Kai Lan leaves and toss well with the stalks. Add 2 tablespoons of water, cover the rice cooker, and allow to simmer for 1 to 2 minutes.

4. Sprinkle with salt and return the shallots to the pot. Toss well in the pot before serving. If mixture appears too dry, add remaining water, cover rice cooker, and simmer for about 1 to 2 minutes, then serve.

Swiss Chard with Raisins

Add some toasted nuts to complement the sweet and tender raisins.

INGREDIENTS | SERVES 2

2 tablespoons extra-virgin olive oil
½ cup thinly sliced onions
½ pound Swiss chard, leaves and stems separated, both coarsely chopped
¼ cup golden raisins, divided use
½ cup water, divided use

Do You Know?
Mature chard leaves and stalks are typically cooked to reduce the bitter flavor, especially in the stems. Lemon juice may be added to offset the bitterness of the dish.

1. Add the oil to the rice cooker, cover, and set to Cook. When the base of the cooker pot gets warm, add the onions and fry about 5 minutes until soft, covering rice cooker occasionally in the process of frying.

2. Add the chard stems and fry for about 2 minutes. Add half the raisins and ¼ cup of the water and allow to simmer for 3 to 4 minutes, covering the rice cooker, until stems are softened.

3. Add chard leaves and remaining water and simmer, covered, for about 2 to 3 minutes until leaves become tender.

4. Sprinkle the remaining raisins over the vegetables before serving.

Okra Stew

This recipe is adapted from gumbo, using some of the key gumbo ingredients such as onions and bell peppers.

INGREDIENTS | SERVES 2 OR 3

2 tablespoons extra-virgin olive oil
2 cloves garlic, finely minced
1 medium-sized onion, finely chopped
1 cup finely chopped green bell peppers
1 cup finely chopped red bell peppers
½ pound okra, sliced into cubes (about ½-inch cubes)
6 ounces white mushrooms, sliced
½ (14½-ounce) can diced tomatoes, with juice
2 bay leaves
¼ cup water
Salt and ground black pepper, to taste
½ tablespoon all-purpose flour

1. Add the oil to the rice cooker, cover, and set to Cook. When the base of the cooker pot gets warm, add the garlic, onion, and bell peppers. Fry about 5 minutes until tender, covering rice cooker occasionally in the process of frying.

2. Add the okra, mushrooms, diced tomatoes, bay leaves, water, salt, and pepper. Cover rice cooker and allow to reach a slight simmer. Stir occasionally, then switch rice cooker to Warm and simmer for about 30 minutes until mixture reaches a slightly thick stew consistency.

3. About 5 minutes before the end of cooking, add the flour, stirring occasionally to further thicken the stew. Remove the bay leaves before serving.

CHAPTER 18

Mushrooms

Steamed Stuffed Mushrooms
260

Mushroom and Barley Soup
261

Mushroom Stew
262

Mushroom Curry
263

Mushroom Korma
264

Mushrooms and
Green Pea Masala
265

Three-Cup Mushrooms
266

Mushrooms in Ginger and Soy
267

Stir-Fry Mushrooms with
Celery and Carrots
268

Lightly Spiced Mushrooms
with Beef
269

Garlic Mushrooms
270

Buttered Mushrooms with
Onions and Herbs
270

Spicy Mushrooms
271

Steamed Stuffed Mushrooms

Mushrooms absorb moisture quite readily. With the marinated pork stuffing and sauce, the mushrooms become plump, juicy, and moist when steamed.

INGREDIENTS | SERVES 2 OR 3

¼ pound ground pork
½ tablespoon dark soy sauce
1 tablespoon Chinese cooking wine
1 teaspoon grated ginger
1 tablespoon finely chopped green onions, divided use
½ teaspoon sesame oil
Salt and ground white pepper, to taste
½ tablespoon corn flour
½ lightly whisked egg
6 large fresh shiitake mushroom caps
1 teaspoon oyster sauce
½ teaspoon grated ginger
½ teaspoon brown sugar
Ground white pepper, to taste
3 tablespoons water

Cooking Tip

Try to get mushrooms with medium or large caps, to allow room for stuffing. However, a smaller mushroom cap is a good idea if you intend to serve these as appetizers or starters, as they look cute and presentable.

1. In a bowl, combine the pork with soy sauce, Chinese cooking wine, ginger, ½ tablespoon green onions, sesame oil, salt, pepper, corn flour, and egg. Form the mixture into meatballs (1-inch diameter) or a size that will fit into mushroom cavity. Stuff the pork mixture into the mushroom caps and set aside on a plate that will fit into the steamer insert or basket.

2. In a separate bowl, mix the oyster sauce, ginger, brown sugar, pepper, and water into a sauce and ladle over the stuffed mushrooms. Cover the plate of stuffed mushrooms with plastic wrap to prevent excess condensation during steaming.

3. Fill the rice cooker pot with water to about the 3-cup mark. Cover and set to Cook. When the water boils, place the steamer insert or basket that holds the plate of mushrooms into the rice cooker, cover rice cooker, and steam for about 15 minutes until the pork cooks through.

4. Garnish with remaining green onions before serving.

Mushroom and Barley Soup

It is best to use at least two varieties of mushrooms to increase the depth of earthy flavors in this dish.

INGREDIENTS | SERVES 2 OR 3

- 4 cups water
- 2 ounces washed and cleaned pearl barley, soaked about 4 hours before using
- 1 tablespoon extra-virgin olive oil
- 3 shallots, thinly sliced
- 4 fresh shiitake mushroom caps, thinly sliced
- 6 white mushroom caps, thinly sliced
- 6 brown mushroom caps, thinly sliced
- ½ tablespoon butter
- 2 cups Vegetable Stock (page 18)
- 1 bay leaf
- Salt and freshly ground black pepper, to taste
- ½ teaspoon dried oregano, for garnish

1. Fill the rice cooker pot with 4 cups water. Cover the rice cooker and set to Cook. When water boils, add the barley, cover rice cooker, and boil about 25 minutes until barley softens. Strain the barley, reserving 2 cups of barley water. Set aside.

2. Clean out the rice cooker and wipe dry. Add the oil to the rice cooker, cover, and set to Cook. When the base of the cooker pot gets warm, add the shallots and fry about 3 minutes until slightly soft.

3. Add the mushrooms and fry for about 5 minutes or until mushrooms turn slightly tender, covering rice cooker occasionally in the process of frying.

4. Add the butter and mix well with mushrooms. Add the cooked barley and reserved barley water, vegetable stock, bay leaf, salt, and pepper. Mix well, cover rice cooker, and allow to come to boil.

5. Once boiling, switch to Warm and allow to simmer for about 20 minutes until mushrooms become tender. Remove bay leaves before serving.

6. Garnish with oregano and serve with crusty rolls.

Mushroom Stew

Place mushrooms in a vented package (such as a paper bag) and store them in the vegetable drawer of the refrigerator where there is cool air circulation.

INGREDIENTS | SERVES 2 OR 3

2 tablespoons extra-virgin olive oil
1 medium-sized onion, thinly sliced
2 cloves garlic, finely minced
½ pound brown cremini mushroom caps, cleaned and roughly chopped
½ pound fresh shiitake mushroom caps, cleaned and roughly chopped
½ tablespoon butter
1 medium-sized potato, peeled and cubed (about ½-inch cubes)
1 teaspoon finely chopped fresh rosemary
1 teaspoon finely chopped fresh sage
1 teaspoon fresh thyme
2 cups Vegetable Stock (page 18), or enough to immerse the potatoes and mushrooms
1 tablespoon finely chopped fresh parsley
Salt and freshly ground black pepper, to taste

1. Add the oil to the rice cooker, cover, and set to Cook. When the base of the cooker pot gets warm, add the onions and fry about 5 minutes until slightly soft. Add the garlic and fry about 3 minutes until fragrant.

2. Add the mushrooms and fry for about 3 minutes until mushrooms become soft (start to give off their liquid). Stir frequently, covering the rice cooker occasionally in the process of cooking.

3. Add the butter, followed by potatoes, rosemary, sage, and thyme. Mix well. Stir in the vegetable stock, cover rice cooker, and allow to come to a boil.

4. Once boiling, switch to Warm and simmer for about 20 minutes until potatoes are soft and disintegrate when pierced with a fork and the soup slightly thickens.

5. Stir in parsley, salt, and pepper. Mix well and cook at Warm for about 2 to 3 minutes. Serve immediately.

Cooking Tip

If you intend to have leftovers, store the stew covered in an airtight container in the refrigerator for up to three days. If it becomes too thick to be reheated, add some extra stock to thin it down.

Mushroom Curry

Many supermarkets sell prepackaged mixed-variety fresh mushrooms. Be on the lookout for this convenient choice.

INGREDIENTS | SERVES 2 OR 3

2 tablespoons vegetable oil
3 shallots, thinly sliced
1 clove garlic, finely minced
1 teaspoon grated ginger
½ teaspoon ground fennel seeds
1-inch cinnamon stick
3 cloves
1 teaspoon curry powder
¼ teaspoon turmeric
½ teaspoon ground black pepper
½ teaspoon red chili powder
1 tomato, finely chopped
½ pound mixed mushroom caps, roughly chopped
2 cups water (adjust as needed during cooking)
Salt, to taste
1 tablespoon finely chopped cilantro leaves, for garnish

1. Add the oil to the rice cooker, cover, and set to Cook. When the base of the cooker pot gets warm, add the shallots and fry about 3 minutes until slightly soft.

2. Add the garlic, ginger, fennel, cinnamon, and cloves. Fry about 3 minutes until fragrant.

3. Add the curry powder, turmeric, pepper, and chili powder. Mix well.

4. Stir in tomatoes and cook for about 8 to 10 minutes, cover rice cooker occasionally in the process of cooking.

5. Add the mushrooms, water, and salt. Cover the rice cooker and allow to come to a boil.

6. Once boiling, switch to Warm and simmer for 30 minutes until mushrooms become tender.

7. Garnish with cilantro before serving.

Mushroom Korma

Korma is a type of mild curry or stew made by adding milk, cream, yogurt, or coconut milk.

INGREDIENTS | SERVES 2 OR 3

2 tablespoons vegetable oil
1 medium-sized onion, thinly sliced
1 teaspoon grated ginger
1 clove garlic, finely minced
½ teaspoon ground cumin
½ teaspoon ground coriander
2 cardamom pods
½ teaspoon turmeric
½ pound mixed (white and cremini) mushrooms, whole caps without stem
3 tablespoons water
½ cup plain yogurt
Salt and ground black pepper, to taste
1 tablespoon finely chopped cilantro leaves, for garnish

1. Add the oil to the rice cooker, cover, and set to Cook. When the base of the cooker pot gets warm, add the onions and fry about 5 minutes until slightly soft.

2. Add the ginger, garlic, cumin, coriander, cardamom, and turmeric and fry for about 2 minutes, stirring constantly, until fragrant.

3. Add the mushrooms and water, cover rice cooker, and bring to a simmer.

4. Once simmering, add the yogurt, stir gently, switch to Warm, and cook about 20 minutes, stirring occasionally until the mushrooms are tender.

5. Add salt and pepper. Garnish with cilantro leaves.

Cooking Tip

Yogurt is a popular dairy product used in Indian cooking. It can be a good substitute for cream or milk but it does not work in every recipe. It depends on the dish itself. Yogurt tends to be slightly sour, so in a recipe that uses milk and lemon juice as ingredients, yogurt might be a good substitution.

Mushrooms and Green Pea Masala

Ghee is often used in Indian cooking as the cooking oil. You can substitute the vegetable oil in this recipe with ghee, and the flavors brought to the final dish will be different.

INGREDIENTS | SERVES 2 OR 3

2 tablespoons vegetable oil
1 medium-sized onion, thinly sliced
1 teaspoon grated ginger
1 clove garlic, finely minced
¼ teaspoon turmeric
½ teaspoon red chili powder
½ (14½-ounce) can diced tomatoes, with juice
½ teaspoon ground cumin
½ teaspoon ground coriander
¼ teaspoon garam masala
½ pound mixed (white and cremini) mushrooms, whole caps without stem
1 cup frozen peas
½ cup water
Salt and ground black pepper, to taste

1. Add the oil to the rice cooker, cover, and set to Cook. When the base of the cooker pot gets warm, add onions and fry about 5 minutes until slightly soft.

2. Add the ginger, garlic, turmeric, and chili powder. Fry for about 2 minutes, stirring constantly, until fragrant.

3. Stir in tomatoes, cumin, coriander, garam masala, mushrooms, peas, and water. Cover rice cooker and bring to a simmer.

4. Once simmering, lift up rice cooker lid, stir occasionally, and continue to simmer about 10 to 12 minutes until gravy slightly reduces (thickens) and mushrooms are tender.

5. Add salt and pepper, and stir well. Cover rice cooker, switch to Warm, and simmer for about 1 minute.

Three-Cup Mushrooms

You can find oyster mushrooms and trumpet mushrooms in most Asian supermarkets and some other larger supermarkets. These are "meaty" mushrooms and are good substitutes when adapting meat recipes to vegetarian recipes.

INGREDIENTS | SERVES 2 OR 3

¼ cup dark soy sauce

½ cup water

¼ cup Chinese cooking wine, divided use

½ tablespoon brown sugar

¼ cup sesame oil

1 teaspoon grated ginger

2 cloves garlic, finely minced

3 ounces oyster mushrooms

3 ounces trumpet mushrooms, sliced along the stems

3 ounces shiitake mushrooms

½ cup fresh basil leaves

1 fresh red chili pepper, seeded and thinly sliced

1. In a small bowl, mix soy sauce, water, half the amount of Chinese cooking wine, and brown sugar. Set aside as sauce.

2. Add the oil to the rice cooker, cover, and set to Cook. When the base of the cooker pot gets warm, add the ginger and garlic and fry about 3 minutes until fragrant.

3. Add the mushrooms and fry about 5 to 8 minutes until mushrooms turn slightly tender, covering rice cooker occasionally in the process.

4. Add the prepared sauce and stir well. Cover rice cooker and allow it to come to a simmer for 5 to 8 minutes, lifting rice cooker lid and stirring occasionally if mixture bubbles too vigorously. If bubbling too much, switch to Warm and simmer for about 15 minutes until mushrooms cook through and sauce slightly reduces (thickens).

5. Before serving, switch back to Cook. Once simmering, drizzle in remaining Chinese cooking wine and add fresh basil and red chili. Mix well and simmer for about 1 minute. Best served with steamed rice.

Cooking Tip

Oyster mushrooms have caps that look like a fan and have cream-colored gills. The caps grow directly on wood, and so the mushrooms have no stems. If the caps are too big, slice them into halves before using. Trumpet mushrooms look very different from oyster mushrooms. They have thick, fleshy stems and a small cap relative to the size of the stem. While the stems of some species of mushrooms tend to be tough and are not used in cooking, the thick stems of the trumpet mushrooms are firm and constitute the main "flesh" of these mushrooms. Thinly slice the stems before using.

Mushrooms in Ginger and Soy

There is always confusion about whether mushrooms should be washed prior to using. If you prefer not to wash the mushrooms under water to clean off dirt remnants, you can use a clean, damp cloth to gently wipe the caps and stems (if using the stems).

INGREDIENTS | SERVES 2

1 teaspoon grated ginger
1 tablespoon dark soy sauce
1 teaspoon sugar
1 cup water
2 tablespoons vegetable oil
1-inch piece fresh ginger, thinly shredded
½ pound fresh shiitake mushroom caps, sliced into quarters
Salt and ground white pepper, to taste
3 drops sesame oil

1. In a bowl, combine the grated ginger, dark soy sauce, sugar, and water. Mix well and set aside as sauce.

2. Add the oil to the rice cooker, cover, and set to Cook. When the base of the cooker pot gets warm, add the shredded ginger and fry about 3 minutes until fragrant. Add the mushrooms and mix well with the ginger.

3. Stir in the prepared sauce and mix it well with mushrooms. Add salt and pepper, cover rice cooker, and allow to reach simmer. Lift up rice cooker lid and continue to simmer about 5 to 8 minutes until sauce slightly reduces and thickens.

4. When sauce almost reduces, cover rice cooker, switch to Warm, and simmer for 5 more minutes.

5. Drizzle sesame oil over the mushrooms before serving.

Stir-Fry Mushrooms with Celery and Carrots

Japanese beech mushrooms are also known as buna shimeji *mushrooms. The most common varieties found in supermarkets are the brown and white beech mushrooms.*

INGREDIENTS | **SERVES 2**

1 teaspoon dark soy sauce
1 tablespoon oyster sauce
½ cup water
2 tablespoons vegetable oil
2 cloves garlic, finely minced
1 stalk celery, sliced into thin strips similar to the length of the mushrooms
½ carrot, sliced into thin strips similar to the length of the mushrooms
1 (3½-ounce) pack Japanese beech mushrooms
4 fresh shiitake mushroom caps, thinly sliced
¼ teaspoon ground white pepper
1 fresh red chili pepper, seeded and thinly sliced, for garnish

1. In a small bowl, mix soy sauce, oyster sauce, and water. Set aside as sauce.

2. Add the oil to the rice cooker, cover, and set to Cook. When the base of the cooker pot gets warm, add the garlic and fry about 3 minutes until fragrant.

3. Add the celery, carrots, and mushrooms, and fry for 3 to 5 minutes.

4. Add the prepared sauce mixture, mix well, cover rice cooker, and allow to reach a simmer. Once simmering, lift up rice cooker lid and continue simmering about 5 to 8 minutes until sauce slightly reduces (thickens).

5. When sauce almost reduces, add the pepper, cover rice cooker, switch to Warm, and simmer for about 10 minutes until vegetables are just tender and cooked.

6. Garnish with red chili before serving.

Lightly Spiced Mushrooms with Beef

This is not a curry dish and does not have much sauce or gravy, though it should still be moist when served.

INGREDIENTS | SERVES 2

2 tablespoons vegetable oil
3 shallots, thinly sliced
½ pound ground beef
1 (3½-ounce) pack Japanese beech mushrooms
1 teaspoon oyster sauce
1 teaspoon curry powder
Salt and ground black pepper, to taste
4 tablespoons water

Cooking Tip

It is important to cook ground beef thoroughly because it has a larger ratio of surface area to volume than does a whole piece of meat, and therefore is at greater risk of contamination by bacteria in the air.

1. Add the oil to the rice cooker, cover, and set to Cook. When the base of the cooker pot gets warm, add the shallots and fry about 3 minutes until slightly soft.

2. Add the ground beef (break up into smaller bits) and cook about 8 to 10 minutes until beef turns brown on the surface and is partially cooked through. Dish out and set aside.

3. Add the mushrooms to the pot and fry for about 5 minutes, until slightly soft, covering rice cooker occasionally in the process of cooking.

4. Return beef to the pot, mixing well with mushrooms. Add oyster sauce, curry powder, salt, pepper, and water; mix well again. Cover rice cooker and allow to cook for about 10 to 12 minutes, until beef cooks through and mushrooms turn soft and tender. If the mixture bubbles too vigorously or dries out too quickly, switch to Warm to continue cooking for the remainder of the 10 to 12 minutes until mushrooms and beef absorb most of the sauce.

Garlic Mushrooms

Spoon these mushrooms over warm toasted bread to serve. For more garlic flavor, rub crushed garlic on the toast and slather with some butter before topping with mushrooms.

INGREDIENTS | SERVES 2 OR 3

2 tablespoons butter, divided use
2 cloves garlic, crushed whole
½ pound mixed mushrooms, sliced
1 teaspoon finely chopped parsley
Salt and freshly ground black pepper, to taste

1. Add 1 tablespoon butter to the rice cooker and set to Cook. When the base of the cooker pot gets warm, add the garlic and fry about 3 minutes until fragrant.

2. Add the mushrooms and fry for 5 minutes. Add the remaining 1 tablespoon butter, stirring and covering rice cooker occasionally in the process of cooking. If the mushroom mixture dries out too quickly on the Cook setting, switch to Warm and continue to cook the mushrooms.

3. Once the mushrooms turn completely soft, add the parsley, salt, and pepper and mix well.

Buttered Mushrooms with Onions and Herbs

Cremini mushrooms are richer in flavor and nutrients than the white button mushrooms.

INGREDIENTS | SERVES 2

1 tablespoon extra-virgin olive oil
3 shallots, thinly sliced
½ pound crimini mushrooms, sliced
½ tablespoon butter
Salt and ground black pepper, to taste
½ teaspoon dried oregano
½ teaspoon dried basil

1. Add the oil to the rice cooker, cover, and set to Cook. When the base of the cooker pot gets warm, add the shallots and fry about 3 minutes until slightly soft.

2. Add the mushrooms and butter and fry for about 10 minutes, until mushrooms turn soft. Cover the rice cooker occasionally in the process of cooking. If the mushroom mixture dries out too quickly, switch to Warm, and continue to cook the mushrooms.

3. When mushrooms turn completely soft, add the salt, pepper, oregano, and basil. Mix well, cover rice cooker, set to Warm, and simmer for 2 minutes.

Spicy Mushrooms

Using a variety of mushrooms not only adds depth to a dish; it also provides a balanced nutrition profile.

INGREDIENTS | SERVES 2 OR 3

1 teaspoon oyster sauce
1 teaspoon chili sauce
1 teaspoon dark soy sauce
1 teaspoon balsamic vinegar
¼ teaspoon freshly ground black pepper
1 teaspoon sugar
2 tablespoons water
2 tablespoons vegetable oil
1 green onion, green top and white bottom portions separated, finely chopped and set aside separately
2 garlic cloves, crushed whole
½ pound mixed mushrooms, sliced

1. In a small bowl, combine the oyster sauce, chili sauce, soy sauce, vinegar, pepper, sugar, and water. Set aside as sauce.

2. Add the oil to the rice cooker, cover, and set to Cook. When the base of the cooker pot gets warm, add the green onions (white portions), followed by garlic. Fry about 3 minutes until fragrant.

3. Add the mushrooms and prepared sauce mixture and stir-fry for 5 minutes until mushrooms turn soft and cook through, covering rice cooker occasionally in the process of cooking. If the mushroom mixture dries out too quickly, switch to Warm, and continue to cook the mushrooms.

4. Once the mushrooms turn completely soft, garnish with remaining green onions (green portions).

Mushrooms and Nutrition

Different varieties of mushrooms contain different minerals. For example, cremini mushrooms are a rich source of selenium and B vitamins, but their iron content may not be as high as shiitake mushrooms.

CHAPTER 19

Desserts

Sweet Taro Crisps
273

Sweet Corn Pancakes
274

Caramelized All-Spiced Sweet Potato
275

Steamed Egg Cupcakes
276

Steamed Egg and Milk Custard
277

Barley Drink
277

Green Bean Soup
278

Red Bean Soup
278

Taro and Bananas in Sweet Coconut Milk
279

Steamed Black Rice Pudding
280

Sweet Snow Fungus and Ginkgo
281

Pink Lemonade with Basil
281

Honeydew and Snow Fungus in Sweet Coconut Milk
282

Sweet Taro Crisps

For something different, you can substitute chocolate chips for the sugar.

INGREDIENTS | SERVES 4

1 pound taro, cut into small pieces (about 2-inch cubes)
1 teaspoon brown sugar
1 teaspoon honey
4 tablespoons vegetable oil, divided use

Cooking Tip

Steam the taro with the skin on to retain nutrition, flavors, and moisture. The skin can be easily peeled after the taro is steamed.

1. Fill the rice cooker pot with water to about the 4-cup mark. Cover the rice cooker and set to Cook. Place the taro on a plate that will fit into the steamer insert or basket.

2. When the water boils, place the steamer insert or basket that holds the taro over the boiling water. Cover the rice cooker and steam for 15 to 20 minutes until taro softens and cooks through. Dish out.

3. Peel the taro and mash it gently and completely with the back of a fork. Combine with sugar and honey. Add 1 tablespoon oil to the mashed taro and mix well until oil is completely blended with the mashed taro.

4. Add remaining 3 tablespoons oil into the rice cooker, cover, and set to Cook. When the base of the cooker pot gets warm, form flat patties (about 2-inch diameter, 1-inch thick) from the mashed taro mixture and add (in batches) to the rice cooker. Pan-fry each side 3 to 4 minutes, until brown and crisp, covering rice cooker while frying each side.

5. Serve taro crisps with a drizzle of honey or maple syrup.

Sweet Corn Pancakes

To uniformly coat the base of the rice cooker pot with oil, use a food oil spray or a brush. You can also dab a piece of paper towel in vegetable oil and use that to coat the base of the pot.

INGREDIENTS | SERVES 4 TO 6

½ pound self-rising flour, sifted
½ teaspoon salt
3 tablespoons castor sugar
2 egg yolks
1 cup whole milk
½ (16-ounce) can corn kernels, drained
½ cup vegetable oil, divided use

1. In a large mixing bowl, combine sifted flour, salt, and sugar.

2. In another bowl, combine the eggs and milk and whisk gently.

3. Make a well in the center of the flour mixture and slowly pour in egg mixture. Stir to form a thick batter. Gently stir in corn kernels.

4. Add half the oil into the rice cooker, cover, and set to Cook. When the base of the cooker pot gets warm, drop tablespoons of batter (about 2 tablespoons batter to form about 3-inch diameter pancakes) into the pot. When bubbles appear on the surface of the pancakes in about 5 to 8 minutes, flip over to cook for another 1 to 2 minutes, until golden brown, covering pot while cooking each side. Continue until all batter is used up and adding remaining oil if oil added previously has been used up.

5. Serve finished pancakes warm with butter and honey.

Caramelized All-Spiced Sweet Potato

As a taste variation, you can try using five-spice powder instead of cinnamon and nutmeg powder. Five-spice powder is a blend of star anise, cinnamon, cloves, fennel, and Szechuan pepper.

INGREDIENTS | SERVES 4 TO 6

4 tablespoons vegetable oil

2 medium-sized sweet potatoes, peeled and sliced (about ¼-inch thick)

¼ cup brown sugar

½ teaspoon ground cinnamon

½ teaspoon ground nutmeg

Five-Spice or Seven-Spice

While five-spice is mostly related to Chinese cooking, seven-spice is related to Japanese and sometimes Thai cuisines. In Japanese cuisine, seven-spice is a mixture that may include spices such as sesame seeds, dried orange or tangerine peel, poppy seeds, chili, and nori seaweed. In Thailand, seven-spice is a mixture that may be a blend of chili powder, garlic, ginger, coriander, star anise, cloves, and lemon peel.

1. Add oil into the rice cooker, cover, and set to cook. When the base of the cooker pot gets warm, add the sweet potatoes. Fry for 6 to 8 minutes, until sweet potatoes turn crisp on the outside but remain soft inside, covering rice cooker occasionally in the process of frying.

2. Add the brown sugar, switch rice cooker to Warm, and stir gradually and evenly until the sugar melts. When sugar completely caramelizes in about 10 to 12 minutes, sprinkle in cinnamon and nutmeg powder.

3. When entire mixture becomes dry and sticky in about 8 to 10 minutes, dish out and serve warm.

Steamed Egg Cupcakes

The oil called for in this recipe is used to lightly grease the cup molds (ramekins) so that the cupcakes do not stick. It is also easier to remove the cupcakes from the molds (ramekins) after steaming.

INGREDIENTS | YIELDS ABOUT 6 CUPS

1 egg
1 tablespoon castor sugar
¼ cup whole milk
2 ounces self-rising flour, sifted
1 tablespoon vegetable oil

1. Fill the rice cooker pot with water to about the 4-cup mark. Cover the rice cooker and set to Cook.

2. In a medium bowl, lightly whisk the egg and sugar in a bowl. Slowly add the milk and mix to combine. Add the sifted flour and mix well, forming a pourable batter.

3. Use the vegetable oil to grease the molds. Pour the mixture into cup molds, filling about 90 percent full. Cover the cups with foil and set aside on a plate that will fit in the steamer insert or basket.

4. When the water in the rice cooker boils, place the steamer insert or basket that holds the cup molds over the boiling water. Cover the rice cooker and steam for about 15 minutes.

Steamed Egg and Milk Custard

This is a popular dessert in Cantonese cuisine. The specialty dessert stalls in Hong Kong have a steamed milk version made solely from milk and egg white.

INGREDIENTS | SERVES 2 OR 3

2 eggs, lightly whisked
1 cup warm milk
1 tablespoon castor sugar

Cooking Tip
For ginger-flavored custard, add 2 to 3 teaspoons of ginger juice into the milk and warm the milk in microwave. Then proceed as directed in this recipe.

1. Fill the rice cooker pot with water to about the 4-cup mark. Cover the rice cooker and set to Cook.

2. In a separate bowl, slowly add the warm milk to the lightly whisked eggs. Then add sugar and mix well with a fork. Pour the mixture into serving bowls that will fit in the steamer insert or basket and cover the bowls with foil.

3. When the water in rice cooker boils, place the steamer insert or basket that holds the covered serving bowls over the boiling water. Cover the rice cooker and steam for 10 minutes.

Barley Drink

Rock sugar is often used in Chinese sweet dessert soups or drinks. Rock sugar, which is made from large sugar crystals, brings subtle sweetness to a dish. As a substitution, use sugar or honey.

INGREDIENTS | SERVES 4

2 cups raw barley, cleaned, soaked and drained according to package instructions
4 cups water
3 or 4 screwpine leaves, cleaned and knotted
8 small rock sugar crystals

1. Add the water to the rice cooker pot, cover, and set to Cook. Once the water boils, add the barley and screwpine leaves.

2. Allow the mixture to return to a boil. Once boiling, tilt the rice cooker lid slightly to vent excessive steam. Simmer for about 30 minutes, stirring occasionally.

3. Add rock sugar and stir again. Continue to simmer for 15 to 30 minutes until barley is cooked. Drain the barley and screwpine leaves and discard. Retain the barley water to serve as a drink, warm or cold as preferred.

Green Bean Soup

Green beans are also mung beans. The Chinese believe that this is a "cooling" food for the body systems and is best eaten when the weather is warm.

INGREDIENTS | SERVES 4 OR 5

1 cup dried green beans (mung beans), cleaned, soaked overnight, and drained

6 cups water

5 or 6 screwpine leaves, cleaned and knotted together

2 tablespoons sugar or more, to taste

1. Add beans and water to the rice cooker pot. Cover, set to Cook, and bring to a boil.
2. Allow to boil for 15 minutes or more until the beans slightly soften, stirring occasionally and tilting the rice cooker lid slightly to vent off excessive steam.
3. When the beans are slightly softened, switch to Warm and simmer for about 1 hour or more until the beans cook through.
4. Add screwpine leaves and sugar. Stir well and continue to simmer for about 30 minutes or more or until the beans have expanded out of their skins and become soft. Serve warm or chilled.

Red Bean Soup

Red beans can also be made into a sweet dessert soup similar to green beans. However, red beans are considered a "warming" food, different from green beans.

INGREDIENTS | SERVES 4 OR 5

1 cup dried red (azuki) beans, cleaned, soaked overnight, and drained

6 cups water

3 tablespoons brown sugar or more, to taste

Zest of half an orange

Cooking Tip

Before soaking red beans or green beans, rinse a few times over water to remove dirt. Discard discolored beans.

1. Add beans and water to the rice cooker pot. Cover, set to Cook, and bring beans and water to a boil.
2. Allow to boil for 15 minutes or more until the beans slightly soften, stirring occasionally and tilting the rice cooker lid slightly to vent off excessive steam.
3. When the beans are slightly softened, switch to Warm and continue to simmer for about 1 hour or more until the beans cook through.
4. Add sugar and stir until dissolved. Switch to Warm and continue to simmer for about 1 hour or more until the beans have expanded out of their skins and become soft. Add the orange zest and serve warm.

Taro and Bananas in Sweet Coconut Milk

Before the times of "canned" convenience, fresh coconut milk could be bought directly from market vendors. The fresh coconut milk was obtained by finely grating the white coconut flesh, and then squeezing the flesh in a muslin cloth to extract the coconut milk.

INGREDIENTS | SERVES 3 OR 4

½ cup peeled and cubed sweet potato (½-inch cubes)

½ cup peeled and cubed taro (½-inch cubes)

3 cups water

½ cup coconut milk

6 screwpine (pandan) leaves, rinsed and knotted together

2 tablespoons brown sugar or more, to taste

1 teaspoon salt

2 to 3 ripe bananas, cut into ½-inch cubes

Cooking Tip

Screwpine leaves can be used as natural (green) food coloring. Blend 6 to 8 leaves and ¼ cup water in a food processor. Place the blended mixture in a strainer and squeeze out the green juice. This "extract" is often added when making cakes and desserts in Asia.

1. Place the sweet potato and taro on a plate that will fit into the steamer insert or basket.

2. Fill the rice cooker pot with water to about the 4-cup mark. Cover the rice cooker and set to Cook. When the water in the rice cooker boils, place the steamer insert or basket that holds the cubes of sweet potatoes and taro over the boiling water. Cover the rice cooker and steam for about 10 minutes, until sweet potatoes and taro are soft. Remove and set aside.

3. Clean out the rice cooker. Add 3 cups water, coconut milk, screwpine leaves, brown sugar, and salt to the pot. Cover rice cooker, set to Cook, and bring to a simmer.

4. Once simmering, switch to Warm, stir well, and slowly add the bananas and steamed sweet potatoes and taro. Stir gently for about 3 to 5 minutes.

5. Ladle the dessert into serving bowls and serve warm.

Steamed Black Rice Pudding

A popular Asian sweet dessert soup made from glutinous black rice is called Pulut Hitam. *This is a pudding version of that dish.*

INGREDIENTS | SERVES 3 OR 4

1 cup black glutinous rice, rinsed clean and soaked overnight
6 cups water
2 tablespoons honey, divided use
¼ teaspoon salt
4 tablespoons coconut milk
Honey, for drizzling

1. Add rinsed rice and the water to the rice cooker pot, cover, and set to Cook. Allow to come to a boil and continue to boil for about 1 hour, stirring occasionally. When boiling vigorously, tilt rice cooker lid slightly to vent built-up steam, and simmer until rice splits open and becomes fairly soft.

2. With about 5 to 10 minutes to go before draining the rice, stir in 1 tablespoon honey.

3. Drain the rice, place in a bowl, and then mix with salt and remaining honey. Spoon the rice mixture into cups or molds and set aside on a plate that will fit in the steamer insert or basket.

4. Clean out the rice cooker. Fill the pot with water to about the 4-cup mark, cover, and set to Cook. When the water in the rice cooker boils, place the steamer insert or basket that holds the cups over the boiling water. Cover the rice cooker and steam for 1 hour.

5. Remove steamed rice from molds (turn the mold upside down above the plate; with the help of a spoon to lift the rice from the edges of the molds, the rice may just drop gently on the plate) and place on serving plates. Drizzle coconut milk and honey over the steamed rice pudding.

Sweet Snow Fungus and Ginkgo

Do not be appalled by the word "fungus." Snow fungus is just another type of mushroom that is used in Chinese medicines and cooking. It can be found in the dried foods section in Asian supermarkets and must be soaked before use. Snow fungus adds a jelly-like texture to desserts.

INGREDIENTS | SERVES 3 OR 4

2 pieces snow fungus, soaked in water before use

4 honey dates

5 small rock sugar crystals

4 cups water or more, enough to submerge ingredients in the pot

2 screwpine (pandan) leaves, rinsed and knotted together

½ cup canned ginkgo

1 to 2 teaspoons sugar or honey, to taste

1. Add snow fungus, honey dates, and rock sugar to the rice cooker pot. Add the 4 cups water, or enough to submerge the ingredients. Cover rice cooker, set to Cook, and bring to a boil.

2. Once boiling, switch to Warm, add screwpine leaves, and simmer for 30 to 45 minutes.

3. Add the ginkgo and sugar or honey (as preferred). Ladle into dessert bowls to serve.

Pink Lemonade with Basil

You can add the 1 stalk of bruised lemongrass to infuse more aroma into this drink.

INGREDIENTS | SERVES 3 OR 4

4 cups water

1 tablespoon sugar

2 tablespoons honey

½ to 1 cup freshly squeezed lemon juice, adjust accordingly to preference for sourness

1 cup fresh red grapefruit juice

½ cup roughly chopped fresh basil leaves

1. Add the water to rice cooker, cover, and set to Cook. When water boils, add the sugar and honey and stir about 5 to 8 minutes to dissolve. Switch off rice cooker and allow mixture to cool.

2. Add lemon and grapefruit juices into the sugar syrup and mix well. Pour into a jug, for ease of serving the drink later.

3. Add the basil and some crushed ice before serving.

Cooking Tip

If any of the grapefruit was not needed for the juice, you can peel the fruit, remove membranes, and cut the segments into smaller pieces to be added to the lemonade.

Honeydew and Snow Fungus in Sweet Coconut Milk

As a variation, you can use cantaloupe instead of honeydew, or use some of each. These fruits give an added texture to the dessert.

INGREDIENTS | SERVES 3 OR 4

2 pieces snow fungus, soaked in water before use
5 small rock sugar crystals
3 cups water
½ cup coconut milk
½ cup whole milk
1 cup bite sized cubes honeydew melon

1. Add the snow fungus, sugar, and water to the rice cooker pot. Cover, set to Cook, and bring to a boil.

2. Once boiling, switch rice cooker to Warm and simmer for 1 hour. Remove snow fungus and allow to cool. (Leave the remaining water in the pot.) Once cooled, cut snow fungus into small pieces and divide evenly into serving bowls.

3. Cover the rice cooker, set to Cook, and bring remaining water in the rice cooker to a boil. Once boiling, turn off heat and then slowly stir in both milks. Mix well.

4. Ladle milk mixture into the serving bowls with snow fungus and chill in refrigerator for 30 minutes or more, until the mixture is cold.

5. Before serving, add the honeydew cubes.

CHAPTER 20

Tips, Leftover Tricks, and More . . .

Fried Ginger Strips
284

Fried Golden Shallots
284

Fried Garlic Slices
284

Pickled Pineapple Salad
285

Mango Chutney
285

Chili Sambal
286

Ginger and Green Onion Sauce
286

Peanut Sauce
287

Toasted Almonds
287

Toasted Pita Pizza
288

Stuffed Egg Rolls with Rice
288

Fried Ginger Strips

Do not use frozen (stored) ginger to make this. Even when thawed, the ginger may contain too much moisture and cause the oil to spit when frying.

INGREDIENTS | YIELDS 2 TO 3 TEASPOONS AS GARNISH

3 tablespoons vegetable oil
2-inch piece fresh ginger, peeled and thinly shredded, set aside on paper towels to drain excess moisture

Add the oil to the rice cooker, cover, and set to Cook. When the base of the cooker pot gets warm, add the ginger and fry for about 8 to 10 minutes, until crisp and golden brown. Cover the rice cooker occasionally in the process of frying and make sure the ginger strips do not burn. Set aside the fried ginger strips on paper towel to drain off excess oil. Stored in an airtight container, they can be left outside at room temperature for about 1 week.

Fried Golden Shallots

Sprinkling fried shallots over Asian soups and noodles will make any dish extra flavorful.

INGREDIENTS | YIELDS 2 TO 3 TEASPOONS AS GARNISH

3 to 4 tablespoons vegetable oil
½ cup thinly sliced shallots, set aside on paper towels to drain excess moisture

Add the oil to the rice cooker, cover, and set to Cook. When the base of the cooker pot gets warm, add the shallots and fry for about 8 to 10 minutes, until crisp and golden brown. Cover rice cooker occasionally in the process of frying and make sure the shallots do not burn.

Fried Garlic Slices

Fried garlic can be stored in an airtight container in the fridge for a few months.

INGREDIENTS | YIELDS 3 TO 4 TEASPOONS AS GARNISH

3 to 4 tablespoons vegetable oil
4 to 6 cloves garlic, thinly sliced

Add the oil to the rice cooker, cover, and set to Cook. When the base of the cooker pot gets warm, add the garlic and fry for about 5 to 8 minutes, until crisp and golden brown. Cover rice cooker occasionally in the process of frying and make sure the garlic does not burn.

Pickled Pineapple Salad

Serve this as an appetizing condiment with steamed rice, coconut-based dishes, or pan-fried fish.

INGREDIENTS | SERVES 2 TO 3

2 tablespoons vegetable oil

2-inch piece ginger, peeled and sliced

1 medium fresh red chili pepper, seeded and thinly sliced

2 cups peeled and sliced fresh pineapples, cut into 1-inch cubes

½ teaspoon salt

¼ teaspoon dark soy sauce

1 to 2 tablespoons brown sugar, to taste

1 tablespoons vinegar

1. Add the oil to the rice cooker, cover, and set to Cook. When the base of the pot starts to get warm, add the ginger and chili and fry about 1 to 2 minutes, until fragrant.

2. Add pineapple, salt, soy sauce, sugar, and vinegar and stir constantly for about 6 to 8 minutes, covering the rice cooker occasionally in the process of cooking, until the pineapple looks shiny and glossy.

Mango Chutney

This mango chutney is a sweet-spicy condiment, mild on the spice and easy to make. Store the chutney in airtight containers in the fridge and consume within five days.

INGREDIENTS | SERVES 4

½ teaspoon mustard seeds

3 medium-sized ripe mangoes, seeds removed, peeled, and diced (about 1-inch cubes)

¼ cup cider vinegar

2 teaspoons brown sugar

1 clove garlic, minced

1 teaspoon grated ginger

½ teaspoon paprika

½ teaspoon freshly ground black pepper

1. Cover the rice cooker and set to cook. When the base of the pot starts to get warm, add the mustard seeds. When seeds start to pop around in about 2 to 3 minutes, add the remaining ingredients and mix well in the pot, stirring occasionally to prevent ingredients from sticking to the bottom of the pot.

2. In about 8 to 10 minutes, when "sticking" is frequent, reduce the heat by switching the rice cooker to Warm. Simmer for 5 to 8 minutes until mixture thickens.

3. Dish out the chutney and allow it to cool.

Chili Sambal

This is an easy chili condiment you can make at home. This chili condiment is also called sambal in Indonesia, Malaysia, and Singapore.

INGREDIENTS | SERVES 4

4 thinly sliced shallots
12 dried red chili peppers, soaked
3 tablespoons vegetable oil
1 teaspoon brown sugar
½ teaspoon salt

1. Combine shallots and chilies in a food processor and blend into a paste.

2. Add the oil to the rice cooker, cover, and set to Cook. When the base of the pot gets warm, add the chili paste and fry about 5 minutes until mixture becomes fragrant, switching the rice cooker to Warm if mixture gets too hot and starts to splatter.

3. Add the brown sugar and salt and cook for another 3 to 5 minutes.

Ginger and Green Onion Sauce

This can be a good dipping sauce for boiled chicken, or lettuce-wrapped chicken rolls.

INGREDIENTS | SERVES 4

1 tablespoon water or Chicken Stock (page 16)
1 teaspoon brown sugar, or to taste
2 tablespoons finely minced green onions
2 tablespoons grated ginger
1 tablespoon vegetable oil

1. Combine water or chicken stock, brown sugar, green onions, and ginger in a small heatproof glass bowl. Set aside.

2. Add the oil to the rice cooker, cover, and set to Cook. Wait for about 5 minutes until the oil gets very hot but is not smoking.

3. Slowly pour the hot oil into the ginger mixture. (It will sizzle for a few seconds.) Allow to sit for 1 to 2 minutes to cool before serving.

Peanut Sauce

Bottled peanut sauce is readily available in Asian supermarkets. However, if you make your own, you can control the ingredients much better. Add some pineapple cubes to the peanut sauce as a variation.

INGREDIENTS | SERVES 5

8 to 10 dried red chili peppers
8 shallots, coarsely chopped
2 cloves garlic, coarsely chopped
1 stalk lemongrass, bottom part bruised
3 tablespoons vegetable oil, divided use
½ cup chunky peanut butter
3 tablespoons coconut milk or more (adjust as needed during cooking, adding 1 or 2 more tablespoons if mixture gets too dry)
¼ teaspoon salt
1 teaspoon brown sugar

1. Blend the chilies, shallots, garlic, lemongrass, and 1 tablespoon oil in food processor until mixture reaches a finely chopped consistency.

2. Add remaining oil in the rice cooker. Cover the rice cooker and set to Cook. When base of rice cooker pot is warm, add the blended mixture and fry for about 3 minutes until fragrant, covering rice cooker occasionally in the process.

3. Add the peanut butter, coconut milk, salt, and sugar. Cover rice cooker and bring to a slight simmer. Switch to Warm when mixture starts to bubble and stir well until sauce thickens.

4. Once thick, transfer to a bowl and allow sauce to cool.

Toasted Almonds

Nuts that need to be toasted can be dry-fried in this way, similar to toasting sesame seeds.

INGREDIENTS | SERVES 4, AS GARNISH

3 cups slivered raw almonds

Cover rice cooker and set to Cook. When the base of the pot gets warm, add the almonds and stir until golden brown.

Toasted Pita Pizza

For topping variations, try canned corn kernels or diced bell peppers.

INGREDIENTS | SERVES 2

4 slices pita bread
4 slices deli ham, chopped
1 cup finely cubed pineapple
½ cup grated Cheddar cheese
½ cup grated mozzarella cheese

1. Cover the rice cooker and set to Cook. When the base of the pot gets warm, add one pita (one pita each batch) to the bottom of the rice cooker; sprinkle ham and pineapple over the top. Cover the rice cooker to heat the pizza for 3 to 5 minutes, until toppings are warmed and pita bread becomes crispy at the base.

2. Toward the end of cooking, add the cheeses, cover rice cooker, and continue to cook about 3 to 5 minutes until the cheese melts. Continue the same for the remaining pita bread. Serve warm.

Stuffed Egg Rolls with Rice

Create stuffed egg rolls with some eggs and leftover fried rice. It brings new life to the leftovers.

INGREDIENTS | SERVES 2

3 or 4 eggs
¼ cup finely chopped green onions
Salt and ground white pepper, to taste
4 tablespoons vegetable oil, divided use (2 tablespoons each batch)
3 cups leftover fried rice, microwaved

1. In a small bowl, whisk the eggs with green onions, salt, and pepper. Set aside.

2. Add half the oil to the rice cooker, cover, and set to Cook. When the base of the cooker pot gets warm, add about half the quantity of the whisked egg (in each batch). Make sure the eggs cover the base of the pot in each batch. Allow the eggs to cook in the oil about 8 to 10 minutes, covering the rice cooker occasionally, until a thin round "plain omelet" is formed (taking care not to let the egg to burn under prolonged cooking). Remove the omelet and set aside on a paper towel to drain the oil. Repeat with remaining whisked egg.

3. To assemble, lay the omelets on a flat surface, place rice in the center of each, fold up the edges, and roll up to enclose the rice.

APPENDIX

Basic Rice Cooker Features

Rice Cooker Size

Rice cookers measure size or capacity by cups, ranging from 1 to 10 cups (10 cups equivalent to about 1.8 liters). The smallest rice cooker is about 0.6 liter and can cook up to 3 cups of rice, whereas the largest rice cookers, typically those for commercial use, are about 4.2 liters and can cook about 23 cups of rice. You should not buy an extremely small or large unit unless you need it. A larger unit also is more expensive to operate because it draws higher voltage and power. The recommended rice cooker size for a family of three to four is 1.8 liter, which can cook up to 10 cups of rice and allows enough real estate within the inner pan to do other cooking besides cooking rice. Generally, because serving size differs in the East and West, the exact measurement of a "cup" in the rice cookers also differs. For example, one Japanese cup is 200 milliliters, as compared to one American cup, which is 240 milliliters. Be aware of such differences and adjust any recipes accordingly.

Rice Cooker Pan

The range of inner pans is almost as varied as that of pans you would choose to use on the stovetop. Rice cookers now come with nonstick pans, anodized aluminum pans, and even stainless steel pans. Choose a rice cooker with the inner pan you prefer to work with. For example, if you do not like to spend too much time cleaning, choose a rice cooker with a nonstick pan. An anodized aluminum pan may allow better dissipation of heat for cooking.

Rice Cooker Lid

The basic models usually come with a metal lid. If there is no extra cost for it, a clear glass or plastic lid is best, as this helps you to "eyeball" cooking or steaming without lifting up the lid and losing heat while cooking.

Steamer Trays

Depending on the model, rice cooker units may come with a steamer basket or perforated metal tray that sits above the rice so that steaming can be done as the rice cooks. The inner pan can also be filled with water to boil, and in effect, steam the food in the steamer tray. There are other models that even have a small tray or pot that sits right at the bottom of the rice cooker pan, above the cooking element. A steamer tray is considered a very useful accessory, allowing the rice cooker to serve "double duty" as a steamer.

Cook and Warm Switch

This switch automatically switches to Warm when the inner thermostat in the rice cooker detects the temperature exceeding a pre-designated Cook temperature limit (usually 100°C to 120°C or 212°F to 248°F). The Keep Warm mode usually operates at about 65°C or above, which means some rice cookers can safely keep rice warm for up to twelve hours. This switch can be intentionally turned to the Keep Warm mode when cooking other food and when heat (temperature) control will be helpful. For example, when you stir-fry in the pan, start with Cook function. When the next step calls for simmering at slightly lower heat, switch the cooker manually to Keep Warm. Most basic Cook and Keep Warm rice cooker models allow you to do this. Read the rice cooker manual to learn what can or cannot be done.

Fuse Protector

Nothing is more important than safety when operating an appliance, especially an appliance such as the rice cooker, which might be left unattended during cooking. This will trip the fuse and prevent possible fires.

Index

Note: Page numbers in **bold** indicate recipe category lists.

Almonds, Toasted, 287
Asparagus
  about: cooking, 154
  Halibut and Asparagus Soup, 47
  Stir-Fried Asparagus with Scallops, 248
  Stir-Fried Shrimp with Asparagus, 154

Bananas, in Taro and Bananas in Sweet Coconut Milk, 279
Barley. *See* Grains
Basics. *See* Essential basics
Basil
  about: types of, 176
  Black Pepper Basil Beef, 200
  Pink Lemonade with Basil, 281
  Spicy Shrimp with Basil, 146
  Thai Basil Chicken, 176
  Three-Cup Mushrooms, 266
Beans. *See* Legumes and beans
Beef, **191**–204
  Beef and Shiitake Pasta, 92
  Beef Fried Rice, 71
  Beef in Honey Caramelized Onions, 202
  Beef in Mushroom Sauce, 201
  Beef Stew, 193
  Beef with Ginger and Green Onions, 199
  Black Pepper Basil Beef, 200
  Dim Sum: Steamed Meatballs, 31
  Ground Beef and Mushrooms Yaki-udon, 113
  Ground Beef and Rice Soup, 79
  Ground Beef with Peas, 198
  Lightly Spiced Mushrooms with Beef, 269
  Macaroni with Chinese Meat Sauce, 102
  Mild Beef Curry with Potato and Peas, 194
  Mini Beef Burger, 204
  Pumpkin and Beef Curry, 195
  Rice Noodles with Beef, 123
  Spicy Ground Beef, 197
  Spicy Ground Beef with Tomato and Egg, 196
  Steamed Beef and Cabbage Rolls, 192
  Stir-Fried Beef in Garlic Black Bean Sauce, 203
Black pepper, "tempering," 153
Broccoli
  about: cooking/blanching/shocking, 93
  Tofu Casserole, 236
Brussels Sprouts
  about: cooking, 253
  Brussels Sprouts in Oyster Sauce, 253
  Buttered Brussels Sprouts, 254
Butternut Squash, Tofu with, 241

Cabbage
  about: benefits of, 35
  Cabbage and Cauliflower with Peas, 251
  Cabbage and Tomato Soup, 39
  Easy Chinese Vegetable Stew, 246
  Meatballs and Napa Cabbage Soup, 41
  Potato, Cabbage, and Spicy Sausage Soup, 55
  Rice Salad, 75
  Savory Cabbage Rice, 68
  Seafood Napa Cabbage Rolls, 35
  Steamed Beef and Cabbage Rolls, 192
  Steamed Napa Cabbage with Ham, 244
  Stir-Fried Chinese Cabbage, 248
  Stir-Fry White Pepper Noodles, 120
  Tofu Cabbage Rolls, 36
Cardamom, about, 78
Carrots
  about: slicing and dicing, 214
  Corn, Carrot, and Pea Congee, 89
  Curried Carrot and Ginger Soup, 54
  French Green Beans and Carrots with Herbs, 255
Cauliflower
  Cabbage and Cauliflower with Peas, 251
  Indian Potato and Cauliflower (*Aloo Gobi*), 250
  Tofu Casserole, 236
  Udon in Mildly Spiced Cauliflower, 111
Chicken, **159**–76
  about: clear chicken soup, 42; cooking, 164, 171; reducing cooking time, increasing moisture, 171
  Asian "Paella," 76
  Chicken and Daikon Soup, 42
  Chicken and Shrimp Pasta, 93
  Chicken Barley Stew, 163
  Chicken Congee, 84
  Chicken Herbal Soup, 49
  Chicken in Wine and Shallot Sauce, 171
  Chicken Jalfrezi, 167
  Chicken Macaroni, 94
  Chicken Mushroom Noodles, 122
  Chicken Rice, 64
  Chicken Satay, 25
  Chicken Soup with Sweet Corn and Carrot, 42
  Chicken Stock, 16
  Chicken with Spicy Tomatoes, 166
  Cider Chicken Stew, 164
  Citron Honey Chicken, 173
  Coconut Chicken Soup, 48
  Dim Sum: Healthy Chicken Siu Mai, 32
  Easy Chicken Curry, 165
  Japanese Chicken Donburi, 58
  Lychee Chicken, 174

Orange Chicken, 172
Sesame Oil Chicken, 170
Steamed Chicken with Carrots and Onions, 161
Steamed Chicken with Ginger and Green Onions, 160
Steamed Dark-Sauce Chicken with Mushrooms, 162
Stir-Fried Black Pepper Chicken with Sugar Snap Peas, 175
Stir-Fry Black Pepper Chicken Udon, 112
Tea-Flavored Chicken with Chinese Spices, 165
Thai Basil Chicken, 176
Thai Ginger Chicken, 168
Three-Cup Chicken, 169

Chickpeas. *See* Legumes and beans
Chilies. *See* Peppers
Chili Sambal, 286
Chinese herbal packs, 49
Cilantro, about, 197
Citron, 173
Clams. *See* Shrimp, scallops, and clams
Coconut
  about: milk, 138; storing milk, 147
  Coconut Chicken Soup, 48
  Fragrant Coconut Rice, 60
  Ginger and Coconut Sauce, 138
Congee (rice porridge) and grains, 14, **81**–89
  about, 5–6; cooking, 86; healing properties of, 88
  Chicken Congee, 84
  Corn, Carrot, and Pea Congee, 89
  Fish Congee, 82
  Gojiberry Congee, 87
  Pork Congee, 85
  Pumpkin Congee, 86
  Rice Congee, 14
  Seafood Congee, 83
  Sweet Potato Congee, 87
  Taro and Spinach Congee, 88
  Tuna and Corn Congee, 84
Coriander, about, 197
Corn
  Clam and Corn in Herby Broth, 158
  Corn, Carrot, and Pea Congee, 89
  Hotshot Sweet Corn, 31
  Mini Ham and Corn Omelets, 29
  Pork with Potatoes, Peas, and Corn, 186
  Sweet Corn Pancakes, 274
  Tuna and Corn Congee, 84
Cucumber Raita, 62
Cumin, about, 146
Curry, about, 149
Curry leaves, about, 151

Dashi stock, 58
Desserts, **272**–82
  Barley Drink, 277
  Caramelized All-Spiced Sweet Potato, 275
  Green Bean Soup, 278
  Honeydew and Snow Fungus in Sweet Coconut Milk, 282
  Pink Lemonade with Basil, 281
  Red Bean Soup, 278
  Steamed Black Rice Pudding, 280
  Steamed Egg and Milk Custard, 277
  Steamed Egg Cupcake, 276
  Sweet Corn Pancakes, 274
  Sweet Snow Fungus and Ginkgo, 281
  Sweet Taro Crisps, 273
  Taro and Bananas in Sweet Coconut Milk, 279
Dim Sum
  Healthy Chicken Siu Mai, 32
  Steamed Meatballs, 31
  Steamed Tofu, 33
Drinks
  Barley Drink, 277
  Pink Lemonade with Basil, 281

Eggplant
  about: cooking, 245
  Indian Eggplant Stew, 252
  Steamed Eggplant, 245
Egg Rolls with Rice, Stuffed, 288
Eggs, **218**–31
  about: boiling, 223; buying and storing, 222; cooking, 221, 223; frying omelets, 227; seasonal frittatas, 231
  Easy Chinese Savory Egg Custard, 219
  Egg and Shrimp Fried Rice, 72
  Egg Curry, 223
  Eggs with Caramelized Onions, 222
  Egg with French Beans, 224
  Egg with Pork and Cilantro, 226
  Green Onion and Potato Frittata, 230
  Indian Cheese Omelet, 229
  Japanese Tea-Bowl Egg (*Chawanmushi*), 220
  Mini Ham and Corn Omelets, 29
  Onion and Green Chili Omelet, 227
  Scrambled Eggs with Spices, 228
  Shrimp and Tomato Fried Eggs, 155
  Shrimp Foo Yong, 225
  Steamed Egg and Milk Custard, 277
  Steamed Egg Cupcake, 276
  Stuffed Egg Rolls with Rice, 288
  Summer Frittata, 231
  Tea-Flavored Eggs, 221
Egg tofu, 33
Essential basics, **11**–18. *See also* Pasta; Stocks
  Brown Rice, 12
  Long-Grain White Rice, 12
  Marinara Sauce, 15
  Rice Congee, 14
  Sushi Rice, 13
  Warm Oats, 14

Fish, **124**–41. *See also* Shrimp, scallops, and clams; Starters
  about: cooking more quickly, 45; leftovers, 22, 80; sustainable seafood sources, 128
  Chinese Fish Soup, 44
  Cod and Shiitake Mushrooms in Wine Sauce, 131
  Codfish with Ginger and Coconut Sauce, 138
  Fishball (Dumpling) Soup, 46
  Fish Burger, 141
  Fish Congee, 82
  Fish Curry, 139

INDEX 291

Fish—continued
　Fish in Creamy Pistachio Pesto Sauce, 136
　Fish Kedgeree, 80
　Fish Pasta, 91
　Halibut and Asparagus Soup, 47
　Halibut with Mango Salsa, 135
　Korean Bibimbap, 59
　Lemongrass Steamed Fish, 128
　Pan-Fried Fish in Chinese Black Bean Sauce, 132
　Pan-Fried Fish in Soy and Ginger Sauce, 134
　Pan-Fried Salmon, 130
　Pasta and Tuna Salad, 103
　Salmon Fillet with Oyster Sauce, 133
　Smoked Salmon with Soba, 110
　Steamed Fish in Spicy Thai-Style Yogurt Sauce, 129
　Steamed Fish in Tangy Ginger Sauce, 125
　Steamed Fish with Ginger and Green Onions, 130
　Steamed Halibut with Mushrooms and Tofu, 126
　Steamed Whole Fish with Ham and Shiitake Mushrooms, 127
　Stir-Fried Fish Slices with Ginger and Green Onions, 137
　Tandoori Fish, 140
　Tuna and Corn Congee, 84
Five-spice, about, 275

Garam masala, about, 229
Garlic
　about: changing flavors of, 206; frying, 116; marinating, 240; optimizing flavor of, 240
　Fried Garlic Slices, 284
　Garlic Bean Soup, 206
Ghee, about, 265
Ginger
　about: benefits of, 130; storing, 54; Thai (*galangal*), 249
　Curried Carrot and Ginger Soup, 54
　Fried Ginger Strips, 284
　Ginger and Coconut Sauce, 138
　Ginger and Green Onion Sauce, 286
　Ginger Dressing, 106
　Soy and Ginger Sauce, 134
　Tangy Ginger Sauce, 125
Gojiberry Congee, 87
Grains. *See also* Congee (rice porridge) and grains; Rice
　about: benefits of barley, 163; buckwheat flour and soba noodles, 105
　Barley Drink, 277
　Chicken Barley Stew, 163
　Mushroom and Barley Soup, 261
　Warm Oats, 14
Green beans. *See* Legumes and beans

Hash
　Bacon, Onion, and Potato Hash, 26
　Potato, Bell Pepper, and Mushroom Hash, 27
Honeydew and Snow Fungus in Sweet Coconut Milk, 282

Kaffir lime/leaves, 37, 216, 237
Kai Lan, Buttered, with Shallots, 256
Kale with Mushrooms, 254
Kimchi
　Kimchi Pork, 180
　Kimchi Soba Soup, 109
　Kimchi Tofu Soup, 52

Leeks
　about, 201
　Pasta and Leek Stir-Fry, 97
Legumes and beans, **205**–17
　about: garbanzo beans, 209; lentils, 208; pinto beans, 212; reducing gas-causing properties, 210
　Beans and rice, 73
　Black Bean Casserole in Tomato Gravy, 210
　Black Bean Patties, 217
　Cabbage and Cauliflower with Peas, 251
　Chickpeas with Peppers, 215
　Chinese Black Bean Sauce, 132
　Corn, Carrot, and Pea Congee, 89
　Curried Chickpeas, 213
　Egg with French Beans, 224
　French Green Beans and Carrots with Herbs, 255
　Garlic Bean Soup, 206
　Garlic Black Bean Sauce, 203
　Green Bean Soup (dessert), 278
　Ground Beef with Peas, 198
　Lentil Soup, 208
　Lentil Soup with Pasta, 99
　Mild Beef Curry with Potato and Peas, 194
　Mushrooms and Green Pea Masala, 265
　Pork with Potatoes, Peas, and Corn, 186
　Potato and Pea Soup, 207
　Quick Chick-A-Pea, 215
　Quick Pea Curry, 209
　Red Bean Soup (dessert), 278
　Snow Peas with Bell Peppers, 244
　Spicy Green Beans, 211
　Spicy Pinto Beans with Onions, 212
　Stir-Fried Black Pepper Chicken with Sugar Snap Peas, 175
　Stir-Fried Long Beans, 247
　Stir-Fried Mixed Beans, 214
　Thai-Style Lentils, 216
　Vegetable Soup with Pinto Beans, 208
Lemon
　Easy Lemon Buttered Rice, 77
　Lemon Pasta, 101
　Pink Lemonade with Basil, 281
Lemongrass, about, 57
Lentils. *See* Legumes and beans
Lychee Chicken, 174

Mangoes
　Mango Chutney, 285
　Mango Salsa, 135
Minestrone, 52
Miso
　about: benefits of, 50
　Green Tea Miso Soup, 50
　Miso Soup, 49
Mortar and pestle, 166
Mushrooms, **259**–71

about: nutritional value of, 271
Beef and Shiitake Pasta, 92
Beef in Mushroom Sauce, 201
Buttered Mushrooms with Onions and Herbs, 270
Chicken Mushroom Noodles, 122
Cod and Shiitake Mushrooms in Wine Sauce, 131
Cream of Mushroom Soup, 53
Creamy Mushroom Pasta, 96
Garlic Mushrooms, 270
Ground Beef and Mushrooms Yaki-udon, 113
Ground Pork with Mushrooms, 185
Honeydew and Snow Fungus in Sweet Coconut Milk, 282
Hot and Sour Soup, 44
Kale with Mushrooms, 254
Lightly Spiced Mushrooms with Beef, 269
Mushroom and Barley Soup, 261
Mushroom Curry, 263
Mushroom Korma, 264
Mushroom Pasta, 101
Mushrooms and Green Pea Masala, 265
Mushrooms in Ginger and Soy, 267
Mushroom Stew, 262
Seaweed Soup with Enoki and Meatballs, 43
Shrimp and Shiitake Curry, 147
Spicy Mushrooms, 271
Spinach Tofu in Mushroom Sauce, 235
Steamed Dark-Sauce Chicken with Mushrooms, 162
Steamed Halibut with Mushrooms and Tofu, 126
Steamed Stuffed Mushrooms, 260
Steamed Whole Fish with Ham and Shiitake Mushrooms, 127
Stir-Fry Glass Noodles with Mushrooms and Celery, 115
Stir-Fry Mushrooms with Celery and Carrots, 268
Summer Soba with Spinach and Mushrooms, 108

Sweet Snow Fungus and Ginkgo, 281
Three-Cup Mushrooms, 266
Tofu with Shrimp, Meat, and Mushrooms, 239
Warm Soba and Japanese Mushrooms in Ginger Dressing, 106

Noodles, **104**–23. *See also* Pasta
about: buckwheat flour and soba noodles, 105; cooking, 111, 114; glass, 114; sauces/toppings for, 117; udon, 111; yakiudon and yakisoba, 113
Black Vinegar Ground Meat Noodles, 117
Chicken Mushroom Noodles, 122
Chilled Soba in Green Onion Dressing, 105
Garlic-Infused Glass Noodles with Tiger Shrimp, 116
Ground Beef and Mushrooms Yaki-udon, 113
Kimchi Soba Soup, 109
Noodles in Creamy Egg Gravy, 119
Nyonya-Style Noodles, 121
Rice Noodles with Beef, 123
Smoked Salmon with Soba, 110
Soba in Tahini Sauce, 107
Spicy Bean Noodles, 118
Stir-Fry Black Pepper Chicken Udon, 112
Stir-Fry Glass Noodles with Mushrooms and Celery, 115
Stir-Fry White Pepper Noodles, 120
Summer Soba with Spinach and Mushrooms, 108
Tom Yum Glass Noodles, 114
Udon in Mildly Spiced Cauliflower, 111
Warm Soba and Japanese Mushrooms in Ginger Dressing, 106
Nori, about, 109

Okra
Indian Braised Okra, 251
Okra Stew, 258
Onions

about: types of, 76, 199
Ginger and Green Onion Sauce, 286
Green Onion Dressing, 105
Onion and Green Chili Omelet, 227

Pandan (screwpine) leaves, 60, 279
Pasta, 15, **90**–103. *See also* Noodles
about: cooking, 15, 99; sauces for, 91; shapes, 96; sticking, 15
Beef and Shiitake Pasta, 92
Chicken and Shrimp Pasta, 93
Chicken Macaroni, 94
Creamy Mushroom Pasta, 96
Easy Shrimp and Celery Pasta Salad, 98
Fish Pasta, 91
Lemon Pasta, 101
Lentil Soup with Pasta, 99
Macaroni with Chinese Meat Sauce, 102
Marinara Sauce for, 15
Minestrone, 52
Mushroom Pasta, 101
Pasta and Leek Stir-Fry, 97
Pasta and Tuna Salad, 103
Pasta Arrabiata, 97
Spicy Italian Sausage Pasta, 100
Spinach and Pine Nut Pasta, 103
Tomato and Shrimp Pasta, 95
Peanut Sauce, 287
Peas. *See* Legumes and beans
Peppers
about: reducing heat in chilies, 167
Chili Sambal, 286
Easy Spiced Rice with Peppers and Pine Nuts, 78
Marinated Scrambled Tofu with Peppers and Onions, 240
Onion and Green Chili Omelet, 227
Potato, Bell Pepper, and Mushroom Hash, 27
Shrimp with Colored Bell Peppers, 156
Snow Peas with Bell Peppers, 244
Pineapple
Pickled Pineapple Salad, 285
Sweet and Sour Shrimp, 150

INDEX   293

Pineapple—*continued*
  Tangy Shrimp Curry with Pineapples, 144
Pink Lemonade with Basil, 281
Pizza, Toasted Pita, 288
Pork, **177**–90
  about: cooking, 185, 187; shaping meatballs, 181; slicing before cooking, 188
  Bacon, Onion, and Potato Hash, 26
  Black Vinegar Ground Meat Noodles, 117
  Braised Fragrant Pork (*Babi Chin*), 188
  Chinese Pork Dumpling (Wonton) Soup, 183
  Chinese Stewed Meatballs, 181
  Dim Sum: Steamed Meatballs, 31
  Egg with Pork and Cilantro, 226
  Ground Pork with Mushrooms, 185
  Hot and Sour Soup, 44
  Kimchi Pork, 180
  Mapo Tofu, 238
  Meatballs and Napa Cabbage Soup, 41
  Mini Ham and Corn Omelets, 29
  Pork Congee, 85
  Pork in Tomato Sauce, 190
  Pork Rib Curry, 182
  Pork Stock, 16
  Pork with Potatoes, Peas, and Corn, 186
  Potato, Cabbage, and Spicy Sausage Soup, 55
  Pumpkin Rice, 67
  Savory Cabbage Rice, 68
  Seaweed Soup with Enoki and Meatballs, 43
  Spicy Bean Noodles, 118
  Spicy Italian Sausage Pasta, 100
  Steamed Pork Patty, 180
  Steamed Ribs with Garlic in Chinese Black Bean Sauce, 178
  Steamed Savory Pork with Sweet Pumpkin, 179
  Steamed Tofu with Ground Pork, 234
  Steamed Whole Fish with Ham and Shiitake Mushrooms, 127
  Stir-Fried Pork with Ginger, 187
  Tamarind Pork Slices, 189
  Thai Meat Patties, 184
  Tofu with Shrimp, Meat, and Mushrooms, 239
Porridge. *See* Congee (rice porridge) and grains
Potatoes. *See also* Taro
  about: taro and, 70; varieties/starchiness of, 27
  Bacon, Onion, and Potato Hash, 26
  Green Onion and Potato Frittata, 230
  Indian Potato and Cauliflower (*Aloo Gobi*), 250
  Mild Beef Curry with Potato and Peas, 194
  Mini Indonesian Potato Cakes, 34
  Pork with Potatoes, Peas, and Corn, 186
  Potato, Bell Pepper, and Mushroom Hash, 27
  Potato, Cabbage, and Spicy Sausage Soup, 55
  Potato and Pea Soup, 207
Protein sources, 126
Pumpkin
  about: seeds (pepitas), 195
  Pumpkin and Beef Curry, 195
  Pumpkin Congee, 86
  Pumpkin Rice, 67
  Steamed Savory Pork with Sweet Pumpkin, 179

Rice, **56**–80. *See also* Congee (rice porridge) and grains
  about: basmati, 74; combining grains, 14; cooking, 7–8; cooking fried rice, 72; cuisine and, 4–6; digesting, 2; "fanning" for sushi, 13; grain length, 3–4; history of, 2, 4–5; long-grain, 4; medium grain, 4; milled, 3; parboiled, 4; polished, 3; processing steps, 2; rinsing, 12; short-grain, 4; storing, 82; varieties, 3–4; white, 3
  Asian "Paella," 76
  Asian "Risotto," 66
  Beans and rice, 73
  Beef Fried Rice, 71
  Brown Rice, 12
  Chicken Rice, 64
  Chinese "Clay-Pot" Rice, 65
  Easy Lemon Buttered Rice, 77
  Easy Spiced Rice with Peppers and Pine Nuts, 78
  Egg and Shrimp Fried Rice, 72
  Fish Kedgeree, 80
  Fragrant Coconut Rice, 60
  Ground Beef and Rice Soup, 79
  Indian Vegetable Biryani, 61
  Japanese Chicken Donburi, 58
  Korean Bibimbap, 59
  Long-Grain White Rice, 12
  Pumpkin Rice, 67
  Rice Salad, 75
  Savory Cabbage Rice, 68
  Savory Taro Rice, 70
  Seafood Fried Rice, 69
  Seafood Tom Yum Rice, 57
  Shrimp Pilaf, 74
  Steamed Black Rice Pudding, 280
  Stuffed Egg Rolls with Rice, 288
  Sushi Rice, 13
  Tomato Rice, 62
  Yellow Rice, 63
Rice cookers
  anatomy of, 9
  as complementary tools, 1
  cooking tips, 153
  features of, 9, 289
  origin of, 8
  types of, 10
  uses of, 9

Salads
  Easy Shrimp and Celery Pasta Salad, 98
  Fish Salad, 24
  Pasta and Tuna Salad, 103
  Pickled Pineapple Salad, 285
  Rice Salad, 75
Salmon. *See* Fish; Starters
Sauces

about: bottled, sodium content, 91
Chinese Black Bean Sauce, 132
Creamy Pistachio Pesto Sauce, 136
Fish Salad Dressing, 24
Garlic Black Bean Sauce, 203
Ginger and Coconut Sauce, 138
Ginger and Green Onion Sauce, 286
Ginger Dressing, 106
Green Onion Dressing, 105
Mango Chutney, 285
Mango Salsa, 135
Marinara Sauce, 15
Mushroom Sauce, 201, 235
Peanut Sauce, 287
Soy and Ginger Sauce, 134
Tahini Sauce, 107
Tangy Ginger Sauce, 125
Thai-Style Yogurt Sauce, 129
Tomato Gravy, 210
Wine and Shallot Sauce, 171
Wine Sauce, 131
Scallops. *See* Shrimp, scallops, and clams
Screwpine leaves, 60, 279
Seafood. *See* Fish; Shrimp, scallops, and clams
Seaweed Soup with Enoki and Meatballs, 43
Seven-spice, about, 275
Shallots
　about, 76
　Buttered Kai Lan with Shallots, 256
　Fried Golden Shallots, 284
　Wine and Shallot Sauce, 171
Shrimp, scallops, and clams, **142**–58
　about: cooking clams, 158; cooking scallops, 157; saving up for shrimp stock, 17; sustainable seafood sources, 128
　Asian "Paella," 76
　Asian "Risotto," 66
　Black Pepper Shrimp, 153
　Buttered Scallops, 157
　Chicken and Shrimp Pasta, 93
　Chinese Steamed Shrimp with Ginger, 143
　Clam and Corn in Herby Broth, 158
　Easy Shrimp and Celery Pasta Salad, 98
　Easy Thai-Style Shrimp Cake, 156
　Egg and Shrimp Fried Rice, 72
　Fishball (Dumpling) Soup, 46
　Garlic-Infused Glass Noodles with Tiger Shrimp, 116
　Herb and Garlic Shrimp, 152
　Indian Shrimp Curry, 148
　Noodles in Creamy Egg Gravy, 119
　Nyonya-Style Noodles, 121
　Pasta Arrabiata, 97
　Salt and Pepper Shrimp, 152
　Seafood Congee, 83
　Seafood Fried Rice, 69
　Seafood Napa Cabbage Rolls, 35
　Seafood Tom Yum Rice, 57
　Shrimp and Shiitake Curry, 147
　Shrimp and Tomato Fried Eggs, 155
　Shrimp Foo Yong, 225
　Shrimp in Spicy Milk Sauce, 151
　Shrimp in Wine Ginger Broth, 145
　Shrimp Pilaf, 74
　Shrimp Stock, 17
　Shrimp with Colored Bell Peppers, 156
　Shrimp with Spicy Tomatoes, 145
　Spicy Shrimp with Basil, 146
　Stir-Fried Asparagus with Scallops, 248
　Stir-Fried Shrimp with Asparagus, 154
　Sweet and Sour Shrimp, 150
　Tangy Shrimp Curry with Pineapples, 144
　Thai Green Curry with Shrimp, 149
　Tofu with Shrimp, Meat, and Mushrooms, 239
　Tomato and Shrimp Pasta, 95
　Tom Yum Soup, 51
Soba noodles. *See* Noodles
Soups and stews, **38**–55
　about: clear chicken soup, 42
　Bean Sprouts and Tomato Soup, 40
　Beef Stew, 193
　Cabbage and Tomato Soup, 39
　Chicken and Daikon Soup, 42
　Chicken Barley Stew, 163
　Chicken Herbal Soup, 49
　Chicken Soup with Sweet Corn and Carrot, 42
　Chinese Fish Soup, 44
　Chinese Pork Dumpling (Wonton) Soup, 183
　Cider Chicken Stew, 164
　Coconut Chicken Soup, 48
　Cream of Mushroom Soup, 53
　Curried Carrot and Ginger Soup, 54
　Easy Chinese Vegetable Stew, 246
　Fishball (Dumpling) Soup, 46
　Garlic Bean Soup, 206
　Green Bean Soup (dessert), 278
　Green Tea Miso Soup, 50
　Ground Beef and Rice Soup, 79
　Halibut and Asparagus Soup, 47
　Hot and Sour Soup, 44
　Indian Eggplant Stew, 252
　Kimchi Soba Soup, 109
　Kimchi Tofu Soup, 52
　Lentil Soup, 208
　Lentil Soup with Pasta, 99
　Meatballs and Napa Cabbage Soup, 41
　Minestrone, 52
　Miso Soup, 49
　Mushroom and Barley Soup, 261
　Mushroom Stew, 262
　Okra Stew, 258
　Potato, Cabbage, and Spicy Sausage Soup, 55
　Potato and Pea Soup, 207
　Red Bean Soup (dessert), 278
　Seaweed Soup with Enoki and Meatballs, 43
　Spinach and Tofu Soup, 40
　Tom Yum Soup, 51
　Vegetable Soup with Pinto Beans, 208
Soy. *See* Tofu (and soy)
Soy sauces, 134
Spices, 78, 146, 149, 151, 229, 275
Spinach
　Creamed Spinach, 255
　Spinach and Pine Nut Pasta, 103
　Spinach and Tofu Soup, 40

INDEX 295

Spinach—*continued*
   Spinach Tofu in Mushroom Sauce, 235
   Summer Soba with Spinach and Mushrooms, 108
   Taro and Spinach Congee, 88
Sprouts
   Bean Sprouts and Tomato Soup, 40
   Tofu with Bean Sprouts and Spices, 241
Starters, **19**–37. *See also* Dim Sum
   Bacon, Onion, and Potato Hash, 26
   Chicken Satay, 25
   Fish Cakes, 20
   Fish Salad, 24
   Hotshot Sweet Corn, 31
   Mashed Sweet Potatoes, 28
   Mini Fish Kebabs, 23
   Mini Ham and Corn Omelets, 29
   Mini Indonesian Potato Cakes, 34
   Potato, Bell Pepper, and Mushroom Hash, 27
   Salmon Patties, 22
   Savory Taro Patties, 29
   Seafood Napa Cabbage Rolls, 35
   Spicy Fish Custard, 37
   Stuffed Tomatoes, 30
   Tofu Cabbage Rolls, 36
   Tuna-Cheese Patties, 21
Stocks
   about: dashi stock, 58
   Chicken Stock, 16
   Pork Stock, 16
   Shrimp Stock, 17
   Soybean Stock, 18
   Vegetable Stock, 18
Sushi Rice, 13
Sweet potatoes. *See also* Taro
   Caramelized All-Spiced Sweet Potato, 275
   Mashed Sweet Potatoes, 28
   Sweet Potato Congee, 87
Swiss Chard with Raisins, 257

Tamarind, 144, 189
Taro
   about, 70; cooking, 273
   Savory Taro Patties, 29
   Savory Taro Rice, 70
   Sweet Taro Crisps, 273
   Taro and Bananas in Sweet Coconut Milk, 279
   Taro and Spinach Congee, 88
Tea-Flavored Chicken with Chinese Spices, 165
Tea-Flavored Eggs, 221
Tips, leftover tricks, and more, **283**–88
Toasted Almonds, 287
Tofu (and soy), **232**–42
   about: cooking, 233, 235; draining, 235; edamame benefits, 102; egg tofu, 33; moisture content and firmness, 233
   Dim Sum: Steamed Tofu, 33
   Easy Chinese Vegetable Stew, 246
   Kimchi Tofu Soup, 52
   Mapo Tofu, 238
   Marinated Scrambled Tofu with Peppers and Onions, 240
   Miso Soup, 49
   Soybean Stock, 18
   Spinach and Tofu Soup, 40
   Spinach Tofu in Mushroom Sauce, 235
   Steamed Halibut with Mushrooms and Tofu, 126
   Steamed Tofu Balls, 233
   Steamed Tofu with Ground Pork, 234
   Tofu Cabbage Rolls, 36
   Tofu Casserole, 236
   Tofu Curry, 237
   Tofu Patties, 242
   Tofu with Bean Sprouts and Spices, 241
   Tofu with Butternut Squash, 241
   Tofu with Hot Shallot Oil, 236
   Tofu with Shrimp, Meat, and Mushrooms, 239
   Tom Yum Glass Noodles, 114

Tomatoes
   about: lycopene in, 39
   Bean Sprouts and Tomato Soup, 40
   Black Bean Casserole in Tomato Gravy, 210
   Cabbage and Tomato Soup, 39
   Chicken with Spicy Tomatoes, 166
   Marinara Sauce, 15
   Shrimp with Spicy Tomatoes, 145
   Stuffed Tomatoes, 30
   Tomato and Shrimp Pasta, 95
   Tomato Rice, 62
Tuna. *See* Fish; Starters
Turmeric, benefits of, 212

Vegetables, **243**–58. *See also specific vegetables*
   about: slicing and dicing, 214
   Buttered Kai Lan with Shallots, 256
   Curry Vegetables, 249
   Easy Chinese Vegetable Stew, 246
   Indian Vegetable Biryani, 61
   Swiss Chard with Raisins, 257
   Vegetable Soup with Pinto Beans, 208
   Vegetable Stock, 18

Wine
   about: cooking with, 169
   Wine and Shallot Sauce, 171
   Wine Sauce, 131
Wonton wrappers, 183

Yogurt
   about: in Indian cooking, 264; as substitute for cream or milk, 264
   Cucumber Raita, 62
   Thai-Style Yogurt Sauce, 129
Yuzu, 173